Dissertation
zur Erlangung des akademischen Grades
Doctor rerum politicarum

An Economic Analysis of the University
University Governance and the Effects of Faculty Participation in University Decision-Making

Fachbereich:	Betriebswirtschaftslehre
Hochschule:	European Business School
Name:	Dipl.-Kffr. Jutta Merschen
Geburtsort:	Eschweiler
Referenten:	Prof. Ulrich Hommel, Ph.D.
	Prof. Dr. Joachim Ahrens
Einreichungstermin:	4. November 2005
Prüfungstermin:	16. Dezember 2005
Erscheinungsort:	Stuttgart
Erscheinungsjahr:	2006
Hochschulkennziffer:	154

Jutta Merschen

AN ECONOMIC ANALYSIS OF THE UNIVERSITY

University Governance and the Effects of Faculty
Participation in University Decision-Making

ibidem-Verlag
Stuttgart

Bibliografische Information Der Deutschen Bibliothek

Die Deutsche Bibliothek verzeichnet diese Publikation in der Deutschen Nationalbibliografie; detaillierte bibliografische Daten sind im Internet über <http://dnb.ddb.de> abrufbar.

∞

Gedruckt auf alterungsbeständigem, säurefreien Papier
Printed on acid-free paper

ISBN: 3-89821-649-7

© *ibidem*-Verlag
Stuttgart 2004
Alle Rechte vorbehalten

Das Werk einschließlich aller seiner Teile ist urheberrechtlich geschützt. Jede Verwertung außerhalb der engen Grenzen des Urheberrechtsgesetzes ist ohne Zustimmung des Verlages unzulässig und strafbar. Dies gilt insbesondere für Vervielfältigungen, Übersetzungen, Mikroverfilmungen und elektronische Speicherformen sowie die Einspeicherung und Verarbeitung in elektronischen Systemen.

Printed in Germany

Für meine Eltern und meinen Bruder
Und für Johannes

Foreword

Universities play an important role in modern information and knowledge societies. In order to fulfill their mission successfully, universities not only need sufficient financial resources, and the brightest faculty and students, they must also be equipped with functional organizational structures.

The public debate about the adequacy of the management and governance structures of German universities has been going on for the last decade. Policy think tanks, the German Rectors' Conference, politicians, and professors alike have voiced calls for more autonomy, and management and decision structures with a clear allocation of responsibility, thereby strengthening the university management. In this context, the participative element in university decision-making enters centre stage of the debate: is it still propitious to grant faculty members and other stakeholders far-reaching decision rights in the university?

In seeking an answer to this question, this dissertation addresses a research gap in the management and economic sciences. So far, theoretically sound general conclusions have been established, whilst the specific matters of how decisions are initiated and implemented, ratified and monitored in universities have been largely ignored. Bridging this gap through both theoretical economic analysis and a practical study of university governance in Germany, this dissertation can be regarded as the first step towards an integrated theory of university governance, thereby making a valuable and distinctive contribution to the debate. Taking a three-fold approach, it combines the merits of theoretical analysis, mathematical modeling, and empirical investigation in the study of universities and their organizational structures.

From the theoretical perspective, this dissertation analyzes the internal players of the university and their relationships with each other. It examines the nature of their conflicts of interests, in particular the principal-agent problem between a typical professor and university management. Against this background, it explains the theoretical rationale for faculty participation in university decision-making by drawing on its governance function. Consequently, the theoretical impact of faculty participation on the university and its performance are identified, proposing a trade-off between positive and negative effects.

These theoretical implications are complemented by an economic model that relates faculty participation to the delegation of authority from the university manager to the individual faculty member. The results of the model show that the incentives of the professor to become engaged in decision-making increase when the formal right to decide is officially delegated to him. In an extension, the model further demonstrates that formal authority is not the only determinant of decision-making: real authority, i.e. effective control over the decision, becomes more and more important as the costs of participating in decision-making increase.

Turning from theory to practice, the empirical investigation presents the insights from interviews conducted with experts in the field of university governance and university decision-making. In sum, the existence of positive and negative effects of faculty participation is largely confirmed. The dissertation identifies the characteristics of faculty members and university managers, and the design of the decision structures as explanatory conditions for the emergence of the observed effects of faculty participation in university decision-making. On this empirical basis, the author recommends reorganizing the university so that decision authority and responsibility are collocated in strengthened management bodies. At the same time, the consultative function of faculty members should be retained.

The policy recommendations, which the author puts forward, can be viewed as an innovative impulse towards overcoming the problematic aspects of the traditional university management and governance structures, preserving at the same time their benefits. This dissertation lays a sound basis for forthcoming work in this area and will appeal not only to scholars of management science and economics, but also to practitioners in university management, politics, and think tanks.

Oestrich-Winkel, January 2006　　　　　　Professor Ulrich Hommel, Ph.D.

Rudolf-von-Bennigsen-Foerder-Foundation Professor of Finance and
Rector of the EUROPEAN BUSINESS SCHOOL

Preface

My master thesis written in 2002 at the European Business School under the supervision of Professor Ulrich Hommel, PhD, who would later become my "Doktorvater", introduced me to the economic study of universities and their governance structures. Since that time, I have been fascinated by their complexity. Thus, it seemed only natural to pursue this research interest as a doctoral student.

During the three years it has taken me to complete this thesis, I have learned a lot: About universities, about academia, about doing research, about writing a doctoral thesis, and about myself. A number of people have accompanied me over this time and I would like to acknowledge their support.

First of all, I would like to thank my thesis supervisor, Professor Ulrich Hommel. He was not only most supportive in discussing ideas, commenting drafts of my papers, setting up interview appointments, and encouraging my academic progress, but was also very helpful and encouraging in my applications for scholarships, summer schools, and internships, thus enabling me to pursue my extracurricular objectives.

I am also deeply indebted to Professor Dr Joachim Ahrens, who agreed to serve as my second supervisor. His enthusiasm for my topic and his feedback were very valuable at various stages of my dissertation process.

Professor Dr Jean-Paul Thommen shaped my way of thinking about organizations during my final year as a master's student at the ebs. He helped me to secure my doctoral scholarship, for which I am very grateful.

This scholarship was provided by the Friedrich-Naumann-Foundation, Germany's foundation for liberal policies, with funds from the German Federal Ministry of Education and Research. I am very grateful to the Friedrich-Naumann-Foundation and the German Federal Ministry of Education and Research for this scholarship and all the possibilities it provided me. Particularly, I would like to thank Mrs Marie-Luise Wohlleben and Mrs Marie-Luise Simon of the Friedrich-Naumann-Foundations for the trust and faith they had in my capabilities.

Christine Jahn, Vera Koerschgen, Isabel Welpe, Peter Jaskiewicz, and Tim Mundhenke repeatedly provided valuable feedback to my papers, references to interesting literature and helpful hints for mastering the various software packages that make life much easier. Dr Schermelleh-Engel and Wolfgang Rauch from the Department of Psychological Research Methods and Evaluation of the University of Frankfurt as well as Dr Dirk Schwinger were very supportive in providing advice on conducting expert interviews and analyzing qualitative data. Dr Florian Englmaier of the University of Munich provided inspiration for my theoretical modeling efforts and gave valuable feedback along the way. Philipp N. Baecker of the European Business School developed the 'ebsthesis' class which greatly facilitated writing this thesis in LaTeX and also provided a lot of helpful support in problem solving, for both of which I am very very grateful.

I would also like to thank the experts who agreed to participate in the interviews. They provided me with immensely valuable information, background, and analysis. Conducting the empirical study of faculty participation in university decision-making in Germany would not have been possible without their help. The conclusions and recommendations of this thesis are based on their expertise. I am very grateful for their time and readiness to share their knowledge.

During the last year of writing this thesis, many friends had to bear my short attention span and my - at times - exclusive dedication to the dissertation that left little time for everything else. I want to thank all of them for their patience, their mental support, and for their continuous friendship.

All of the above, however, was only possible due to four very special people: My brother Julian, who has developed into an academic counterpart who patiently gave advice on my mathematical endeavors; my parents Bea and Toni, who have always been there when I needed them, providing feedback on my dissertation, the speed of the progress, and my life in general. I owe them all the chances I have had during my (academic) life. They have been staunch, yet critical, supporters of the choices I have made. Finally, I want to thank Johannes. For his love, for his intellectual support, for his eternal understanding, and for always believing in me.

Summary of Contents

List of Figures   XXV

List of Tables   XXVII

List of Abbreviations   XXIX

List of Symbols   XXXI

1 Introduction   1
     1.1 Motivation 1
     1.2 Focus of the Dissertation and Research Questions 2
     1.3 Methodological Approach and Outline 3

Part I: The Theoretical Analysis

2 A Survey of Theoretical Frameworks   9
     2.1 Introduction 9
     2.2 The Foundations of New Institutional Economics 9
     2.3 The Principal-Agent Framework 17
     2.4 Governance Theory 22
     2.5 Conclusion 27

3 The University as an Economic Organization   29
     3.1 Introduction 29
     3.2 The University as an Object of Analysis 30
     3.3 The Relevant Players in the University and Their Conflicts 38
     3.4 University Governance as a Mitigation Mechanism 48
     3.5 Faculty Participation as a Measure of University Governance ... 54
     3.6 Conclusion 70

Part II: The Economic Model

4	**A Survey of Economic Modeling**	**75**
	4.1 Introduction	75
	4.2 Foundations of Economic Models	76
	4.3 Economic Models on Universities	79
	4.4 Conclusion	86
5	**Modeling Faculty Participation in University Decision-Making**	**89**
	5.1 Motivation and Overview	89
	5.2 Reference Models on Strategic Delegation	90
	5.3 An Initiative Model - Base Case	97
	5.4 A Proposal Model - Extension	125
	5.5 Conclusion	155
	5.6 Appendix	157

Part III: Empirical Insights

6	**The Methodology of the Empirical Study**	**173**
	6.1 Introduction	173
	6.2 Empirical Background	174
	6.3 The Set-up of the Empirical Study	175
	6.4 The Data Collection	184
	6.5 Evaluating and Interpreting Qualitative Research	194
	6.6 Conclusion	197
	6.7 Appendix	198
7	**Empirical Insights into University Decision-Making**	**205**
	7.1 Introduction	205
	7.2 Overview of the Governance Systems in Practice	205
	7.3 The Effects of Faculty Participation	207
	7.4 The Explanatory Value of the Variables	215
	7.5 A First Classification of the Underlying Reasons of Faculty Participation	225

7.6	Conclusion	230
8	**Final Conclusion**	**233**
8.1	Summary	233
8.2	Limitations	238
8.3	Policy Recommendations	239

Bibliography   **247**

Table of Contents

List of Figures   **XXV**

List of Tables   **XXVII**

List of Abbreviations   **XXIX**

List of Symbols   **XXXI**

1 Introduction   **1**
    1.1 Motivation 1
    1.2 Focus of the Dissertation and Research Questions 2
    1.3 Methodological Approach and Outline 3

Part I: The Theoretical Analysis

2 A Survey of Theoretical Frameworks   **9**
    2.1 Introduction.................................. 9
    2.2 The Foundations of New Institutional Economics 9
       2.2.1 Introduction 9
       2.2.2 Four Basic Assumptions of NIE 10
       2.2.3 The Research Branches of NIE 14
    2.3 The Principal-Agent Framework 17
       2.3.1 Introduction 17
       2.3.2 Principals, Agents, and the Structure of Their Relationships   18
       2.3.3 The Defining Elements of a Principal-Agent Problem 19
    2.4 Governance Theory.............................. 22
       2.4.1 The Necessity for Organizational Governance 22
       2.4.2 Mechanisms of Corporate Governance 24
    2.5 Conclusion 27

3 The University as an Economic Organization   **29**
    3.1 Introduction.................................. 29
    3.2 The University as an Object of Analysis 30

	3.2.1	Definition and Categorization	30
	3.2.2	Why Universities Exist as Organizations	32
	3.2.3	Special Characteristics of the University	33
	3.2.4	The Concept of University Performance	35
3.3	The Relevant Players in the University and Their Conflicts		38
	3.3.1	The Players	38
	3.3.2	The Preferences	39
	3.3.3	The Conflicts between the Players	41
	3.3.4	Synopsis	47
3.4	University Governance as a Mitigation Mechanism		48
	3.4.1	Definition of University Governance	48
	3.4.2	The Applicability of Corporate Governance Mechanisms in the University Context	49
3.5	Faculty Participation as a Measure of University Governance		54
	3.5.1	Introduction and Definition	54
	3.5.2	The Rationale for Faculty Participation as a Governance Mechanism	57
	3.5.3	Positive Effects of Faculty Participation	59
	3.5.4	Negative Effects of Faculty Participation	64
	3.5.5	Synopsis	69
3.6	Conclusion		70

Part II: The Economic Model

4	**A Survey of Economic Modeling**		**75**
4.1	Introduction		75
4.2	Foundations of Economic Models		76
4.3	Economic Models on Universities		79
	4.3.1	Introduction	79
	4.3.2	Faculty Models	80
	4.3.3	Organizational Models	82
	4.3.4	Tenure Models	84

4.4	Conclusion			86

5 Modeling Faculty Participation in University Decision-Making 89

- 5.1 Motivation and Overview 89
- 5.2 Reference Models on Strategic Delegation 90
  - 5.2.1 Introduction 90
  - 5.2.2 Aghion/Tirole (1997) 92
  - 5.2.3 Baker/Gibbons/Murphy (1999) 94
  - 5.2.4 Burkart/Gromb/Panunzi (1997) 96
  - 5.2.5 Synopsis 97
- 5.3 An Initiative Model - Base Case 97
  - 5.3.1 Set-up 97
    - 5.3.1.1 The University Context 97
    - 5.3.1.2 The Decision-Making Process 99
  - 5.3.2 The Model 103
    - 5.3.2.1 Introduction 103
    - 5.3.2.2 University Management Authority 103
    - 5.3.2.3 Faculty Authority 112
    - 5.3.2.4 Comparative Analysis 120
  - 5.3.3 Synopsis from the Initiative Model 123
- 5.4 A Proposal Model - Extension 125
  - 5.4.1 Modeling Idea 125
  - 5.4.2 Set-up 126
    - 5.4.2.1 The University Context 126
    - 5.4.2.2 The Decision-Making Process 126
  - 5.4.3 The Model 129
    - 5.4.3.1 University Management Authority 129
    - 5.4.3.2 Faculty Authority 134
    - 5.4.3.3 Comparative Statics 137
    - 5.4.3.4 Comparative Analysis 148
  - 5.4.4 Synopsis from the Proposal Model 154

5.5	Conclusion			155
5.6	Appendix			157
	5.6.1	Conditions for the Initiative Model		157
	5.6.2	Comparative Statics for the Initiative Model		158
		5.6.2.1	University Control	158
		5.6.2.2	Faculty Control	161
	5.6.3	Comparative Statics for the Proposal Model		163
		5.6.3.1	University Control	163
		5.6.3.2	Faculty Control	166

Part III: Empirical Insights

6 The Methodology of the Empirical Study   **173**

6.1	Introduction			173
6.2	Empirical Background			174
6.3	The Set-up of the Empirical Study			175
	6.3.1	The Research Question		175
	6.3.2	Methodology		176
		6.3.2.1	The Objective of Empirical Research	176
		6.3.2.2	Quantitative vs. Qualitative Approaches	178
		6.3.2.3	The Rationale for a Qualitative Study	179
	6.3.3	A Conceptual Model of Influencing Factors		182
6.4	The Data Collection			184
	6.4.1	Defining the Sample		184
	6.4.2	Expert Interviews as a Data Collection Method		186
	6.4.3	Selecting Interview Partners		189
	6.4.4	Questionnaires as a Data Collection Tool		190
	6.4.5	Conduct of Data Collection		193
6.5	Evaluating and Interpreting Qualitative Research			194
6.6	Conclusion			197
6.7	Appendix			198
	6.7.1	Letter to Interview Partners		198

	6.7.2	Interview Questionnaire	200
	6.7.3	Evaluation Sheet	203
	6.7.4	Summary Sheet	204

7 Empirical Insights into University Decision-Making — 205

- 7.1 Introduction — 205
- 7.2 Overview of the Governance Systems in Practice — 205
- 7.3 The Effects of Faculty Participation — 207
  - 7.3.1 Overview — 207
  - 7.3.2 The Effects on the Academic Working Environment — 208
  - 7.3.3 The Effects on Academic Quality — 210
  - 7.3.4 The Effects on Managerial Professionalism — 213
  - 7.3.5 Summary of the Effects — 214
- 7.4 The Explanatory Value of the Variables — 215
  - 7.4.1 The Impact of the Factor 'Faculty' — 215
  - 7.4.2 The Impact of the Factor 'University Management' — 218
  - 7.4.3 The Impact of the Factor 'Decision Structures' — 220
  - 7.4.4 The Impact of Other Factors — 222
- 7.5 A First Classification of the Underlying Reasons of Faculty Participation — 225
  - 7.5.1 Conditions and Relationships between Influence Factors and Effects — 225
- 7.6 Conclusion — 230

8 Final Conclusion — 233

- 8.1 Summary — 233
- 8.2 Limitations — 238
- 8.3 Policy Recommendations — 239

Bibliography — 247

List of Figures

3.1	Principal-Agent Relationships in the University	42
3.2	Forms of Faculty Participation	55
5.1	The Best Response Functions of University Management and Faculty Under University Management Authority	106
5.2	New Equilibrium after an Exogenous Change in λ	108
5.3	Direct and Indirect Effects of λ	108
5.4	New Equilibrium after an Exogenous Change in R	110
5.5	New Equilibrium after an Exogenous Change in b	112
5.6	The Best Response Functions of University Management and Faculty Under Faculty Authority	115
5.7	New Equilibrium after an Exogenous Change in λ	116
5.8	New Equilibrium after an Exogenous Change in R	118
5.9	New Equilibrium after an Exogenous Change in b	119
5.10	The Best Response Functions of University Management and Faculty Under University Management Authority	133
5.11	The Best Response Functions of University Management and Faculty Under Faculty Authority	137
5.12	New Equilibrium after an Exogenous Change in λ	138
5.13	New Equilibrium after an Exogenous Change in μ	141
5.14	New Equilibrium after an Exogenous Change in α	142
5.15	New Equilibrium after an Exogenous Change in λ	143
5.16	New Equilibrium after an Exogenous Change in μ	146
5.17	New Equilibrium after an Exogenous Change in α	147
5.18	The Difference between Total Welfare under University Control and under Faculty Control in Equilibrium dependent on α	151
5.19	Equilibrium University Welfare dependent on α	152
5.20	Equilibrium Faculty Welfare dependent on α	153
6.1	Types of Variables in Empirical Research	177
6.2	A Conceptual Model of the Effects of Faculty Participation	182

6.3	An Overview of the Interview Partners	190
6.4	The Interview Questionnaire - I	200
6.5	The Interview Questionnaire - II	201
6.6	The Interview Questionnaire - III	202
6.7	An Evaluation Sheet for the Variable 'Faculty'	203
6.8	The Summary Sheet for the Variable 'Faculty'	204
7.1	The Effects of Faculty Participation in University Decision-Making	214
7.2	The Conditions Underlying Effects of Faculty Participation in University Decision-Making	228

List of Tables

5.1	The Project Payoff Structure in the Initiative Model	100
5.2	The Adapted Project Payoff Structure	100
5.3	The Project Payoff Structure in the Proposal Model	128
5.4	The Conditional Probabilities of the Payoffs (Management Proposal)	128
5.5	The Conditional Probabilities of the Payoffs (Faculty Proposal)	128

List of Abbreviations

AAUP	American Association of University Professors
BRF	Best response function
CEO	Chief Executive Officer
ed	Editor
edn	Edition
eds	Editors
e.g.	Exempli gratia (for example)
EV	Expected value
FOC	First-order condition
HRK	Hochschulrektorenkonferenz
i.e.	Id est (that is)
NCES	National Center for Education Statistics
NIE	New Institutional Economics
NPO	Non-profit organization
p.	Page
pp.	Pages
PR	Private
SAT	Scholastic Aptitude Test
SP	Special Public
TP	Typical Public

List of Symbols

α	Cost efficiency parameter of faculty effort
λ	Measure of congruence between university management and faculty (for good payoff)
μ	Measure of congruence between university management and faculty (for bad payoff)
A	Effort level of the principal under Agent-formal authority
a	Effort level of the agent under Agent-formal authority
A^*	Equilibrium effort level of the principal under Agent-formal authority
a^*	Equilibrium effort level of the agent under Agent-formal authority
b	Project payoff to faculty
$c(E)$	Cost function with respect to principal effort
$c(e)$	Cost function with respect to agent effort
D	Difference between total payoffs under Principal-formal and Agent-formal authority
E	Effort level of the principal
e	Effort level of the agent
F	Total payoff to faculty
F^A	Payoff to the agent under Agent-formal authority
F^P	Payoff to the agent under Principal-formal authority
n	Number of alternatives
P	Effort level of the principal under Principal-formal authority
p	Effort level of the agent under Principal-formal authority
P^*	Equilibrium effort level of the principal under Principal-formal authority
p^*	Equilibrium effort level of the agent under Principal-formal authority
R	Project payoff to the university manager

S	Decision alternative
T	Total payoff to the principal and the agent
T^A	Total payoff to the principal and the agent under Agent-formal authority
T^P	Total payoff to the principal and the agent under Principal-formal authority
U	Total payoff to the university manager
U^A	Payoff to the principal under Agent-formal authority
U^P	Payoff to the principal under Principal-formal authority

1 Introduction

1.1 Motivation

The human asset 'knowledge' plays an essential role in economic growth. A substantial part of this knowledge is being produced and transmitted in universities. In the last decade, Germany's higher education landscape has witnessed an increasing withdrawal of the state from control over university policy and operation. The state has continuously downsized its role from an interventionary to a facilitatory state (Eurydice (2000), p. 19).

During the course of the reform process, Germany's federal and state legislations have passed laws that open possibilities for implementing more individual management and governance structures. Since 1997, the "Berliner Hochschulgesetz" (Berlin State Act on Higher Education) encompasses a trial endorsement, allowing the Berlin universities to deviate from certain regulations of the state law in order to experiment with new governance and management structures. In 2003, the State of Rhineland-Palatinate granted its universities increasing decision rights over the organization and realization of management and governance functions (Fedrowitz/Müller-Böling (1998)). In 2004, the State of Hesse passed a special law for one of its universities, handing over many of the control and decision rights formerly held by the State Ministry of Higher Education to the university and a newly founded board of trustees. In August 2005, the state of Bavaria initiated a legal reform aimed at giving its universities more autonomy over decision-making and decision control.

The promotion of decentralization and delegation of decision power to the universities has led to rising autonomy for the university during the last years (Müller-Böling/Küchler (1998), pp. 18-23). In return for the granted self-government and independence, the state demands institutional responsibility and accountability for the performance of the university. In order to adapt to this new situation and its challenges, universities are increasingly looking at management structures, decision-making systems, and governance mechanisms as fundamental performance drivers (Mora (2001), p. 95). Especially universities in Germany are recognizing that their participatory, democratic governance structures may hinder them from effectively responding to the social and financial challenges of current times (Mittelstraß (2003); Müller-Böling/Küchler (1998), pp. 27-29). The question that arises with the introduction of flexible legal structures and increasing performance pressure is that of optimal design of the organizational structures for the university.

Growing demands concerning both the effectiveness and the efficiency of the university require an in-depth analysis of the university. Organizational structure and organizational performance can only be improved with an understanding of the internal organization of the university (Faria (2002), p. 187). While the study of organizational behavior is one of the main research fields of economics and management science, very few accounts employ an economic approach to studying management and governance structures of the university.[1] Most of the literature available stems from the social sciences, or has a practical, policy-based background that lacks academic rigor.

The motivation for this dissertation therefore is to provide an economic insight into the inner workings of German universities in order to answer the question how universities in Germany should organize in order to persist in times of economic, organizational, and competitive challenges.[2]

1.2 Focus of the Dissertation and Research Questions

The economic analysis of the university focuses on the governance structures as an important driver of university performance. Governance structures refer to those mechanisms that control the management and day-to-day running of the university. Empirical studies in the US and casual observations in Germany have proposed that the widespread participatory management and governance systems are not only beneficial for the university, but also come with significant disadvantages. Anecdotal evidence suggests that positive effects are expected for academic

---

[1] Accounts that take an economic perspective to the university as an organization include Borooah (1994), Brennan/Tollison (1980), Brown (1997, 2001), Ehrenberg (1999), Garvin (1980), Hoenack/Collins (1990), James/Neuberger (1981), and Toma (1986).

[2] Most of the existing economic literature on universities focuses on US institutions. While the analysis is conducted in a rather abstract fashion, a link to phenomena observed in reality is essential. The German university system will serve as the source of practical insight.

quality, while the negative effects mainly point to inefficient decision-making structures and avoidance of necessary reform steps. The core of the dissertation is the academic investigation of these propositions from a theoretical, a mathematical, and an empirical perspective.

The governance structures of the university cannot be analyzed without taking into account the internal workings of the university, i.e. the economic agents of the university, their preferences, and their interactive relationships. The explanation of the rationale for the existence of the governance mechanisms of the university and the economic evaluation of their effects can only be performed on the basis of a systematic presentation of the organizational behavior of the university.

Three key questions guide the research process throughout the course of this dissertation:

1. What is the theoretical explanation for the existence of participatory governance structures in German universities?

2. What are the effects of this particular governance system on the university?

3. How should an optimal governance system of the university be designed and what are the requirements for the implementation of an optimal governance system for the university?

The claim of this dissertation is to deliver theoretically valid results and to derive implications for practice. The different parts of this thesis are linked by an overarching question that implicitly drives the research interest of this dissertation: How could the institutional and organizational framework in which universities operate be improved?

1.3 Methodological Approach and Outline

A broad research program as outlined by the three research questions requires a comprehensive methodological approach. From a methodological perspective, the dissertation adheres to the following research process: An observation from the real world is abstracted and analyzed within a certain research paradigm of existing theories. On the basis of deductive logic, inferences are drawn to explain the observed phenomenon within a theoretical framework. These theoretical insights provide the starting point for the empirical validation of the theoretical conclusions. The result of the empirical studies feeds back into the theoretical body and possibly requires the adaptation of the theoretical framework.

Following this process, the dissertation is divided into three parts, each consisting of two chapters. Parts I and II are concerned with theoretical analysis, and part III provides the link to the real world. The three parts can be regarded as self-contained, independent pieces of work. The cross-references between the chapters as well as the underlying research questions compose the storyline of this dissertation by linking the three parts into a comprehensive study of faculty participation in university governance. Faculty participation is regarded as the right of faculty members to take certain decisions in the university or to influence their outcome.[3]

In part I, the theoretical foundations of the dissertation are outlined and then applied to the university. The analysis follows the tradition of the research paradigm of the New Institutional Economics (NIE). Principal-agent theory and governance theory constitute the framework for the examination of the internal organization of the university and its governance mechanisms. At its core, principal-agent theory is concerned with the study of delegation relationships, and governance theory provides a set of mechanisms for alleviating potential conflicts that arise in such relationships. In the university, both of these concepts play an important role, so that these reference theories provide a sensible starting point for the economic analysis. Chapter 2 presents the economic tools that are applied in chapter 3. The first part of the dissertation can thus be regarded as the application of economic theory to the university. The analysis results in a set of propositions that show how economic theory predicts the university to function. From a methodological viewpoint, the hypotheses are derived through

---

[3] Faculty participation is thus an intermediate decision-making system, located between faculty determination, where faculty members make all the decisions in the university, and management determination, where the university manager holds all decision rights.

1.3 Methodological Approach and Outline

deductive reasoning by applying general economic theory to a particular type of organization, the university.

Part II of the dissertation seeks to explain the effects of faculty participation in university governance by illustrating them in a mathematical model of university decision-making. This model is the first of its kind to address the question of who should hold authority over university decisions - the university management or faculty members. By explicitly expressing the assumptions on the preferences and benefits of the economic agents in mathematical notation, an understanding of the interdependencies of the actions of the economic agents is generated. Within part II, chapter 4 provides an overview of economic modeling in general and presents previous models that were built to examine aspects of university organization. Chapter 5 presents the economic model concerned with decision-making in the university on the basis of reference models on strategic intra-firm delegation.

In part III of the dissertation, the link is established between theory and the real world with an empirical study on university governance in Germany. Based on a series of expert interviews, qualitative empirical data is collected and analyzed in order to describe and explain the effects of faculty participation in university decision-making in Germany. Chapter 6 provides a brief insight into the methodology of empirical research with a focus on the methods applied in the context of the research objectives. The research process is illustrated, including the design and conduct of data collection and data analysis. The results of the interpretation of the extracted information are presented in chapter 7. From a methodological point of view, both deductive as well as inductive logical reasoning are applied. The propositions derived in part I and the insights provided by the mathematical model in part II are the starting point for the design of the empirical research process in part III. On the basis of the data collected and the information extracted, relationships between the factors are identified. In order to generalize the results, inductive inferences are drawn, illustrating how the statements derived from the selected cases are applicable to universities in general.

As the final step to answering the research questions outlined above, chapter 8 synthesizes the implications from parts I to III into a conclusive statement. It provides policy implications as well as an outlook on further research that can be conducted in the field of university governance.

This thesis seeks to generate new knowledge about the inner workings of the university and its governance and decision-making structures from a positive as well as a normative methodological standpoint. The description of the governance structures (positive methodology) is complemented by an analysis of how they should be designed in order to improve the organizational framework of the university (normative methodology). Ultimately, this dissertation is a further contribution to an economically founded discussion of how the university of the 21st century should organize.

Part I
The Theoretical Analysis

2 A Survey of Theoretical Frameworks

2.1 Introduction

The economic analysis of the university is carried out in line with the currently dominating research paradigm in economic theory, the New Institutional Economics.[1] As NIE was developed in the context of the firm, an understanding of the original economic concepts is essential in order to identify the differences between the firm and other organization such as the university. On this basis, the established theories can be expanded to incorporate the special characteristics of the university where required.

The following sections therefore outline the theoretical foundations of the New Institutional Economics and two bodies of theory belonging to its research program: Principal-agent theory and governance theory. An exhaustive presentation of NIE and of its research branches would go beyond the scope and focus of this dissertation. The following discussion is of theoretical nature and deliberately does not bear reference to the university in order to keep apart general theory and its application to the university. The latter follows in chapter 3.

2.2 The Foundations of New Institutional Economics

2.2.1 *Introduction*

The core of the New Institutional Economics is the economic analysis of the design of institutions and the effects they have on the behavior and interactions of economic agents. Based on the decisions of individuals, NIE seeks to explain the functioning of markets, organizations, and political systems. Institutions are defined as any kind of regulation system, i.e. formal and informal, explicit and implicit rules that influence the actions of the different economic agents (Homann/Suchanek (2000), p. 118; Mantzavinos (2001), p. 83). Examples of insti-

---

[1] Kuhn (1969) pioneered the term 'paradigm' in his account on the philosophy of science. A paradigm refers to the set of practices that define a scientific discipline during a particular period of time. In essence, it tells the researchers what is to be studied, the questions that are supposed to be asked, how these questions are to be formulated, and how the results of scientific investigations should be interpreted.

tutions are markets, legal regulations, organizations, decision-making hierarchies, incentive contracts, etc. (Erlei et al. (1999), pp. 23-27).

Institutions have been a focus of the economic science since the times of Adam Smith and David Hume.[2] In Europe scholars such as Carl Menger, Ludwig von Mises and Friedrich August von Hayek influenced economic thinking during the late nineteenth and throughout the twentieth century.[3] They established what has been termed the Austrian School of Economics, a school of thought concerned with the emergence of institutions. In Germany, a related approach was developed by the Freiburg economists Walter Eucken and Franz Böhm.[4] With the objective of building a new economic order for Germany in mind, they were interested in the effects of rules and institutions.[5]

The term 'New Institutional Economics' was originated by Oliver Williamson (1975). Its foundations are attributed to Ronald Coase and his seminal papers (Coase (1937, 1960)), Hayek's writing on knowledge (Hayek (1937, 1945)), and Chandler's history of industrial enterprise (Chandler (1962)). The NIE research paradigm draws on a set of basic assumptions that are discussed in the following section.

2.2.2 Four Basic Assumptions of NIE

According to Lakatos' notion of the philosophy of science, a paradigm consists of four elements: Basic assumptions, auxiliary hypotheses, and positive and negative heuristics that guide the research program (Lakatos (1974), pp. 89-140). The four basic assumptions that underlie the research paradigm of New Institutional Economics and that define the way research is conducted within NIE are outlined in the following.[6] These assumptions provide the implicit basis for the economic analysis of the university and the economic model in chapters 3 and 5, so that

---

[2] See for example Smith (1776) and Hume (1739).
[3] See for example Menger (1871, 1883), von Mises (1933, 1949), von Hayek (1960, 1973).
[4] See for example Eucken (1947, 1952), Böhm (1933), and Böhm et al. (1937).
[5] For a detailed historical overview, see Erlei et al. (1999), pp. 27-40.
[6] See Erlei et al. (1999), pp. 52-55 for a complete overview of the elements of the NIE paradigm.

2.2 The Foundations of New Institutional Economics

it is important to clarify their implications at this point (Erlei et al. (1999), pp. 51-55).[7]

1. Methodological individualism

    Methodological individualism builds on "[...] the simple fact that all social interactions are after all interactions among individuals." (Arrow (1994), p. 3). Decisions, actions, and the impact of institutions are analyzed from the perspective of the individual, his preferences, and his actions. With the application of the methodological individualism, the analysis of the behavior of collective bodies such as groups, organizations, states, or entire societies can be performed on a new level since the interaction problems of the individuals within the respective unit are taken into account. This individualistic perspective builds on the insight that "[o]rganizations do not have preferences, and they do not choose in the conscious and rational sense that we attribute to people." (Jensen (1983), p. 327). The rise of the methodological individualism constitutes a reversal from the formerly widespread notion of treating the firm, or any collective unit, as a 'black box'.

    Methodological individualism should not be mistaken as a concept that makes individualistic behavioral predictions. In general, the economic science does not offer any conjectures of how a certain event influences the behavior of one particular person. The relevant research dimension is always the representative behavior of the average individual in a certain situation (Erlei et al. (1999), pp. 5-6, 53).

2. Individual utility maximization and opportunism

    Each economic agent is assumed to possess a set of personal preferences. Through decisions and actions he strives to maximize the utility that he derives from the satisfaction of his preferences (Wolff (1999), pp. 136-137). Utility can be derived from a great variety of objectives that do not necessarily have to be tangible or self-interested.[8]

---

[7] For a detailed presentation of the main elements of the NIE, see for example Erlei et al. (1999), North (1990), Richter/Furubotn (2003), and Williamson (1975).

[8] For example, the act of donating money to a good cause can increase the utility of the donor if his preferences are altruistic.

In order to be able to quantify utility, a joint measure must be found. In economics, this measure is monetary because "[...] the condition that there is some monetary amount that would compensate for a change of circumstances holds widely for many of the most common kinds of business decisions." (Milgrom/Roberts (1992), p. 35)

Opportunism enforces the concept of utility maximization. An opportunistic actor is assumed to behave strategically in his pursuit of utility, implying that he is prepared to act against the interest of other players if this is to his personal benefit. By incorporating opportunistic behavior into the NIE framework, moral or ethical behavior is no longer assumed to be exogenously given. Instead, it must be achieved through appropriate motivation and coordination mechanisms (Wolff (1999), pp. 140-141).

3. Rationality

The individual is commonly assumed to be a rational player. "The 'model of man' underlying [...] organizational economics is that of the self-interested actor rationally maximizing their own personal economic gain." (Donaldson/Davis (1991), p. 51). Rationality assumes that the individual seeks to fulfill his desires by estimating the expected utility of different alternatives and by comparing them with each other in order to find the one yielding the highest utility. According to Laver (1997, pp. 23-25), there are only two ways not to behave rationally: The first is to be counter-rational, i.e. to choose an alternative or an action that is known to yield lower utility than some other alternative or action. The second way to be non-rational is to behave recklessly by consciously refusing to evaluate the outcome of an alternative or an action.

The rationality assumption does not imply that individuals are perfectly rational. Due to the limited information processing capacity and the uncertainty of future events, individuals make imperfect rational decisions (Wolff (1999), pp. 138-140). The concept of imperfect, or bounded rationality, was first studied by Simon (1955, 1957) and has recently found its way into the formal models of mainstream economics (see for example Rubinstein (1998)).

4. Incomplete contracts
From an economic point of view, a contract can be regarded as an agreement or a set of promises between two or more parties to carry out a certain transaction. Whether or not such a contract can be regarded as complete has important implications for the analysis of the contractual relationship.

In NIE, complete contracts are assumed to be infeasible due to the bounded rationality of individuals that prevents the prediction of future contingencies with certainty.[9]. This implies that a contract that tells an economic agent exactly what to do in all states of the world cannot be written (Schmitz (2001), p. 2; Shleifer/Vishny (1997), p. 741).

Transaction costs lie at the core of the contracting problem. They include costs such as thinking about all possible information and states of the world, negotiating the terms and conditions, and writing the contract in a fashion that allows third-party verification. These costs prohibit writing long-term complete contracts (Hart (1995), pp. 679-680; Shleifer/Vishny (1997), p. 741). The contracting notion in NIE therefore turns away from the Arrow/Debreu (1954) framework of complete contracts which relied on complete information and perfect rationality. Rather, NIE is based on the notion of incomplete concepts. At best, contracts can be regarded as comprehensive, implying that they build on all observable information and need not be revised, renegotiated or completed (Holmström/Tirole (1989), p. 68). In some situations, however, not even comprehensive contracts can be written because the main parameter of the contract may change in the future, making renegotiation beneficial.

In general, contracts can be of formal (i.e. enforceable by a third party), or informal nature. Informal contracts have also been termed 'relational

---
[9] This notion was first discussed by Williamson (1975, 1985).

contracts'.[10] Baker et al. (2002) define that "[...] a relational contract can be based on outcomes that are observed by only the contracting parties ex post, and also on outcomes that are prohibitively costly to specify ex ante." (p. 39). In line with Hayek (1937, 1945), relational contracts make use of situation-specific knowledge and can be adapted as new knowledge becomes available. Since they cannot be enforced by third parties, relational contracts have to be self-enforcing, implying that they are especially applicable in long-term relationships where the value of future benefits provides sufficient incentives to both parties not to renege on the contract.

In sum, these four basic assumptions of the New Institutional Economics research paradigm constitute the 'homo oeconomicus'. The homo oeconomicus refers to an analytical construct, consisting of a set of simplifying presumptions that enable the economic analysis of human behavior (Williamson (1996), p. 6). Contrary to recent criticism, the homo oeconomicus does not depict a pessimistic model of man, but constitutes a tool of economic analysis (Wolff (1999), p. 133).

2.2.3 The Research Branches of NIE

Three interrelated research branches have developed on the basis of the underlying assumptions of NIE: Transaction cost economics, property rights theory, and agency theory (see Picot (1991) for this classification).[11] This dissertation predominantly draws on the principal-agent framework since it is especially applicable for analyzing the internal organization of the university. In the following, only a brief overview is given of transaction cost theory and property rights theory. Principal-agent theory is discussed in greater detail in section 2.3.

---

[10] The concept of relational contracts was first described by Macneil (1974), and was introduced into organizational economics by Williamson (1976) and Goldberg (1976).

[11] These three fields relate to the study of market institutions. The NIE paradigm can also be considered as a cornerstone for the analysis of institutions in politics, which has come to be known as New Political Economy, Rational Choice Theory, or Public Choice Theory. The discussion of this field of NIE lies outside the scope of this dissertation. The groundbreaking works in rational choice theory are attributed to Downs (1957), Buchanan/Tullock (1962) and Olson (1965). See Laver (1997) and Shepsle/Boncheck (1997) for an overview.

1. Transaction cost theory

    Transaction cost theory starts with the basic question why firms exist and why economic transactions are organized through them (Coase (1960)). The term 'transaction costs' was first used by Arrow (1969), who defined them as the "[...] costs of running an economic system." (p. 48). The objective of transaction cost theory is to analyze how economic transactions can be organized in a cost-minimizing way, depending on the nature of the transaction (Williamson (1975, 1985, 1986, 1996)).

    Transaction cost theory identifies two extreme alternatives of organizing transactions: Markets and hierarchies (Robbins (1990), p. 313). Organizational structures can help to reduce transaction costs between economic agents because they serve as a substitutive contractual setting, allowing for long-term contracts and for governance mechanisms that mitigate opportunistic behavior (Williamson (1985), pp. 30-32).[12] Governance mechanisms are necessary because even writing an ex-ante efficient contract does not necessarily imply that the transaction will be optimally executed ex-post. In order to determine the most efficient institutional arrangement, the costs and benefits of using hierarchies versus markets have to be evaluated (Erlei et al. (1999), p. 182. See also Williamson (1991)).

    In summary, transaction cost theory is concerned with the study of transactions and the choice of the optimal organizational setting and ex-post governance mechanisms. Frictions arise from incomplete contracts in which bounded rationality, uncertainty, and asset specificity are important drivers of the transaction-cost minimizing conditions.

---

[12] One important argument for the existence of the firm in the context of incomplete contracts and relationship-specific investments is the hold-up problem. The hold-up problem refers to a situation in which the contracting parties face post-contractual opportunism by the other party. When both parties have to make relationship-specific investments which cannot be contracted due to the incompleteness of contracts, then a situation can arise where neither party actually makes the necessary investment, thus reducing the welfare of both parties. Alternatively, the hold-up problem refers to a situation where one party to the contract is forced to accept a disadvantageous change in the terms of the contract after an investment has been sunk. The party forced to accept the worsening of the conditions has been 'held up'. The term was first originated by Williamson (1975, 1985) as opportunistic behavior.

2. Property rights theory

Property rights are defined as the right to use an asset, the right to change its form or substance, the right to earn income from it, and the right to sell or rent the asset (Furubotn/Pejovich (1972), pp. 1139-1140). Based on Coase (1959, 1960), two strands of property rights literature evolved: The classical form, emphasizing the context that shapes and changes property rights, and the modern form with a focus on ownership and incentive structures (Kim/Mahoney (2005), p. 224).[13] At the core of modern property rights theory lies the hold-up problem that is inherent in relationship specific investment (see footnote above).

As an extension of the classical insights from property rights theory, Grossman/Hart (1986) and Hart/Moore (1990) ask the question of optimal asset ownership. In equating ownership rights to residual control rights, they go beyond the notion of Alchian/Demsetz (1972), who propose that ownership is the right to residual income. By taking into account the allocation of property rights, the corresponding ex-ante investment incentives, and the respective bargaining positions, a consistent theory of firm integration is derived.

To sum up, property rights theory studies the allocation of ownership rights and their institutional effects. The objective is to derive an ex-ante efficient property rights assignment in order to minimize ex-post conflicts over the distribution of the benefits. Problems arise from vaguely defined property rights, negative externalities, and vested interest which impede the evolution of efficient ownership allocations.

Transaction cost and property rights theory provide the theoretical context for discussing the third research of the New Institutional Economics, the principal-agent theory. While it is related to and draws on the insights of transaction cost

---

[13] The earliest works in classical property rights theory are attributed to Alchian (1965, 1969), Alchian/Demsetz (1972, 1973), Cheung (1968, 1969, 1970), Demsetz (1964, 1966, 1967), Davis/North ((1971) and Furubotn/Pejovich (1972, 1973, 1974). Modern property rights theory follow the seminal papers by Grossman/Hart (1986) and Hart/Moore (1990).

and property rights theory, the focus of agency theory lies on the problems that arise in delegation relationships between the principal and the agent.

2.3 The Principal-Agent Framework

2.3.1 Introduction

Since its first accounts due to Spence/Zeckhauser (1971) and Ross (1973), the theory of agency has developed into two directions. Both normative and positive agency theory are essentially concerned with "[...] the contracting problem between self-interested maximizing parties and both use the same agency minimizing tautology [...]" (Jensen (1983), p. 334).

Normative principal-agent theory, also called contract theory, follows a mathematical approach to studying the nature of incentive contracts that determine the hierarchical interactions within and between organizations. The focus lies on the ex-ante design of the optimal contract under different informational structures and under various organizational settings.[14]

Positive agency theory, on the other hand, generally follows a non-technical, empirical methodology. Based on the belief that an organization is best defined as a nexus of contracts, it concentrates on aspects of the contracting environment and tries to explain the organizational mechanisms for controlling agency problems. Positive agency theory is more closely related to the theory of the firm, addressing questions such as the allocation of decision and control rights, the role of residual claims, the degree of vertical integration, and asset ownership.[15] The focus of the following discussion lies on the normative part of agency theory since this will be relevant for the analysis of the internal organization of the university in chapter 3.

---

[14] The earliest accounts of normative agency literature include Mirrlees (1976), Harris/Raviv (1978), Holmström (1979), Harris/Townsend (1981), Grossman/Hart (1983).

[15] The seminal papers on positive agency theory include Alchian/Demsetz (1972), Jensen/Meckling (1976), Fama (1980), Barzel (1982), and Fama/Jensen (1983a, 1983b, 1985). The fundamental question of the separation of ownership and control dates back to Adam Smith (1999, 1st edn 1776) and was taken up again by Berle/Means (1932).

2.3.2 Principals, Agents, and the Structure of Their Relationships

A principal-agent relationship is regarded as a bilateral relationship between two parties where the first party, the principal (she), delegates a task to the second party, the agent (he).[16] The principal hires an agent to perform a task on her behalf. The main reason for the division of tasks that is achieved through a principal-agent relationship is the expected gain from specialization (Smith (1999, 1st ed. 1776), pp. 110-117).

Principal-agent relationships are omnipresent in everyday economic life. They are as diverse as shareholder – manager, manager – employee, client – lawyer, parents – teacher, creditor – debtor relationships. The terms and conditions of delegation are formalized in a contract between principal and agent. "An agency relationship [arises] between two (or more) parties when one, designated as the agent, acts for, on behalf, or as representative for the other, designated the principal, in a particular domain of decision problems." (Ross (1973), p. 134).[17]

The central feature in principal-agent relationships is the contract, which can be regarded as "[...] a reliable promise by both parties, in which the obligations of each, for all possible contingencies are specified." (Macho-Stadler/Pérez-Castrillo (1997), p. 5). This definition includes all institutions that can influence and coordinate the behavior of the agent (Schweizer (1999), p. 6). The contract specifies the task the agent has to fulfill and the compensation he will get from the principal.

From the structure of the principal-agent relationships it is already evident that principal and agent will not necessarily have the same interests in their interaction (Jensen/Meckling (1976), p. 308). The next section illustrates the three key factors that complicate the relationships between principal and agent.

---

[16] Using the female pronoun for the principal and the male pronoun for the agent follows conventional practice in the literature and solely serves the purpose of verbally differentiating between the two players.

[17] The standard principal-agent model considers one principal and one agent. This simple model has been extended to incorporate multiple agents (team production), multiple principals (called common agency), multitask job design, and repeated interactions in a dynamic framework. See for example Holmström (1982) for a team production model, Dixit (1997) for a common agency model, Holmström/Milgrom (1991) for a multitask model, and Holmström/Milgrom (1987) for a dynamic agency model.

2.3.3 The Defining Elements of a Principal-Agent Problem

The utility-maximizing principal requires high performance on the task delegated while offering minimal payment to the agent. The agent, on the other hand, wants to maximize his compensation while exerting as little costly effort as possible. The agent therefore has an incentive for opportunistic behavior, i.e. actions that are to his benefit but detrimental to the principal.[18] This constitutes the basic conflict of interest between the principal and her agent. Consequently, the principal will structure the contract so that the agent's reward is higher for good performance than for bad performance (incentive-compatibility constraint).

A conflict of interest alone is not the decisive problem in principal-agent relationships. If the principal can observe the actions of the agent during their interaction, the agent would behave in the interest of the principal since the principal could otherwise refuse to compensate the agent. However, the fundamental assumption of principal-agent theory is that information is distributed asymmetrically, the agent being the informed party and the principal the uninformed party (Pratt/Zeckhauser (1985), p. 2).

It is intuitive that the joint occurrence of diverging interests and asymmetric information is the cause of the agency problem: Without diverging interests, the agent would reveal all private information he holds about his intentions and actions (Macho-Stadler/Pérez-Castrillo (1997), p. 6). Without asymmetric information, contracts could be written on the behavior of the agent rather than on his output. Such a contract would sufficiently motivate the agent to act in the interest of the principal since he would not receive his compensation otherwise.

---

[18] This refers to the basic assumption of NIE concerning the rational and opportunistic behavior of economic actors. See section 2.2.2 for a detailed discussion.

Yet, even under asymmetric information and in the presence of a conflict of interest, the principal could write an optimal contract if one of the following assumptions were to hold (Jost (2001), p. 21):

1. The output of the agent is solely determined through the agent's effort, i.e. there is no random influence in the 'production function' of the agent. In such a case, the principal could derive the precise level of effort from the observed level of output despite asymmetric information. She could thus contract the activities of the agent directly instead of only being able to contract the output of the agent.

2. The agent is risk neutral and has unlimited wealth. In such a setting, the principal can make the agent the full residual claimant of his effort by offering him a franchise contract that sells the cash-flow of the task to the agent in return for a lump sum payment or a fixed fee. Any residual profit above the franchise fee accrues to the agent.

In order to arrive at a situation where the strategic interaction of principal and agent becomes relevant, these two situations are ruled out. It is common in principal-agent theory to assume either the existence of random effects, or to presume that the agent is risk neutral and wealth-constrained, or entirely risk averse (Schmidt (1995), p. 19).

To summarize, the principal-agent problem is characterized by a bilateral relationship between principal and agent with the following three features: Firstly, the interests of principal and agent diverge, and subsequently there exists a conflict of interests in the principal-agent relationship. Secondly, information is distributed asymmetrically so that the principal cannot observe relevant characteristics and/or actions of the agent. And thirdly, either random effects prevent a contract contingent on behavior, or the risk aversion and wealth constraint of the agent prevent franchise contracts.

In general, principal-agent problems can be classified into two different categories, depending on the structure of private information (Salanié (1997), pp. 7-8). Private information can bear on what the agent does, i.e. the decisions he takes

2.3 The Principal-Agent Framework

and the actions he carries out, or on the type of the agent, i.e. his characteristics. Depending on the timing, two types of problems can thus be distinguished:

- Adverse selection
  Adverse selection problems arise when the agent holds private information about his characteristics before the principal-agent relationships is initiated.[19]

- Moral hazard
  Moral hazard problems arise when private information is gained after the relationship has been initiated, e.g. when the effort of the agent cannot be observed, or verified.[20]

In adverse selection situation, two strategies are available to mitigate the effects from asymmetrically distributed information. On the one hand, the agent can communicate his private information to the principal ex-ante (signaling). On the other hand, the principal can screen the agent by offering different contracts, thus motivating the agent to reveal his private information (Salanié (1997), p. 8).

The contractual mechanism for mitigating a moral hazard agency problem in normative principal-agent theory is an incentive contract contingent on a proxy for the unobservable action of the agent. It conditions on the observable and verifiable outcome of his efforts since the effort level is unobservable and non-verifiable. Comprehensive contracts aim at minimizing the diverging interests between principal and agent by giving the agent both an incentive to behave in accordance with the principal's preferences and insurance from the income risk (Holmström/Tirole (1989), p. 68). In contrast to complete contracts, comprehensive contracts do not condition on each and every contingency of the world.

Incentive contracts are one way of mitigating moral hazard incentive problems, but they face two key difficulties. Firstly, a performance measure that is highly

---

[19] Adverse selection in markets was pioneered by the seminal papers of Akerlof (1970) and Spence (1974). In organizational applications, the classic papers include Mussa/Rosen (1978), Baron/Myerson (1982), Hart (1983), Laffont/Tirole (1986, 1988, 1990).

[20] The seminal account on the moral-hazard problem stems from the insurance industry and was first discussed by Spence/Zeckhauser (1971). Other classical papers include Holmström (1979, 1982), Shavell (1979), Grossman/Hart (1983), and Sappington (1983).

correlated with the quality of the agent's actions has to be found. Secondly, the optimal structure of the performance-based compensation has to be designed. It is therefore "[...] problematic to argue that incentive contracts completely solve the agency problem." (Shleifer/Vishny (1997), p. 745).

Due to the incompleteness of contracts and the difficulty in designing optimal incentive contracts, another measure to mitigating agency problems comes into play. Governance structures address the post-contractual conflicts that arise from the bounded rationality and the opportunism of the economic agents (Ahrens (2002), p. 125). In the next section, the necessity of governance is explained and an overview is given of the different governance mechanisms developed to mitigate the agency conflicts in the firm. Understanding the origin of the governance discussion is a prerequisite for the discussion of the governance of the university that follows in chapter 3.

2.4 Governance Theory

2.4.1 *The Necessity for Organizational Governance*

Regardless of the type of organization in question, Hart (1995, p. 678) specifies two conditions that must be fulfilled in order for a governance structure to become necessary: Firstly, the presence of an agency problem, and secondly, the existence of transaction costs so that a complete solution of this conflict of interest through contracts is not feasible.

In section 2.3.3, an agency problem is defined as a principal-agent relationship complicated by asymmetric information and diverging interests. Agency problems are omnipresent in economic interactions, so that the first of the two conditions for the necessity of governance is easily satisfied.

The second condition for the necessity of governance structures depends on the contractual framework. If contracts were complete, the principal could simply specify the behavior to be realized by her agent, provide the agent with the optimal allocation of incentives and insurance for the required action, and expect the desired outcome. In the framework of incomplete contracts adopted by NIE,

2.4 Governance Theory

this is not feasible due to the difficulty of writing long-term contracts that are contingent on the relevant performance indicators and comprehensive in the sense that they do not need to be renegotiated.

In such a context, governance structures have a very specific role: They "[...] can be seen as a mechanism for making decisions that have not been specified in the initial contract." (Hart (1995), p. 680). Governance structures constrain the agent from pursuing his own agenda and from taking actions that are beneficial to himself but detrimental to the principal. Governance can be regarded as the sum of the mechanisms designed to act as checks and balances on agent behavior.

The question that remains unanswered is who implements and realizes governance measures. In general, any utility maximizing constituency has an incentive to engage in governance when the benefits of governance outweigh the costs of governance. Especially the residual claimants, i.e. those constituencies who do not receive a fixed share of the profit, will participate in governance since their payoff increases as agency costs decrease. In the corporation, the stockholder is considered to be the primary residual claimant. Other stakeholders such as creditors and employees can be regarded as partial residual claimants. In theory, both principals and agents have incentives to ensure that governance mechanisms are implemented (Brown (2001), p. 129). In reality, the costs of governance (time, effort, etc.) often lead to free-riding behavior on the governance efforts of the primary residual claimant or principal (Burkart et al. (1997), pp. 698-699).

In order to give an insight into how governance is effectively realized in the corporate world, the next section briefly presents the main governance mechanisms for solving the corporate agency conflict.

2.4.2 Mechanisms of Corporate Governance

Corporate governance measures mitigate the moral hazard agency problem between shareholders as the principal and the manager as her agent.[21] Shareholders essentially want to ensure that their funds are being optimally allocated in the firm and are not expropriated by the manager. "[C]orporate governance mechanisms are economic and legal institutions [...]" (Shleifer/Vishny (1997), p. 738). Due to its reference of governance mechanisms as institutions, governance theory plays an important role in the framework of New Institutional Economics (Erlei et al. (1999), pp. 193-225).

Corporate governance mechanisms are distinguished based on who the governing party is. Bonding mechanisms can be regarded as a form of commitment by the agent. In market mechanisms, the driving force of governance is the competitive pressure on the agent. Monitoring mechanisms refer to those mechanisms where one party checks on the performance of the other party, and both principal and agent can play the role of the monitor.[22]

1. Bonding mechanisms

    Bonding mechanisms refer to governance mechanisms that induce the agent to commit himself to good behavior. In the firm, one such mechanism is the use of debt which increases the risk of bankruptcy. The higher the debt level, the higher the risk of insolvency, and the higher is the manager's risk of losing his job. Consequently, the threat of liquidation encourages managers to show a high degree of effort and to run the firm as efficiently and effectively as possible.[23] The use of debt as a financing instrument serves as a bonding

---

[21] In addition to the classical principal-agent conflict between shareholders and management, there exist further agency problems in the corporations, e.g. between debtors and management, managers and employees, or among employees in team-production situations. Some of the mechanisms discussed in the following are also applicable to mitigate these problems. The focus of corporate governance measures, however, lies on the agency conflict between shareholders and management.

[22] Incentive contracts, including such elements as pay-for-performance, stock holding by management, and management option plans are often regarded as governance mechanisms in the literature. Under the definition of governance provided above, they do not qualify as a governance mechanism since these contracts are incomplete. Due to the incompleteness of contracts, corporate governance mechanisms become necessary in the first place.

[23] As a side effect, the use of debt also encourages active monitoring by lenders (Agrawal/Knoeber (1996), p. 377).

or commitment device, increasing the ex-ante credibility of the management not to engage in shirking or rent seeking (Hart (1995), p. 685).

As a second bonding mechanism, a high dividend payout can also have disciplining effects on management: The more profit distributed, the less cash flow is available to management for financing opportunistic or bad projects (Hommel/Pritsch (1997), p. 21).

2. Market mechanisms

Market mechanisms affect the behavior of management indirectly through market signals. Three markets play a role in corporate governance: The market for managerial labor, the market for corporate control, and the product market.

A manager who performs badly risks being dismissed, which is associated with a lower value of his human capital on the job market (Hommel/Pritsch (1997), p. 20). Internal competition also plays a role: "Lower managers perceive that they can gain by stepping over shirking or less competent managers above them." (Fama (1980), p. 293). Managers know that low firm performance makes them assailable from within and from without. This threat provides a motivation to act in the shareholders' interest and to show good performance.

On the market for corporate control, the risk of becoming a takeover target provides another incentive to the manager to act in the interest of the shareholder. If management failure leads to a low market valuation of the company, a new owner might be attracted by the prospect of achieving superior returns by acquiring the company. Following a change in ownership, management is usually replaced and the firm is restructured. In order to avoid becoming a take-over candidate and losing his job, a manager is motivated to increase shareholder value (Hommel/Pritsch (1997), pp. 26-28).

The third market that can have governance effects is the product market on which the firm operates. Competition between firms also poses a threat to incumbent management since a firm "[...] that does not minimize costs will eventually be driven out of the market." (Schmidt (1997), p. 191). The reduction of the profits for each competitor, resulting from effective competition, increases the probability that the firm will go into bankruptcy if its costs are too high. Leading a company into bankruptcy also lowers the value of the manager's human capital on the managerial labor market, which provides an incentive to keep the company profitable and competitive (Schmidt (1997), p. 193; Shleifer/Vishny (1997), p. 738).

3. Monitoring mechanisms

    Monitoring measures can be regarded as intervening and controlling mechanisms. Interventionary, or ex-ante, monitoring takes place before and during the agent exerts effort. Controlling or ex-post monitoring takes place after an agent has exerted effort. While ex-ante monitoring can be regarded as a corrective measure, possibly preventing bad actions, ex-post monitoring can only penalize the agent after he has already performed badly. Cont (2001) refers to ex-ante monitoring as supervision and to ex-post monitoring as auditing. In order for a supervisor to effectively influence the actions of the agent, he must have veto rights, i.e. the supervisor can be regarded to have ultimate control over the decisions the agent takes and the actions he pursues. The auditor, on the other hand, reports the wrongdoing of the agent, and thus influences the set-up in which the agent conducts his tasks in the future.

    In corporate governance, two monitor groups exist: The Board of Directors and large shareholders. Both types of monitoring can take the form of supervision or audit, depending on the allocation of rights to become involved in decision-making and on the intensity of monitoring activity. The Board of Directors has the task to review and approve the decisions of the management ex-ante and to monitor the consequences of these decisions ex-post (Hommel/Pritsch (1997), p. 23; Colesa et al. (2001), p. 29).

    On the other hand, large shareholders play an important role in corporate monitoring since the monitoring costs for small shareholders are usually higher than their expected gains from monitoring. Therefore "[...] only the large shareholders engage in monitoring." (Burkart et al. (1997), p. 698). Small shareholders rely on the control activities of large shareholders, effectively free-riding on their monitoring effort (Hommel/Pritsch (1997), p. 24).

Research on the effectiveness of corporate governance mechanisms has shown that usually no single mechanism is able to fully mitigate the agency problem (Hart (1995), pp. 681-686). Thus, in practice, they often appear together within a comprehensive governance framework.

2.5 Conclusion

Economic research conducted within the paradigm of the New Institutional Economics is concerned with the study of institutions and their effects on economic behavior. NIE builds on the principles of methodological individualism, opportunistic utility maximization, rationality, and the incompleteness of contracts. The research program of NIE has developed along three branches: Transaction cost economics, property rights theory, and principal-agent theory. In order to answer the research questions this dissertation has posed, principal-agent theory is most suitable as an analytical tool since it provides a systematic approach to studying the relationships between economic actors in organizations. A principal-agent problem is defined as a contractual interaction between principal and agent that is characterized by diverging interests, asymmetrically distributed information, and risk aversion.

In an incomplete contract framework, governance measures are identified as a mechanism to mitigate the agency problems. The different mechanisms developed in the corporate world are outlined as a reference point for the analysis of university governance. This will be the focus of the next chapter: The insights of NIE, principal-agent theory and governance theory are applied to the university. The objective is to derive implications about the rationale for the existing organizational structures of the university, and to examine the effects these governance structures have on university performance.

3 The University as an Economic Organization

3.1 Introduction

Organizations need effective governance systems in order to reach their objectives and to deliver high performance. In this regard, the university as an organization is no different. Compared to business firms, however, universities are different both in key characteristics and in their governance requirements.

Three questions arise in this context:

1. What are the defining elements of the university?

2. What is university governance and which measures can be observed?

3. What are the benefits and drawbacks of these measures for the university?

These three questions guide the structure of this chapter. Section 3.2 discusses the nature of the university, its output objective, its organizational characteristics, and its constituencies in order to generate an understanding of what a university is. Section 3.3 then analyzes the internal organization of the university with the methodological approach of principal-agent theory. On the basis of the principal-agent conflicts identified in the university, the governance system of the university is examined as a mitigation mechanism. Its merits in alleviating the principal-agent conflicts in the university are evaluated in section 3.4. Following this general account on university governance, the focus of section 3.5 lies on faculty participation in university decision-making as a mechanism of university governance. The impact this mechanism has on the university is studied, and its advantages and disadvantages are considered from an economic perspective.

This chapter is both theoretical and applied. It is theoretical because it abstracts from the phenomena observed in universities in practice. Hypotheses are derived from the economic theories outlined in the previous chapter by deductive logic rather than by inductive, evidence-based reasoning. On the other hand, the applied nature of this analysis stems from the application of economic theory to a new unit of analysis - the university. The economic methods and tools for analyzing organizational behavior are tested on the university.

3.2 The University as an Object of Analysis

3.2.1 Definition and Categorization

Two approaches can be distinguished to define what a university is: On one hand, the university can be characterized by its functions and products. On the other hand, it can be defined by a comparative assessment of its characteristics with those of other organizational forms. Both approaches contribute to a complete understanding of what a university is.

Perkins (1973, p. 3) defines a university as an institution of higher education that has four key functions: Teaching, research, service to society, and creating an ideal democratic community. The output of the university is regarded as "[...] the discovery, refinement, and transmission of knowledge [...]" (Bailey (1973), p. 130). Classic input factors of the university include labor, capital and property (Bolsenkötter (1976), p. 5; Stuchtey (1999), p. 3). Stegner (2000, p. 8) identifies four demands that universities face in general. Firstly, they provide skills and competencies to students. Secondly, they develop the current level of knowledge through innovation. Thirdly, universities preserve traditional knowledge, and lastly, universities legitimate the model of society in which they are embedded. Depending on the political system, governments place different weights on these four functions, so that diverse higher education and university systems have evolved.[1]

The comparative approach contrasts the university with other organizations such as expert associations, bureaucracies, service companies, or non-profit foundations (see for example Müller-Böling (1994)). The university is defined positively by the characteristics it has in common with other institutions, and distinguished negatively in terms of the features of these organizations it does not possess. Different models of university behavior, such as the collegial and the political model are also compared in order to discover the core of the organizational characteristics of the university (Garvin (1980), pp. 2-5). While this methodology

---

[1] See Stegner (2000) for a detailed overview of the historical development of the university and the university systems of different countries.

has yielded important insight and has helped to classify the university in the organizational taxonomy, the main conclusion is that the university is a combination of different stereotype organizational models. It shows the characteristics of a bureaucracy in some areas, while other areas are best characterized as a service company. No consistent definition of the university has been derived through this approach, but the complexity of the university is well illustrated through these attempts (see also Bailey (1973), Besse (1973), and Corson (1973) for detailed comparisons).

One common element in almost all definitions of the university is its non-profit character (Stegner (2000), p. 1). Non-profit organizations (NPOs) are subject to the non-distribution constraint, which implies that any surplus generated cannot be distributed to external parties (Hansmann (1980), p. 838). Thus, the university does not yield transferable, or alienable cash-flows.[2]

For the purpose of this dissertation, universities are defined as non-profit degree-granting organizations providing research, and undergraduate, graduate and post-graduate, teaching. Research can be regarded as the individual act of creating specialized knowledge by building upon existing implicit and explicit knowledge.[3] Teaching implies the transfer of explicit knowledge and abilities from faculty to students. This definition summarizes the key points that are relevant for the following analyses.

---

[2] Although there have been successful foundations of for-profit universities, these are mostly pure teaching institutions. The majority of the universities providing both research and teaching in Germany and the US are non-profit organizations under public or private sponsorship (Hochschulrektorenkonferenz (HRK) (2005); National Center for Education Statistics (NCES) (2001), p. 3). One example of a for-profit teaching university is the University of Phoenix, owned by the Apollo Group, Inc.

[3] Explicit knowledge is of objective nature, it can be priced without difficulty, and can therefore be transferred easily. Implicit knowledge, on the other hand, refers to the private, intangible knowledge of an individual. Consequently, implicit knowledge cannot be transferred without social interaction. Only when implicit knowledge is formalized can it be transformed into explicit knowledge (Osterloh et al. (1999), pp. 1248-1250).

3.2.2 Why Universities Exist as Organizations

One question that has not been answered so far is why the provision of higher education is realized through organizational structures rather than in a market setting. The rationale for the existence of universities in their current organizational form draws on transaction cost theory (see section 2.2.3).

Within transaction cost theory, a knowledge-based approach to explaining the existence of organizations has evolved over the past decade (Foss (2001), p. 1). In essence, this approach proposes that organizations exist because they have common rules and a common knowledge, which increase the efficiency of coordination and creation of new knowledge. As long as an organization can use knowledge more effectively than the respective members of the organization could use their knowledge individually in the market, its existence is justified (Osterloh et al. (1999), p. 1247f). Fundamental to the knowledge-based approach is the presumption that the primary input factor of the organization is knowledge. The second premise for the existence of an organization according to the knowledge-based approach is the existence of gains from specialization (Grant (1996), pp. 112-113).

From the two key products of the university, research and teaching, it is evident that knowledge is the decisive input factor of the academic production process. The specialization argument also holds for universities since faculty members are experts in relatively narrow fields of science and thus possess highly specialized knowledge. In order to offer the service 'teaching', faculty knowledge must be integrated into comprehensive degree curricula aimed at obtaining a degree. Individual professors, for example, usually cannot teach the entire curriculum due to the fact that their knowledge is specialized and limited.

In terms of the production of research output, knowledge integration is not necessarily required since conducting research is basically an individual process. Often, however, research projects are realized in teams, and research output results from the effective integration of specialized knowledge and analytical skills in these groups of researchers.

To sum up, a high degree of knowledge integration is needed to produce the products universities deliver, especially teaching. The decisive point is that the market cannot perform the necessary coordination more efficiently, since significant transaction costs would arise (e.g. cost of contracting with different professors, achieving the necessary standardization of curricula and degrees, etc.). In general, the market cannot "[...] create conditions under which multiple individuals can integrate their specialist knowledge." (Grant (1996), p. 112). Therefore, universities have emerged in organizational structures and persist as such in modern educational societies.

As much as a university may be comparable with a firm from the point of view of their existence, the university is a unique organization with particular characteristics and a special production process that influence the behavior of its agents. The next section outlines these special features of the university.

3.2.3 Special Characteristics of the University

Universities are organizations "[...] with two extraordinary characteristics: Its chief product - education - defies [easy] measurement, and its major staff members - professors - defy [easy] regulation." (Cowley (1980), p. 64). While this quote focuses on the complexity of measuring teaching, the observation is also applicable to research, the second main product of the university.

Both products of the university are difficult to evaluate because they cannot be measured adequately by input factors (e.g. number of professors, computers, books), nor by output factors (e.g. number of hours taught, number of degrees granted, number of pages written). Instead, outcome and impact indicators are more applicable for judging the quality of the products of the university. Outcome indicators such as type of publication, job finding rate of graduates, faculty salary development, academic prizes, patents registered, etc. evaluate the objective effects of output. Impact indicators such as faculty and student satisfaction, reputation of the university, etc. take into account the subjective effect of output (Schenker-Wicki (1996), pp. 59-60). The problem of measuring the quality of the university's products is complicated by the lack of functioning markets, which prevents the emergence of truly objective outcome and impact measures.

The first point Cowley makes in his quote on the nature of the universities is concerned with its products. The second source of complexity in the university lies in the academic staff. The academic production process is very labor intensive, and consequently the overall performance of the university and the quality of its products greatly depends on highly specialized and trained human capital (Oster (2000), p. 14).[4] Two special features characterize the academic production process: Academic freedom, and tenure or civil servant status.

Academic freedom grants faculty members a high degree of independence, autonomy and authority over decisions concerning the subjects and methods of their research and teaching activities. This implies that faculty members are under no obligation to accept orders concerning their research and teaching (Garvin (1980), p. 3; Mora (2001), p. 107; Tropp (2002), pp. 48-50). Although there are some constraints that have to be respected, e.g. teaching loads and core curricula, faculty is principally free to decide upon their research topics and the content of their lectures. In Germany, the freedom of research and teaching is guaranteed by article 5 of the "Grundgesetz" (German Constitution).

Tenure and the civil servant status of faculty can be considered as long-term labor relationships that can only be terminated in case of a crisis, such as the closing of an academic department or of an entire school.[5] In general, tenured faculty and civil servant professors are guaranteed employment independent of their academic performance in research and teaching.

As a result of the extremely specialized nature of academic production, the high degree of autonomy faculty enjoys over the academic production process and the job security provided to academic staff, the university is characterized by a high degree of decentralization and delegation (Tropp (2002), p. 36). Decisions concerning their personal research and teaching program are made by faculty directly, and the actual academic production process is carried out by faculty

---

[4] In Germany in 2003, 60,9% of all university costs accrued to personnel. See Statistisches Bundesamt (2003), p. 38.)

[5] There are a number of accounts that analyze the benefits and costs of tenure. See for example McPherson/Schapiro (1999); Brown (1997); Stuchtey (1999); Carmichael (1988); McPherson/Winston (1983); Ehrenberg et al. (1999);Bess (1998)). See section 4.3.4 for an overview of economic models dealing with tenure.

independently. Faculty members of the same field of science organize in academic departments that operate as largely autonomous units of the university. This decentralized structure is one of the reasons that the principal-agent theory as a theoretical framework for analyzing the university is applicable for the economic analysis of the university.

The discussion above already pointed out that the university's academic production process is very particular, thus preventing easy evaluation of the quality of the products of the university. These problems of performance measurement exist at the level of the individual faculty member, at the level of the academic department, and on a university-wide scale. Developing a concept of university performance, however, is important for evaluating the effects of governance mechanisms on the university. The next section therefore devotes some more thought to this issue.

3.2.4 The Concept of University Performance

The fundamental problem of measuring university performance is the necessity to reduce different outcome indicators into one easily quantifiable measure. The university has no equivalent of the profit function of the firm, and thus lacks an obvious performance measure such as profitability. Therefore, university performance has to be defined and a system of performance indicators needs to be created (Schenker-Wicki (1996), p. 104). The aggregation of this indicator system to one single measure could then be used to depict university performance. Such a procedure raises the questions of who defines performance and identifies the set of indicators, and of how the weighting and aggregation of the different indicators is assigned.

The lack of ownership in the university implies the absence of an "[...] authority-granting group [...] parallel to shareowners." which would streamline the university (Besse (1973), p. 108). Instead, the multitude of objectives intensifies the problem of performance measurement (Coelho (1976), p. 416).

The lack of ownership of the university and its non-profit status have another important implication in regard to the existence of a residual claimant. The residual claimant is the person or group that receives the residual profit, and is therefore interested in ensuring that the university is run as efficiently and effectively as possible (Alchian/Demsetz (1972), p. 782). Due to the fact that the typical university does not have a clearly defined owner and does not generate alienable cash-flows, the university lacks a natural residual claimant (Glaeser (2002), p. 2).

As a consequence of these impediments, so far, no standardized set of universally accepted indicators to measure university performance exists (Schenker-Wicki (1996), p. 169). In general, it is simply assumed "[...] that there is some overall measure of university performance or prestige and that each interest group benefits from an increase in this performance/prestige" (Brown (2001), p. 131). Prestige can be regarded as a signal for the overall quality of a university, and also incorporates reputational elements that are not included in the notion of quality (Ben-David (1971), p. 1; Vladeck (1976), pp. 94-96).[6] Brown (2001, p. 131) asserts that university reputation is a good signal of university performance since only universities with high performance are able to build a good reputation. The measure of the overall prestige of a university can be formalized as a function of the prestige of its individual departments, which depend on the quality and quantity of faculty members (Garvin (1980), pp. 22-24).

The notion of university prestige proposed by Garvin (1980), however, ignores the impact of management and governance structures as well as administrative university policy on the performance of the university. Therefore, for the purpose of this dissertation, the prestige function is adapted to depend on two aspects: Academic quality on the one hand and managerial professionalism on the other hand. Academic quality is determined through the quality of faculty output and the number of faculty members. Managerial professionalism summarizes how efficient and effective the university is run from a managerial perspective, including the quality and length of decision processes, the acceptance of decisions, the degree to which they are successfully implemented, and the efficiency and effectiveness of the administration.

---

[6] The concept of signaling was pioneered by Akerlof (1970), and Spence (1973, 1974). For a distinction between quality and prestige, see Gross/Grambsch (1974), pp. 100-101.

3.2 The University as an Object of Analysis

Academic quality and managerial professionalism are not substitutive 'inputs' to the prestige functions. Rather, a subsistence minimum of both academic quality and managerial professionalism is required. In the long run, university prestige can only be increased when both academic quality as well as managerial professionalism improve.

One important reason for employing prestige as the measure for university performance is that most of the other possible performance measures are positively influenced by the prestige of the university: The quality and quantity of students a university attracts, the amount of research grants and other external financing it secures, the infrastructure and working environment the university can provide will all increase with raising prestige. A higher prestige also positively impacts the financial viability of the university.[7] Therefore, the measure 'prestige' can be regarded to subsume the relevant performance dimensions. A precise mathematical formulation of the prestige function of the university does not exist and its development lies outside the scope of this dissertation. For the purpose of the following analyses, it will suffice that university performance is a function that is positively influenced by academic quality and managerial professionalism.

All constituencies of the university benefit directly or indirectly from a higher prestige. For university management, the overall institutional prestige is the essential measure of personal success. Faculty benefit from the prestige of their departments because it raises their personal reputation and market value, and students have better job opportunities when graduating from a university with high prestige (Garvin (1980), pp. 22-24).

The next section turns to the different constituencies of the university and analyzes their preferences in order to understand their role in the university governance framework.

---

[7] A recent example from Germany illustrates this point: The University of Mannheim has developed a strong reputation for excellence in economics and social sciences over the last decade. As a consequence, the university has received the largest private donation a German university has ever been endowed with: The Hasso-Plattner-Förderstiftung bestowed ten million euros for the expansion of the library (University of Mannheim (2003)).

3.3 The Relevant Players in the University and Their Conflicts

3.3.1 *The Players*

The university consists of a number of constituencies, or stakeholders. In order to derive predictions about their behavior and to understand their role in the governance of the university, their preferences must be examined. In this section, the following two questions are answered:

1. What are the constituencies in the university?

2. What are the preferences of these constituencies?

Two basic categories of constituencies can be distinguished: Internal and external stakeholders. The distinction is based on the academic production process. Only those constituencies that are involved in the production processes of the university are considered as internal constituencies. With this definition, faculty, university management, financial sponsors, and administrative staff can be classified as internal stakeholders (Corson (1973), p. 163). Administrative staff is assumed to comprise all non-academic staff. Faculty, university management, and administrative staff contribute human resources to the academic production process, and the financial sponsors provide the financial funds.

External constituencies are alumni, cooperation partners, employers of graduating students, the local community, society in general, and the state (Stegner (2000), pp. 75-83). The constituency of the students is difficult to classify since students can be considered as customers, input, or output factors (Besse (1973), p. 120; Bolsenkötter (1976), pp. 5-6). For the purpose of this dissertation, students will be treated as customers, therefore belonging to the group of external constituencies.

For the analysis of the effects of internal university governance on the university, only the internal constituencies are relevant. The principal-agent relationships between external stakeholders are of no concern for university governance, and the relationships between external and internal constituencies lie outside the

3.3 The Relevant Players in the University and Their Conflicts

scope of the dissertation. Thus, all external stakeholders are excluded from the following analysis.

Two caveats of the analysis need to be mentioned before proceeding: Firstly, the following characterization of the players is necessarily based on assumptions about prototypical representatives. Not every member of the constituency will behave in the way described below. The degree of abstraction, however, is necessary to facilitate the analysis. It is assumed that "[...] membership in a constituency prevails over individual idiosyncrasies as a predictor of behavior." (Ortmann/Squire (2000), p. 379). Secondly, the evidence cited refers mostly to studies on the preferences of faculty and students of management science, economics, and psychology. Therefore, some limitations to generalizing the insights to all academic fields may apply.

3.3.2 The Preferences

This section analyzes the tasks and preferences of the four internal constituencies faculty, university management, financial sponsors, and administrative staff.

Faculty members have the task of producing the two primary services of the university, research, and teaching. Faculty activities also include administrative duties. Due to their importance in the academic production process, faculty can be regarded as the elite employees of the university (Glaeser (2002), p. 32). It is often assumed that elite employees are motivated primarily intrinsically, i.e. more by work itself than by monetary incentives (Küpper (1997), p. 434; Tropp (2002), pp. 46-49). An empirical study by Hartmann (1998) confirmed that faculty members in management science and psychology are in fact intrinsically motivated by a working environment that allows for autonomy and personal responsibility (pp. 88-89). Consequently, faculty does not necessarily regard work as unpleasant per se, but casual evidence suggests that the monetary interests of faculty are undeniable (Coupé (2003), pp. 2-4; Holmström/Milgrom (1991), pp. 32-34). The utility of a prototypical professor therefore increases with the degree of academic freedom, and with job security, professional reputation, and salary (Garvin (1980), p. 23; Ortmann/Squire (2000), p. 380).

The university manager is responsible for the planning and initiation of academic and administrative university policies. In the context of corporate management boards, Williamson (1963) identifies compensation, job security, power, prestige, professional excellence, and status symbols as the typical objectives of management. Since these objectives are related to overall university prestige, it can be assumed that the utility drivers of university management give rise to a prestige-maximizing behavior.

As pointed out in section 3.2.4, university prestige depends on both academic quality and managerial professionalism. The question arises whether different types of university managers will have different preferences for overemphasizing one of the two elements of university prestige over the other. Judging from casual evidence in Germany and the US, a university manager is either a former faculty member with a full academic education or a former professional business manager. While the former is likely to have a preference for high academic quality, the latter may have a preference for managerial professionalism and the financial bottom line of the university. Precisely differentiating the underlying preference structures of different university management types lies outside the scope of this dissertation as this requires an in-depth study on its own. For the purpose of this analysis, it is assumed that academic quality and managerial professionalism are equally important to a university manager since an improvement in both is needed to increase university prestige.

As the third group of internal constituencies, financial sponsors provide the funds for the operation of the university. Due to the non-distribution constraint of the non-profit university, their return is not monetary and must be interpreted according to the type of financial sponsor. Financial sponsors are a heterogeneous constituency that can be differentiated into governments, research fund granting agencies, and individual and organizational donors. In general, financial sponsors demand the efficient and effective use of the resources provided and derive utility from the performance of the university, i.e. from its prestige. Each group, however, has slightly different preferences. Governments prefer the universities to deliver service to society, while fund granting agencies are interested in the success of the particular project they are supporting. Donors can derive intrinsic benefit, i.e. the utility received from the knowledge of contributing to a good cause, and prestige benefit, i.e. the utility received from the publication of the donation (Harbaugh (1998a), p. 277; Harbaugh (1998b), pp. 271-272). Corporate donors are interested in receiving certain privileges (e.g. preferred recruiting). Their utility from the donation depends on the degree to which corporate demands are met by the university. In general, donors may also get a benefit from impacting university policy through their donation, e.g. by becoming a member of the supervisory board (Glaeser (2002), p. 6).

Administrative staff ensure the administrative and organizational infrastructure needed for conducting research and teaching and are responsible for implementing university policies (Gomez-Mejia/Balkin (1992), p. 923). Comparable to the corporate employee, the administrative staff seeks compensation, job security, personal reputation, and perks, manifesting their status and power (Ortmann/Squire (2000), p. 380; Williamson (1963), pp. 1032-1033).

The four internal constituencies of the university are not isolated players, but interact in principal-agent relationships. The next section identifies the hierarchy of principals and agents in the university and discusses the nature of the principal-agent problems that exist.

3.3.3 The Conflicts between the Players

As described in section 2.3, principal-agent relationships are characterized by the delegation of a task from the principal to the agent. Principal-agent relationships are situation-specific since any economic actor can be a principal or an agent depending on the perspective (Tropp (2002), 37; Meyer (2003), p. 52). Figure 3.1 illustrates the constituencies within the external and the internal context of the university. Within the university, a cascade of principal-agent relationships can be identified.

Financial sponsors can be regarded as the top-level principals of the university since they provide the necessary funds to the university. Financial sponsors delegate two tasks to university management as their agent: Firstly, the task of

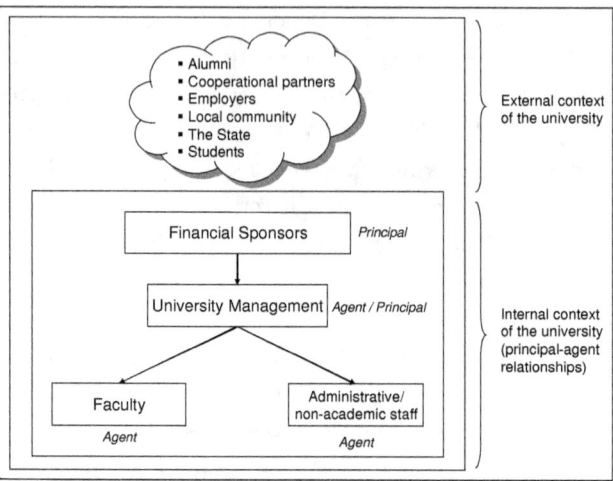

Fig. 3.1 Principal-Agent Relationships in the University

efficiently allocating the funds provided across the university, and secondly, the task of organizing and providing research and education. University management in turn serves as a principal for administrative staff and faculty. The task of implementing university policy is delegated to administrative staff, and the task of providing research and teaching is delegated to faculty.[8]

Thus, three internal principal-agent relationships exist in the university: Financial sponsor – university management, university management – administrative staff, and university management – faculty.[9] The nature of the principal-agent relationships and the existence of conflicts are discussed in the following by drawing on the insights of principal-agent theory as presented in section 2.3. The focus lies on the relationship between university management and faculty since this re-

---

[8] This hierarchy could be expanded to an even finer level of detail by including the different organizational units and subunits of a university's administration, or by incorporating the research and teaching assistants as the agents of faculty. For the purposes of this analysis, the three-level structure is sufficient.

[9] The relationship between faculty and administrative staff cannot be regarded as a principal-agent relationship since it is not characterized by an explicit hierarchical delegation of tasks between the two players.

lationship can be regarded as the decisive agency relationship in the university due to the importance of faculty in the academic production process (Gomez-Mejia/Balkin (1992), p. 923).[10]

1. Financial sponsor – university management

    Financial sponsors delegate the day-to-day tasks of running the university to management while retaining ultimate control over university policy. From the analysis of preferences it can be derived that both financial sponsors and university management are interested in increasing the prestige of the university. Conflicts of interest, however, may arise over the best university policy to reach the common objective. Furthermore, university management also strives for personal benefits, which may come at the expense of the university's prestige since funds may be expropriated.

    The university manager has a certain degree of discretion over the initiation and ratification of university policy, so that an agency problem can be assumed to exist. It is characterized by a moral-hazard situation where the principal cannot observe the actions of her agent. The output of the university management's effort is difficult to evaluate due to a lack of a clearly defined measure for university prestige. Furthermore, the financial sponsors cannot directly observe the development of the university and depend on university management for the relevant information. This also complicates the agency problem.

2. University management – administrative staff

    On the second level of the principal-agent hierarchy, university management serves as the principal of administrative staff. The task of implementing and executing university policy is delegated to the administrative staff. Interest alignment between management and administrative staff is only partial: To the degree that the benefits of the administrative staff are related to the institutional prestige of the university, the administrative staff are inte-

---

[10] The notion that faculty members are the most interesting and distinctive constituency of the university is also reflected in the growing literature on faculty behavior, see for example Backes-Gellner/Sadowski (1991); Tullock (1993); Ortmann/Squire (2000).

rested in enhancing the prestige of the university. The pursuit of personal benefits such as higher salary, lower workloads, and other perks, however, may diverge from the interests of the principal, so that a conflict of interest is predictable. Since university management cannot observe the actions of administrative staff and can only judge their performance based on the outcome, information is distributed asymmetrically. Administrative staff maximize their personal utility and may choose the satisfaction of their own objectives over their duty to increase the prestige of the university, for which they have been hired by the principal.

The agency problem faced by university management and administrative staff can thus be regarded as a moral-hazard problem between a principal who cannot observe the actions of her agents. The principal-agent-problem is complicated by the fact that the outcome of the work of administrative staff is not easily evaluated due to the lack of a precise measure of performance for the university (see also section 3.2.4).

3. University manager – faculty

   In their principal-agent relationship, university management and faculty are likely to have diverging interests over how to fulfill the functions of the university. The conflict of interest between university management and faculty is twofold: Firstly, the problem of overall low performance, i.e. low quality research output or shirking on teaching duties, may arise. By compromising their academic tasks, faculty can take off time for outside activities such as consulting.

   Secondly, differing opinions about the optimal allocation of faculty time between teaching and research can lead faculty to pursue activities that are in their private interests but do not advance the objectives of the university. The principle of academic freedom enhances this potential conflict as it provides faculty members with the right to independence in their academic decisions. Therefore, this second situation does not imply that faculty is shirking in terms of the total level of effort provided. From the perspective

3.3 The Relevant Players in the University and Their Conflicts

of the university manager, however, a certain mix of research and teaching is regarded as optimal and any deviation thus creates an agency problem.[11]

The discussion above suggests the conclusion that the academic production process is characterized by a multitasking context.[12] Faculty not only has to decide how much effort to exert but also how to allocate it to the different tasks. Research and teaching can be considered as substitutive, yet inseparable tasks (Holmström/Milgrom (1991), p. 25). Faculty has to choose doing either research or teaching, and these activities cannot be simply performed by separate faculty members due to the positive externalities that arise from incorporating research results into the preparation of teaching.[13] The principal may prefer available faculty time to be divided evenly between research and teaching, whereas faculty may strive more for research reputation than for excellence in teaching, since research has a greater influence on income, career moves, etc. than teaching (Backes-Gellner (1989), p. 62; Stegner (2000), p. 45).

Due to the specific nature of academic production, university management cannot identify the true effort of faculty (McCormick/Meiners (1988), p. 426). Even through constant monitoring it would be difficult to determine faculty effort since a professor observed staring out the window could be shirking, or thinking hard (Alchian/Demsetz (1972), p. 786). The persisting conflict of interest and the unobservability of effort characterize the relationship between university management and faculty as a moral hazard principal-agent problem (Tropp (2002), p. 38).

---

[11] For example, faculty may spend too much time on research and outside engagement, neglecting teaching duties such as preparing good lectures, developing new teaching methods, or incorporating current research results into classes while still fulfilling the contractually specified minimum teaching load (Tropp (2002), p. 49).

[12] Multitask principal-agent relationships were first studied by Holmström/Milgrom (1991). Further developments include Dewatripont et al. (2000), Feltham/Xie (1994), Holmström/Tirole (1993), Itoh (1994), Olsen (2000), and Sinclair-Desgagné (1999).

[13] While some universities (e.g. in the US) employ faculty only for teaching, the majority of the universities in Germany or the US have not adopted this separation (Tropp (2002), p. 51).

Where effort is unobservable, university management has to rely on observing the output of faculty effort. While this output may be determined fairly easily in terms of quantity (e.g. how many written pages, how many supervised theses and dissertations, how many courses taught), quality is difficult to evaluate. The highly specialized nature of academic production requires experts for monitoring the quality of academic output. Another difficulty in evaluating faculty output is the long period of production in research and the time lag between the completion of research output and its impact, i.e. its publication in a journal or book (McCormick/Meiners (1988), p. 426). The moral hazard agency problem in the relationship between university management and faculty is thus aggravated by the special characteristics of the academic production process and of faculty output (Tropp (2002), pp. 38-45).

In addition to the difficulties of performance measurement and the multitask moral hazard situation, the existence of multiple agents, or team production is the third special characteristic in the relationship between university manager and faculty. Team production arises when "[...] 1) several types of resources are used and 2) the product is not a sum of each cooperating resource" (Alchian/Demsetz (1972), p. 779). The problem with team production is that output is difficult to assign to each input factor by observation only. The creation of university prestige can be regarded as a team production since all internal members of the university, including faculty, are involved in the process.[14]

Generating a high level of university performance is the result of the joint effort by all constituencies of the university. Faculty can be assumed to play a special role due to their dominance in the academic production process.

---

[14] Team production arises in research and teaching. Research is often conducted in teams, so that the incentive for the team members to shirk is higher than when working individually. Team production in research refers to an inter-team problem without direct effects on the university. The performance of the university is influenced indirectly when team production problems lead to lower overall research performance. In teaching, team production arises since faculty jointly teach a certain degree curriculum. The effort exerted and the output of teaching cannot be attributed to individual faculty members, possibly leading to free-riding behavior.

3.3 The Relevant Players in the University and Their Conflicts

Although all faculty members benefit from increased university prestige, its team production nature leaves room for free-riding on the effort of others.

To sum up, university management and faculty face a moral hazard problem complicated by:

- Difficulties in distinguishing and evaluating outcome.
- Inseparable, but substitutive tasks, leading to a multitasking problem.
- Faculty team production in the generation of institutional prestige.

3.3.4 Synopsis

The analysis of the university with the principal agent framework provides an insight into the relevant constituencies of the university, their preferences, and their diverging interests. As a result, three moral hazard principal-agent problems are identified between the financial sponsor and university management, between university management and administrative staff, and between university management and faculty.

Principal-agent problems can be regarded as a cost to the university since they lower organizational performance. Minimizing agency conflicts and the costs associated with them therefore increases the overall prestige of the university. All internal constituencies have an interest in mitigating the agency-problems as they benefit from increasing prestige.

Within the context of governance theory, section 2.4 pointed out that in order to alleviate agency problems, governance structures play an important role. In essence, they aim at ensuring the optimal performance of all economic agents with the objective of increasing overall university prestige. The next section discusses possible governance mechanisms in the university.

3.4 University Governance as a Mitigation Mechanism

3.4.1 *Definition of University Governance*

From an economic perspective, governance comprises all mechanisms that serve to mitigate the conflicts of interests that arise between different constituencies of organizations (Brown (1997), p. 442).[15] University governance refers to the principles of the allocation of control and decision rights in the university (Bowen (1969), p. 518). Brown (1997) describes the problem of university governance as a system of mechanisms for monitoring the agents of the university in order to reduce agency costs and to increase organizational effectiveness. Governance structures are regarded as a substitute for the lack of residual claimants in the university.

In the non-economic literature on the university, the term 'university governance' is used differently. De Groof, Neave et al. (1998) relate governance to the relationship between the federal or state government and the university (p. 9). Here, university governance is regarded as the interaction between external private or public financial sponsors, and the management of the university.

Cowley regards academic governance "[...] as a structure that performs the function of social control" (Cowley (1980), p. 6). In this notion, governance includes both policy control and operational control, implying that the term 'governance' is not used as rigorously in the general literature on the university as in economic discussions of governance (compare for example Brown (1997, 2001), Masten (2000), and McCormick/Meiners (1988) with Barrett (1963), Bowen (1969), Dearlove (2002), Pfnister (1970), and Yoder (1962) in regards to the use of the term 'university governance').

However, governance can be distinguished from management: Management refers to running the university, i.e. the initiation and planning of decisions and the organization of their implementation. Governance, on the other hand, relates to the control of the operations of the university, i.e. the ratification of decisions and the monitoring of their implementation by the internal constituencies of the

---

[15] See section 2.4 for an in-depth discussion of organizational governance.

university (Fama/Jensen (1983a, 1983b)). For the discussion of university governance, the restrictive meaning of the term 'governance' is applied as this relates to the notion of governance used in economic theory.

The core of university governance can consequently be described as a system of mechanisms for mitigating the agency problems in the university (Brown (2001), pp. 130-131). The basis for this definition of university governance is provided by corporate governance. This suggests taking corporate governance as a starting point for the discussion of university governance. In the next section, the governance mechanisms applied in the context of the corporation are tested for their applicability to the three principal-agent conflicts in the university.

3.4.2 The Applicability of Corporate Governance Mechanisms in the University Context

There are two main reasons for starting an analysis of university governance with a comparison to corporate governance. Firstly, there exists no unified theory of university governance, so that the theory on corporate governance is used as a theoretical background. Secondly, it has been pointed out that "[n]on-profit firms have governance problems that resemble the problems in for-profit firms, but are often far more extreme" (Glaeser, 2002, p. 54). This suggests that the application of corporate governance may yield insights into the differences between corporate governance and non-profit governance in general and university governance in particular.

The analysis proceeds along the following lines: First, the nature of the agency problem in the corporation and in the university are compared. In a second step, the applicability of the corporate governance mechanisms discussed in section 2.4.2 is tested.

The nature of the principal-agent problems that the university faces are different from the shareholder – manager agency problem in the corporation. The financial sponsor as the ultimate principal of the university does not act as a residual claimant of the university since she does not aim to secure her return on investment through governance. Instead, the financial sponsor strives to ensure that the funds she provides to the university are optimally allocated. This agency problem is therefore less severe than the owner – manager corporate agency problem since the effects of bad performance of the agent are not as detrimental to the principal since she bears no personal monetary consequences.

The principal-agent problems between university management and administrative and non-academic staff, and between university management and faculty are similar more to the firm-internal manager – employee moral-hazard problem than to the shareholder - manager problem of the firm. Baker et al. (1988) note that "[...] managers in hierarchical organizations, from supervisors to CEOs and board of directors, are not principals in the sense usually modeled in the principal agent literature. Principals in this literature are 100% owners of the alienable residual claims to cash flow [...]. In hierarchies, substitutes for residual claims are allocated to managers in the form of incentive contracts and various direct-monitoring provisions." (pp. 613-614).

From this, two conclusions follow. Firstly, both the financial sponsors in their role as the ultimate principals of the university, and university management as the intermediary principal have lesser incentives to engage in monitoring than the shareholders in a corporation. The incentives of the principal in the university are weakened by the fact that they are not true principals in the sense of full residual claimants and by the difficulty of monitoring with unclear performance measures. Secondly, the governance measures used to alleviate the manager – employees agency conflict are primarily direct monitoring provisions, so that it can be presumed that monitoring mechanisms are most promising in mitigating the agency problems between university management and faculty, as well as between university management and administrative/non-academic staff.

Turning to the corporate governance mechanisms discussed in section 2.4.2, it is evident from the above analysis that the use of dividend policy, the market for corporate control, and block ownership monitoring are inapplicable in the university context due to the non-profit status of the university and the lack of clearly specified owners (Brown (1997), p. 442; Brown (2001), p. 130; Glaeser (2002), pp. 2-3).

3.4 University Governance as a Mitigation Mechanism

Of the bonding mechanisms, debt structure is a feasible governance mechanism in those university systems that allow universities to take on debt.[16] The debt structure can help to alleviate the moral-hazard problem between financial sponsors and university management since it provides an incentive to university management to run the university as efficiently as possible to ensure that interest payments can be met.[17]

Turning to the market mechanisms, the external labor market for faculty, university managers, and administrative staff can mitigate the agency problem between financial sponsors – university management, and between university management – administrative and faculty. In theory, low performance increases the risk of being dismissed. At least for faculty and staff, however, the labor markets have more of a rewarding than a sanctioning function since the majority of university staff are civil servants or enjoy tenure and cannot be fired as a result of low performance. Thus, there is no sanctioning market mechanism. In the case of good performance, the labor market has upside potential because excellent staff will be offered attractive positions at other universities. As a result of this asymmetry in the rewarding and sanctioning function, the impact of the academic labor market on the mitigation of the agency problem is ambiguous. Where staff is mobile and competition for the best talent is high, the labor market may provide incentives to show high performance. In more static markets, this incentive effect is less pronounced because of the limited sanctioning threats the labor market poses.[18]

---

[16] As set forth in the laws governing the universities, public German universities are not allowed to incur debt, whereas private universities and universities operating as a "Stiftungsuniversität" (public law foundation) may do so. In the US, private and public universities may raise debt and use this financing instrument frequently (Ward (1999), p. 1; Williams (2003), p. 30).

[17] In the US, universities often use tax-exempt debt to finance their projects. During the stock boom in the 90s, return on investment was higher than interest rates. The stock market baisse in the last years, however, caused problems for some universities as they had to pay interest that was not covered by earnings from their investments. Especially small universities had to raise tuition and fees to compensate for the losses (Williams (2003), p. 30).

[18] The question also arises of the incentive compatibility between the labor market and the objective of the university. The academic labor market tends to reward faculty with research excellence more than those with distinctive teaching or administrative skills. Therefore, the labor market may motivate faculty to show high performance especially in research while the principal may prefer a more equal allocation of time and effort between research and teaching.

The effects of product competition on the market for higher education and research can also be observed in universities and can help to mitigate all three agency problems prevalent in the university. Although they are non-profit organizations, universities compete with each other for private and public funds, for the brightest students, and for the most renowned faculty.[19] As they strive for the fulfillment of their mission, they have to adapt to the changing requirements of their financial sponsors, customers, and the market environment.

The governance effectiveness of competition between universities necessarily depends on the degree of competitiveness. Bohren/Odegaard (2003) assert that product markets can only unfold their governance potential if markets are fully competitive, which cannot be assumed for the education and research markets. In Germany, universities cannot simply go bankrupt and bad performance is more likely to go undetected due to a lack of an objective performance indicator. Therefore, the governance impact of competitive markets is even smaller for the university than for a corporation.

Turning to the monitoring mechanisms, the institution of a Board of Trustees is a feasible measure in the governance of the university, which is widely observed in practice in Germany and the US. The task of the board members is to monitor the performance of the university and to intervene in cases where the decisions and actions taken by the constituencies of the university do not benefit the university. Supervisory boards combine elements of ex-ante as well as of ex-post monitoring. The difficulty university boards face is the information problem between them and university management since board members need to be very well informed about the activities of the university in order to be effective monitors. The amount and quality of their information depends on transparent and frequent communication of information from university management, which may not be in the best interest of university management. This is a problem that all supervisory boards face, but

---

[19] In Germany, universities have to accept the assignment of students for the largest degree courses through a central agency. For more specialized degrees, they can select students according to their own criteria. The debate about granting universities full rights to select students is ongoing and tends toward further liberalization, so that competition for students will certainly increase. In the UK and the US, fierce competition for students can already be observed.

in the university it is complicated by the complex products of the university, and by the lack of performance criteria and market feedback (Brown (2001), p. 131). Furthermore, the question arises who should appoint university board members in absence of clearly defined owners of the university.

In summary, the traditional bonding and market-based governance mechanisms that help mitigate the agency problems in corporations are only partially applicable in the university.[20] The reason for this lies in the nature of the principal-agent problems the university faces, which are different from the shareholder – manager agency problem of the corporation for which corporate governance mechanisms were designed. The agency problems in the university are more similar to the corporate agency problem between manager and employee, for which only monitoring can provide a governance-based solution. Consequently, ex-ante and ex-post monitoring mechanisms such as the allocation of decision-making rights and decision control appear to be the most suitable governance mechanisms to solve the agency problems in the university.

Hence, the question arises who has an incentive to be the monitor in the university. The two principals in the university - financial sponsors and the university manager - are not the owners of the residual cash flows because there are no residual cash flows in the university. Therefore, "[...] there are no residual claimants to provide the monitoring role normally played by the shareholders." (Brown (2001), p. 130). Thus, monitoring must be performed by 'substitute' residual claimants including the university manager, faculty, and possibly other constituencies.

This argument is also reflected in a formal model on non-profit governance by Glaeser (2002). He comes to the conclusion that the preferences of employees in non-profit organizations tend to be more important than in the for-profit firm. Due to the special characteristics of the non-profit organization, employees of NPOs and in particular the elite employees possess a large degree of influence on decision-making. It is proposed that the increase in stakeholder monitoring through participative decision-making can partially compensate for the lack of a

---

[20] See also Glaeser (2002) for a discussion of the main governance differences between for-profit firms and non-profit organizations.

residual claimant. Efficient organizational governance structures in non-profits thus often result "[...] in different interest groups maintaining control over different types of decisions." (Brown (2001), p. 131). In the university, faculty is the most important human resource in the academic production process. It can be expected that faculty plays an important role in university governance alongside the university manager. In practice, the participation of faculty in the decision-making of the university is widely observed (see sections 1.2 and chapter 7 for more detailed discussions). The analysis of the participative decision structures of the university and its relevance as a governance mechanism is the focus of the next section. A rationale for faculty participation is given and the effects on the performance of the university are examined.

3.5 Faculty Participation as a Measure of University Governance

3.5.1 Introduction and Definition

Faculty participation is defined as the transfer of authority from the principal (university manager) to the agent (faculty). Authority results from "[...] the right to decide on specified matters." (Aghion/Tirole (1997), p. 2). It can be distinguished into formal authority and real authority. Formal authority refers to the theoretical right to decide, and real authority implies having effective control over a decision. Formal and real authority need not necessarily be collocated. Figure 3.2 gives an overview of the different forms faculty participation in university decision-making can take. Endowing faculty with formal authority is regarded as the strongest form of faculty participation since faculty can then take decisions independently or delegate real authority to another constituency.

In Germany, the respective state laws on higher education grant faculty participation rights through the academic body of the senate. The rights range from consultation rights to formal faculty authority depending on the type of decision. In the US, surveys conducted among universities reveal that there exist intermediate types of decision-making such as joint decision-making or faculty consultation rights (American Association of University Professors (AAUP) (1971);

3.5 Faculty Participation as a Measure of University Governance

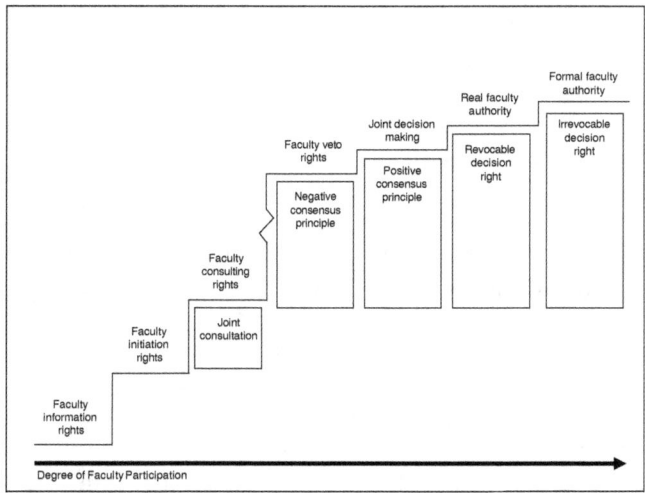

Fig. 3.2 Forms of Faculty Participation

Kaplan (2002)). Where faculty is involved in decision-making, the decisions are usually taken by groups of faculty members, or by academic bodies consisting of different constituencies, including faculty representatives. Therefore, faculty decision-making can be considered as a result of collective action.[21]

The decisions that are regularly made in the university can be classified into different decision groups. McCormick/Meiners (1988), Masten (2000), and Brown (2001) identify eight broad areas of decision-making in universities:[22]

---

[21] Casual evidence from Germany and the US supports this conjecture as faculty takes decisions in committees such as the academic senate or department councils instead of transferring their authority to a single faculty member. For Germany, see e.g. "Bayerisches Hochschulgesetz" (Bavarian State Act on Higher Education), for the US, see e.g. Kaplan (2002).

[22] This list can provide only a schematic overview. Depending on the university systems, not all of these decisions are made on the level of the university. For example, in Germany, final decision power over appointment and tenure decisions for public and publicly accredited universities usually still lies with the State Ministries for Higher Education. The salary level for faculty at public universities is also determined almost entirely through state laws. In recent years, both federal as well as state laws have been reformed, giving the university more autonomy over such decisions. See chapter 7 for a more detailed discussion.

- Faculty status (decisions on appointments, reappointments and renewals, promotions, tenure, and dismissal for cause).

- Academic operation (decisions on curriculum, degree requirements, and the academic performance of students).

- Academic planning and policy (decisions on the types of degrees offered, establishment of new educational programs, admission requirements, relative staff sizes of disciplines, and programs for buildings and facilities).

- Selection of administrators and department chairs (decisions on the president, the academic deans, and the department chairmen).

- Financial planning and policy (decisions on faculty salary scales, individual faculty salaries, short range budgetary planning, long range budgetary planning).

- Professional duties (including decisions on average teaching loads, teaching assignments).

- Organization of faculty agencies (decisions on specification of department committees, membership in department committees, authority of faculty in government, specification of senate committees, and membership in senate committees).

- Student activities (decisions on academic discipline, specification of student extracurricular rules, extracurricular behavior, and student role in institutional government).

The question that arises from the existence of participative decision-making structures in the university is why this particular structure is prevalent in the university, but cannot be observed in most other organizational contexts (exceptions include the Yugoslav firm and the Israeli kibbutz, see James/Neuberger (1981), p. 585). The key proposition raised by this dissertation is to regard faculty participation in university decision-making as a mechanism of governance that addresses

3.5.2 The Rationale for Faculty Participation as a Governance Mechanism

Faculty members have an interest to engage in governance because they can be considered as substitutive residual claimants of the university. This status is due to the nature of academic employment and motivation as faculty reputation, job security, and research funds all depend on the overall prestige of the university. The creation of university prestige is the result of a team production process, so that faculty members have an incentive to ensure that other agents are not shirking on their tasks (Brown (1997), pp. 449-451).

There is a second dimension to the argument in favor of residual claimant status, which is especially relevant in university systems where faculty remuneration depends on the financial well-being of the university and is not regulated or guaranteed by law.[23] The financial situation of the university and faculty salaries thus depend on the team performance of all of the agents of the university. Assuming that wage increases with faculty seniority, faculty wants to ensure that the university is capable of meeting future pay rises. This is especially relevant for compensation schemes which reward faculty at a wage below marginal product in early years and above marginal product late into academic career.[24] As a result of such a wage structure, faculty becomes a residual claimant of the financial well-being of the university and has an incentive to play an even stronger role in the university governance system.

---

[23] In Germany, the wage structure of the civil servant professors of public universities is based on a law called "Bundesbesoldungsgesetz" (Federal Compensation Law). Due to this law, the range for individual salary negotiations or university-specific wage structures was very limited, and salary increased with seniority instead of performance. With the reform of this law in 2002, performance-based compensation components have been introduced and the seniority principle has been waived for all newly appointed professors. Private universities are not subject to this law and can set salaries according to supply and demand.

[24] This kind of pay system is often observed in academia. Young, highly productive faculty are often paid little, while older faculty whose productivity is declining are paid more, especially after tenure has been granted (Brown (1997), p. 451). Also see Lazear (1979); Lazear (1981).

The argumentation to regard faculty participation in university governance as a governance mechanism draws on the expected effect of faculty participation on monitoring the constituencies of the university. By maintaining control over selected types of academic decisions, faculty improves the monitoring of faculty members, i.e. faculty rewards or sanctions the performance of peers. Most of the decisions faculty members take follow indirectly from the observation of the performance of other faculty members. For example, a decision concerning the expansion (or closure) of an academic department or cluster can be interpreted as a form of indirect performance monitoring of the affected faculty members. However, decisions about reappointment or promotion of faculty members as well as decisions on performance-based compensation, if applicable in the specific university, can be regarded as a form of more direct monitoring.[25] In lack of elaborate faculty performance appraisal systems, monitoring by fellow faculty members can thus provide effective checks and balances on faculty performance.

Monitoring faculty performance requires expert knowledge that the university manager and academic staff do not possess to the same extent as faculty. Therefore, faculty can effectively monitor the performance of other faculty members better than any other constituency. Without faculty participation, university manager and administrative staff would not necessarily be able to correctly evaluate the performance of faculty due to the specialized nature of academic production (see section 3.3.3). Compared to a situation without faculty monitoring, faculty participation in decision-making can therefore alleviate the agency conflict between university manager and faculty by providing effective monitoring that is able to detect and correctly evaluate low performance.

The rationale for the existence of faculty participation in university decision-making is thus based on governance considerations. The particular nature of its governance mechanism raises the question what the general effects of faculty participation on the university are beyond the mitigation of the agency problem

---

[25] An example of such a direct monitoring function of faculty participation is the mid-term evaluation that is required in the process of obtaining a "Habilitation" (post-doctoral lecture qualification) in Germany. A number of universities require such an assessment by a faculty committee, which can in fact lead to the termination of a "Habilitation" process if the performance of the candidate is not satisfactory.

3.5 Faculty Participation as a Measure of University Governance

between university manager and faculty. Faculty participation can be assumed to have other effects on the university, both beneficial and detrimental. These benefits and costs need to be analyzed in order to come to a conclusion regarding the net impact of faculty participation on the university and its organizational performance.

The focus of the next two subsections lies on the presentation of theoretical arguments for positive and for negative effects of faculty participation on university performance. These effects are discussed from a theoretical economic perspective. Empirical observations from the German university system follow later in chapter 7.

3.5.3 Positive Effects of Faculty Participation

Faculty participation in university decision-making positively influences university performance in three ways: Firstly, through the monitoring effect, secondly, by enabling effective decision commitment of the university manager, and finally, through improved information processing.

1. Monitoring effects

    When faculty participates in decision-making, the decisions faculty take can have the effect of monitoring fellow faculty members, university management, and administrative staff. Due to their superior knowledge in academic issues, faculty members are assumed to be best capable of monitoring faculty performance, the academic decisions of university management, and the implementation of academic policy by the administrative staff.

    The quality of monitoring will improve especially in faculty self-monitoring. Due to the fact that the output of faculty is difficult to evaluate (see section 3.2.3), university management can only correctly evaluate the performance of faculty at prohibitively high costs. If university management were to increase its monitoring intensity, this could provide a disincentive for faculty to show high effort. Faculty could not be certain that their performance would be judged accurately, so that showing high performance becomes less worthwhile. On the other hand, the probability that shirking is detected is lower when the university manager is the only monitor of faculty.

In order to adequately monitor faculty performance, specific knowledge is necessary which only faculty members of the same academic discipline possess. Faculty self-monitoring is therefore more accurate and should induce faculty members to show higher performance (Bainbridge (1997), p. 30, 40).[26]

These arguments strengthen the notion that faculty participation in university decision-making can be regarded as a governance mechanism for alleviating the moral-hazard problem between university management and faculty. Increased quality of expert monitoring induces higher faculty effort in research and teaching. As a by-product of faculty monitoring, university management and administrative staff are also monitored by faculty. Faculty is also interested in an efficient and effective university management and administration in order to increase university prestige.

2. Commitment effects

The second argument for positive effects of faculty participation in university decision-making relates to the commitment problem of university management. The beneficial effect of faculty participation becomes evident from analyzing the opposite organizational setting. In a decision-making system without faculty participation, all decisions would be made by the university manager. While faculty might have information or consultation rights, from the perspective of faculty, decision-making is autocratic. Autocratic decision-making in this context implies that there are no checks and bal-

---

[26] Aghion/Tirole (1997) distinguish between monitoring models and initiative models. In monitoring models, performance of the monitored party increases with the intensity of monitoring. In initiative models, the opposite is assumed. While monitoring detects bad performance ex-post and is thus beneficial, it is assumed to lower the incentives of the agent to exert high effort at all ex-ante. Transferring this notion to the university, faculty self-monitoring is expected to have usual monitoring effect, i.e. more monitoring means higher effort. In the case of management monitoring, the initiative model seems to hold, implying that higher monitoring effort by the university management results in lower overall effort of faculty.

ances on the behavior of the decision-maker, i.e. the autocrat has unlimited control over decisions.

In economics and politics, the benefits and costs of autocratic governance have been analyzed in detail (see e.g. Olson (1965); Boncheck/Shepsle (1997); Arrow (1963)). One of the main disadvantages of autocracy has come to be known as the commitment problem. This describes the inability of the autocrat to restrain himself from making decisions that are to his own personal benefit, but come at the expense of the common.[27] The consequence of autocracy is the hold-up problem, i.e. the under-provision of specialized investment in production technology, human capital, etc. by the agents. The hold-up problem leads to an outcome where all economic actors are worse off.[28] The core of the commitment problem in the decision-making context refers to "[...] the inability of those with unconstrained authority to commit to exercising that authority non-opportunistically." (Masten (2000), p. 1).

Autocratic, management-dominated decision-making in the university can result in lower performance by faculty since university management cannot commit ex-ante not to make decisions ex-post that are detrimental to faculty (e.g. higher teaching loads, closure of departments or degree programs, stricter performance measurement and more monitoring, etc.).

Faculty participation in university decision-making can provide a solution to the commitment problem: If faculty is involved in decision-making, university management is deterred from taking decisions that are detrimental

---

[27] A comparable issue is raised in team production theory where no team member can commit ex-ante not to shirk on his team members when ex-post profit is divided according to ex-ante sharing rules (see for example Blair/Stout (1999)).
[28] See section 2.2.3 for a discussion of the hold-up problem.

to faculty but beneficial to management.[29] As a consequence, faculty has stronger incentives to show higher relationship-specific effort. Granting authority to faculty in areas which are important to faculty and where faculty members are informed assures faculty members that their interests are being taken into account (Brown (1997), p. 458). This is assumed to increase the incentive of faculty to incur relationship-specific investment.

The argument builds on the welfare disadvantages that arise to faculty when decisions are implemented without their consent. Under autocratic decision-making, it is more likely that decisions are taken that are detrimental to faculty because the autocratic university manager will pursue her own personal interests. When faculty are able to participate in decision-making, the probability of being overruled and the costs associated with it decrease (Masten (2000), pp. 5-6).

In more qualitative terms, faculty participation is assumed to translate into a working environment that strengthens the incentives for high academic effort. Ackroyd/Ackroyd (1999) conclude that "[i]f professional academics have too little influence, [...] then their capacity for intellectual progress is also seriously threatened." (p. 181). Due to the dependence of the academic production process on the performance of faculty, the elite employees of the university, committing the university management to respecting the preferences of the faculty members by granting them decision rights is therefore expected to have a positive effect on academic quality.

---

[29] Two other mechanisms besides faculty participation might mitigate the commitment problem: Management reputation, and the possibility of faculty to inflict punishment on university management in case of unfavorable decisions (Glaeser (2002), p. 4; Masten (2000), p. 9). Both mechanisms work only imperfectly. Reputation may only solve the commitment problem if the time horizon is sufficiently long and if the (long-term) gains from honoring commitment are larger than the (short-term) benefits of defecting. The end game problem in finite relationships approaching the end of their interaction horizon is also a major constraint on reputational enforcement (Milgrom/Roberts (1992), pp. 261-7). The arguments against the functioning of punishment relate to the necessity of collective action. In order to deter management from breaching its commitment, the threat of multilateral action must be credible. However, a group of individuals is not necessarily able to credibly threaten with collective action even if group members share common interests (Olson (1971), pp. 1-3).

3. Information advantages

At the core of both the monitoring and the commitment effect lies the informational advantage faculty has over university management in certain areas (Brown (1997), p. 442). In the university, the principal (i.e. university management) hires faculty primarily to perform research and teaching. As a by-product of these activities, faculty acquires information and knowledge on many university issues, thus creating an informational advantage over other university constituencies in some fields.[30]

In order to mitigate the information asymmetry in decision-making which arises when the decision-maker has less information than other individuals and/or groups in the organization, one mechanism is the delegation of authority to those party/parties with superior information (Jensen/Meckling (1992), p. 253). The better the quality of available information is, the better decision-making will be (Masten (2000), p. 12).

In the context of the use of knowledge in economic decision-making and social planning, Hayek (1945) discovered that "[...] practically every individual has some advantage over all others because he possesses unique information of which beneficial use might be made, but of which use can be made only if the decisions depending on it are left to him or are made with his active co-operation" (p. 520).

The prospect of authority delegation to faculty can be expected to solve the problem of asymmetrically distributed information between the university manager and faculty because it sets incentives for the provision of information. If developing and maintaining expertise is a costly activity, only those constituencies who possess some authority over corresponding decision areas will invest into the generation of specific information. "The need to economize on [information] costs suggests that a potential expert is more likely, ceteris paribus, to acquire and accumulate knowledge in a [...] domain

---

[30] For some areas, e.g. operational or financial decisions, university management can be assumed to possess superior knowledge due to their managerial experience.

in which he possesses procedural prerogatives or other forms of structural authority [...]" (Gilligan (1993), p. 336).

Faculty participation is the mechanism that selectively allocates authority over certain decisions to faculty. The university thus benefits from the informational advantage faculty possesses and the improved quality of decision-making this leads to.

To sum up, the positive effects of faculty participation in university decision-making are based on the increased monitoring, the mitigation of the commitment problem that the university management faces, and the improvement of the quality of university decision-making. Especially as a result of the higher academic quality, faculty participation in decision-making is expected to positively influence the overall prestige of the university. As pointed out in section 3.5.2, a complete assessment of faculty participation in university decision-making is not limited to the discussion of its merits, but must also critically evaluate possible drawbacks. The next section is therefore concerned with an analysis of the two main disadvantages of faculty participation.

3.5.4 Negative Effects of Faculty Participation

One seemingly obvious cost of faculty participation is that it requires faculty time that is not available for the fulfillment of their actual tasks, research and teaching. Such a proposition presumes that faculty spends less time in decision-making under autocratic, management-dominated governance. The concept of influencing activities, however, suggests that faculty will spend time in governance activities even without formal decision-making authority (Milgrom/Roberts (1992), p. 272, see also Milgrom (1988) and Milgrom/Roberts (1988)). In a setting where faculty members do not enjoy formal decision rights, they will try to influence university management in its decision-making process with the objective of realizing personal benefits.

Faculty is thus expected to commit time to university governance under both autocratic and participatory decision-making systems. Without decision authority, faculty members spend time monitoring peers, management and administrators, and then informally advising the university manager on the best decision alternative based on their private knowledge and expertise and personal incentives. When having participation rights, faculty members show the same monitoring effort, but then take the respective decision themselves. Thus, the time costs of monitoring are incurred under both authoritative settings and the time lost on governance activities cannot be the primary source of negative effects of faculty participation on university performance (McCormick/Meiners (1988), p. 428).

Instead, the primary costs of faculty participation are the disadvantages of collective decision-making. Faculty participation usually comes with collective decision-making by committees rather than individual decision-making by one single faculty member (Masten (2000, pp. 11-12). The second source of costs of faculty participation are the costs associated with conflicting interests between faculty and other constituencies, which may lead to decisions that are not in the best interest of the university.

1. The costs of collective decision-making

    As soon as faculty consists of three or more individual faculty members, aggregating individual preferences is necessary and may be problematic.[31] Arrow (1963) identifies two basic mechanisms for aggregating the preferences of multiple individuals and converting them into decisions: Consensus and authority.

    Authority is characterized by a central decision-making agency that collects the information transmitted by the different individuals and then makes binding decisions. In order for consensus decision-making to yield stable results, identical information allocation and identical interests are required. However, these conditions are not necessarily fulfilled in the university. Es-

---

[31] In the discussion of principal-agent conflicts (section 3.3.3), faculty was assumed to have homogeneous preferences in comparison to other constituencies. It was presumed that "[...] faculty had a team objective function, common to all faculty members." (James/Neuberger (1981), p. 599). Within the broad framework of common preferences of faculty members, however, heterogeneous interests on specific topics are expected and are compatible with the assumption made above. The preferences of faculty as a constituency can be regarded as the outcome of a voting process that aggregates individuals' preferences.

pecially in university-wide collective bodies where faculty members of different academic disciplines have to make joint decisions, interest conflicts are predictable (Bainbridge (1997), p. 68-73).

Compared to concentrated decision-making in an autocratic framework, collective participatory decision-making may thus lead to instability and inconsistency (Masten (2000), p. 1). Voting procedures may have to be repeated, implying a loss of time for all parties involved. The case may also arise that individual preferences are defined so that cyclical group preferences prevail, prohibiting decision-making under certain voting systems.[32] Decisions are also dependent on the voting system since they are not necessarily robust to changes of the rules of preference aggregation or the order of voting (Boncheck/Shepsle (1997), pp. 167-173).

Collective decision-making is also susceptible to strategic voting such as log rolling (James/Neuberger (1981), p. 600). The idea behind log rolling is for different subgroups within a decision-making committee to form alliances in order to implement projects for which they alone would not have a majority. The problem of log rolling behavior is that it can exploit minorities while actively reducing the overall well-being of the entire group (Dunleavy (1991), pp. 39-42). Faculty coalitions can fend off decisions that would be beneficial to the entire university, but bear certain disadvantages to faculty. Over time, such detrimental decisions may reduce the prestige of the university. Log rolling behavior could arise for example when faculty has to decide which courses are included in the core curriculum. These courses require more resources and more funds, which benefits the reputation of the individual professor. Coalitions of self-interested faculty groups could be formed, leading to decisions that are not necessarily in the best interest of the university and have negative effects on overall university prestige.

---

[32] The cycling problem appears when preferences are double-peaked, which arises when returns of specialization are increasing, or when a decision has more than one attribute and individuals place different weights on the attributes (James/Neuberger (1981), p. 599).

Another problem of log rolling processes is that they require complex procedures and influence activities that consume faculty time and effort. The time spent with the design of the decision process and with politicking can be seen as another source of inefficiency compared to decisions made by autocratic management (Gibbons (2003), pp. 770-773). This point serves well to illustrate the dilemma of faculty participation in university governance: Democratic collective decision-making has higher costs due to its voting systems, but eventually may lead to higher quality decisions.[33] On the other side, autocratic decisions are less costly, but may lead to decisions with detrimental effects on the university.

2. Incentive conflicts and the resistance to change

   The second main problem of faculty decision-making is that faculty's incentives and interests may not always be fully aligned with the preferences of the principal. This is known as the incentive problem (McCormick/Meiners (1988), p. 425). Faculty has an incentive to make decisions that increase the overall prestige of the university since they are partial residual claimants of the university. Being a rational agent, faculty is also inclined to making decisions that advance their own personal interests more than those of the university (Brown (2001), p. 132). When the personal benefits of entrenched decision-making are greater than the benefit faculty would receive from improving overall university performance, faculty decisions may be biased. Like an autocrat, faculty members may be tempted to take advantage of their decision authority for their personal causes, leading to a negative impact of faculty decision-making on the university.

   Detecting such shirking on decision-making duties and holding the responsible faculty members accountable for their behavior is complicated. Team production nature of collective decisions prevents determining an individual's contribution to a specific decision or a specific outcome (Alchian/Demsetz (1972), p. 779). Also, due to tenure or the civil servant status, faculty

---

[33] The problems inherent in group decision-making in the university are studied in depth by James/Neuberger (1981).

are protected from being dismissed even when bad decision-making is obvious.

The universities of Oxford and Cambridge in the 12th and 13th centuries provide an example for the problems of faculty-dominated decision-making. A faculty-dominated governance evolved in the colleges of Cambridge and Oxford as a form of self-governance. Faculty elected faculty members and administrative officers into governance bodies, controlled the university property, and acted as their own board of trustees. Although formal control over the activities of each college was held by an external visitor, this seldom translated into real control. Therefore, decisions such as appointment and promotion decisions were only subject to peer review by faculty. Despite the fact that their residual claimant status should encourage faculty members to practice good governance, the faculty-dominated governance structures did not serve well to mitigate the conflicts of interests inherent in a team production situation, such as the problem of faculty shirking on its tasks. Oxford and Cambridge developed into "[...] clubs for lackluster and lazy academic remittance men" (Cowley (1980), p. 19), seeking to exploit the private advantages of their function. The lack of external control ultimately led to the institution of governance commissions in the 19th century in order to reform the colleges and their governance structure.

The incentive problem can become especially pronounced when it comes to implementing change. Compared to autocratic decision-making, a change in university policy is more difficult to achieve under a system with faculty participation. This is due to the fact that in collective, participative decision-making, the decision to change the status quo must be vested in the change of the priorities of a group. In contrast, the shift in the preferences in autocratic decision-making only has to occur within the individual preference set of the autocrat. Depending on the rule of vote, necessary change projects may thus be forestalled. Consequently, faculty participation in university decision-making can make the institution "[...] slow, cumbersome and protective of entrenched interests [...]" (Masten (2000), p. 3), preventing the implementation of reform projects, and thereby endangering the prestige of the university.

In summary, the negative impact of faculty participation in university decision-making stems from the downsides of collective decision-making (politicking, unstable decision, log rolling behavior, etc.) and from a lack of interest alignment of faculty preferences with the preferences of the entire university. While these issues seem to lower especially managerial professionalism, indirect negative effects on academic quality cannot be ruled out.

3.5.5 Synopsis

Faculty participation in university decision-making comes with benefits, but also with costs. The existence of this particular decision-making structure in universities can be explained with the governance function of faculty participation. The possible positive effects this has on academic performance and the quality of decision-making, however, are countered with the potential negative effects on the efficiency of decision-making. Inefficient decision-making also hinders the university management from effectively fulfilling its task of developing the university and enhancing its performance.

The hypothesis this analysis puts forward is that faculty participation in university decision-making gives rise to a trade-off. The gains from increased monitoring, faculty effort, and quality of decision-making are set off by the costs of collective decision-making, and the resistance to implementation of change, or reform projects. A set of hypotheses can be derived from the suggested trade-off. The higher the degree of faculty participation, the more decisions are controlled by faculty, and

- the higher is faculty monitoring of academic peers, university management, and administrative staff. This results in less shirking and higher academic performance by faculty and leads to better administrative and management performance.

- the more influence faculty has over its work environment, and consequently, the more motivated faculty will be to show good performance.

- the better is the quality of information that is incorporated into the decision-making process, leading to higher managerial efficiency and effectiveness.

On the downside of the trade-off, higher faculty participation leads to

- an increase in the time spent for politicking by faculty. This reduces the time available for research and teaching.

- the opportunity for faculty members to make decisions that are in their best interests, but come at the expense of the entire university.

- greater resistance against the implementation of projects that change the status quo significantly.

To sum up, the trade-off of faculty participation in university decision-making refers to the difficulty of maintaining a high degree of participation while carrying on as efficiently as possible with the management function (Pfnister (1970), p. 434).

3.6 Conclusion

Like most economic organizations, the university faces principal-agent problems. Based on a definition of the university and its special characteristics, this chapter analyzed the principal-agent conflicts in the university with special focus on the relationship between university management as the principal and faculty as the agent. The problem that exists between them can be considered as a moral hazard problem complicated by multi-tasking, team production, and difficult performance measurement. In an incomplete contracts framework, governance structures emerge as a solution for mitigating agency conflicts.

Faculty participation in university decision-making can be regarded as such a governance mechanism since it induces faculty to engage in monitoring. This monitoring mitigates the principal-agent problem between university management

3.6 Conclusion

and faculty. Faculty participation comes with additional benefits, such as the improvement of the quality of decision-making, but it also comes with costs, centering around the argument that collective decision-making is less efficient compared to autocratic, management-dominated decision-making. On the basis of these arguments, a trade-off of faculty participation in university decision-making on university performance is identified. In the optimal allocation of decision rights over the different decision types, the positive effects compensate the negative effects of faculty participation and yield the maximum university performance.

The question that cannot be answered on the basis of the theoretical economic analysis is what the optimal degree of faculty participation in university governance is. The remaining two parts of the dissertation address this question in further detail: Chapters 4 and 5 are concerned with modeling the effects of faculty participation in university decision-making in a setting of strategic delegation. Chapters 6 and 7 present practical evidence and insights from the German university system.

Part II
The Economic Model

4 A Survey of Economic Modeling

4.1 Introduction

Theoretical models have always been omnipresent in microeconomic theory and in the focus of New Institutional Economics. They help to analyze specific aspects in various organizations, ranging from profit maximizing firms to non-profit organizations, the public sector and universities.[1] Microeconomic models examine the inner workings of organizations, i.e. the conduct and relationships of the different organizational agents, and the interaction of organizations with each other and with third parties in economic environments. The common characteristic of all models within the NIE framework is the economic analysis of institutions and their effects on the behavior and interactions of individuals within organizations.

In particular, so-called principal-agent models have come to play a prominent role in recent years. Their focus lies on the assessment of the impact of incentives in situations of informational asymmetries. Principal-agent models provide a theoretical framework for the formal mathematical deduction of optimal incentive design.[2]

By way of principal-agency theory, economic models have found their way into business administration and management science. Jost (2001) gives an overview of the models applied in such fields as finance, strategic management, marketing, human resource management, controlling, and organizational design and delegation. Most of these models consist of the following basic elements (Varian (1997)): Economic agents, their preferences and objectives, the choices they make to achieve these objectives, and the constraints they face in the process.

This chapter and the following chapter explore how economic modeling can be applied to the university and its decision-making processes. To date, most economic analyses of the university have been conducted on a non-technical level.

---

[1] For papers on models of the firm, see for example Hart/Holmström (2002) and Holmström/Milgrom (1994). For models on non-profit organizations, see for example Glaeser (2002), Glaeser/Shleifer (1998). Burgess/Metcalfe (1999a) and Burgess/Metcalfe (1999b) give an overview of the economic literature on incentives in the public sector. See also Dewatripont/Jewitt/Tirole (1999). Section 4.3 of this thesis presents accounts of economic models on the university.

[2] This branch of principal-agent theory is often called normative agency theory in contrast to the less formal field of positive agency theory. For a more detailed account of the distinction between positive and normative principal-agent theory see chapter 2.

To illustrate the merits economic modeling has in general, section 4.2 provides an insight into the basic thoughts of the philosophy of economic modeling. A definition of economic models is proposed, and it is demonstrated why they are needed and what can be learned from them. Section 4.3 gives an overview of existing microeconomic models concerned with aspects of university organization in order to show that even though economic modeling has not been the predominant methodology for analyzing the university, the formal approach has clear benefits.

Following the explanation of the general purpose of economic modeling and the presentation of examples of models on the university, chapter 5 develops a new theoretical model for decision-making in the university with special regard to the role of faculty participation.

4.2 Foundations of Economic Models

Three central questions structure this section:

1. What are economic models (definition)?

2. Why are they needed (purpose)?

3. What is their relation to reality and what can be learned from them about reality (realism)?

An economic model can be defined as a theoretical, stylized construct that represents economic processes by a set of variables and a set of logical and mathematical relationships between them (Mankiw (2001), p. 22-23). To distinguish an economic model from an economic theory, Dohmen (2002) defines the latter as an organized body "[...] of ideas about the truth and the functioning of the economy." (p. 192). A model refers to the simplified structure of a theory and it depends on the assumptions the theory proposes. Assumptions filter out the multitude of details of the real world, thus reducing the complexity of the economic phenomenon and making it susceptible for economic modeling.

In terms of their purpose, economic models serve to explore and communicate the economic theory they are embedded in, as Dohmen (2002) and Hausman

(1992) note. Morgan/Morrison (1999) point out that economic models not only illustrate theory, but mediate between theories and the real world: Theory provides the *structure* and reality provides the *story* of the model. Already Gibbard/Varian (1978) note that a model "[...] is a story with a specified structure." (p. 666). Morgan (1999) specifies that stories determine the central questions of a model. Economists "[...] choose and pose the question, and use the mathematics or other resources [...]" in order to answer them (p. 367).

The question concerned with the relationship of models with reality is the most difficult to answer. By means of economic models, characteristics, structures, and processes that otherwise would not have been distinguishable are idealized and made accessible for explicit analysis (Mankiw (2001), p. 22-23). Economic analysis always goes hand in hand with a certain degree of abstraction that facilitates the processing of the mass of data, information, and facts available in reality (Samuelson (1973), p. 8-9).

In his seminal essay on the methodology of positive economics, Friedman (1953) also addresses the connection of economic theory to the observations in reality. "A completely 'realistic' theory of the wheat market would have to include not only the conditions directly underlying the supply and demand for wheat but also the kind of coins or credit instruments used to make exchanges; the personal characteristics of wheat-traders such as the color of each trader's hair and eyes, his antecedents and education, the number of members of his family, their characteristics, antecedents, and education, etc. [...]. Any attempt to move very far in achieving this kind of "realism" is certain to render a theory utterly useless." (p. 32). Theories and models will always and necessarily be simpler and more abstract than the reality they are trying to depict (Koopmans (1957); Gordon (1991)).

The trade-off in assessing the importance of the degree of realism of economic models is whether they "[...] only facilitate theory development or also inform our understanding of the real world [...]" (Dohmen (2002), p. 196). Friedman (1953) argues that "[t]he ultimate goal of positive economics is the development of a "theory" or "hypothesis" that yields valid and meaningful (i.e. not truistic) predictions about phenomena not yet observed" (p. 7). In Friedman's view, the assumptions that underlie a theory or a model should not be judged by their conformity with reality. Only the resulting theories and models should be evaluated based on the predictive power with regard to the phenomenon they are trying to explain. Assumptions must not be in-sync with reality, while the conclusions of a model should deliver testable implications about the real world. Samuelson (1973) argues that the value of a theory or model is derived from the usefulness of its explanation of the reality observed. Hausman (1992) agrees that the ultimate objective of models is "[...] to make true and reliable assertions about the world." (p. 27), while admitting that any single model will not necessarily help to understand the world.

Robbins (1984) and Koopmans (1957) take a slightly different position by requiring that a theory should be developed with an increasing degree of realism. Evidence from the real world enters the assumptions of theoretical models via induction, whereas the implications from the model for the real world are derived by deductive reasoning. Morgan/Morrison (1999) maintain the intermediate position that through the creation and application of models, both theory and reality can be explored.

To summarize, a model can be regarded as a simplified representation of reality, yet interconnected with the real world. On one hand, the objective of building a model is to provide a rather abstract account of the relevant issue. On the other hand, a model should also allow to draw conclusions for the real-world question studied.

Now that the three central questions on economic models that were posed at the beginning of this section have been answered, the next section gives an overview of three categories of microeconomic models concerned with the economic analysis of the university. The objective is to give an impression of the different modeling approaches and the research questions that have been addressed in the literature. Economic modeling makes the university accessible to rigorous analysis, and thus yields valuable insights.

4.3 Economic Models on Universities

4.3.1 Introduction

Due to a "[...] surprising dearth of analysis by economists of their institutional environment [...]", the university lacks a comprehensive economic theory (McCormick/Meiners (1988), p. 423). This may be one reason why there exist only a limited number of formal economic models on the university.[3] James/Neuberger (1981) note that "[t]here is a danger in writing about something [economists] are all familiar with: the simplifications inherent in an abstract model are harder to accept." (p. 592).

Among the existing formal models on university issues, three categories can be distinguished:

1. Faculty models, dealing with the preferences and objective functions of professors and academic staff

2. Organizational models, analyzing resource problems at the level of departments or the entire university

3. Tenure models, concerned with the economic rationale of tenure

Both faculty and organizational models can be regarded as classical microeconomic models where problems of informational asymmetry are not yet at the focus of the analysis. In contrast, the tenure models follow a principal-agent approach and illustrate how principal-agent relationships in the university can be formally represented. The next three sections briefly present the relevant models in each category, the technical approaches used, and the conclusions that can be drawn from them.

---

[3] The economic theory of the university should not be confused with the economics of education. For the latter, see for example Hoenack (1994), Lazear (1979), Psacharopoulos (1985, 1987) and Váradi (2001).

4.3.2 Faculty Models

In one of the earliest accounts of formal modeling of university agent behavior, Becker (1975) presents a professorial decision-making model. To overcome the "[...] conflicting verbal speculations as to the possible means of improving instruction." (p. 108), he develops a comparative statics model where time is a variable input.

In his model, faculty derives utility from research output, teaching output, and from consumption. Faculty members can freely allocate their time between these activities. Research and teaching outputs depend on the time spent for each activity and the respective technology coefficients. Consumption depends on the available income and the time available for consumption. The professor tries to maximize his utility subject to the time constraint, the production functions, and the income determination function.

The model analyzes the effect of an improvement in teaching technology on teaching output compared to an increase in the wage accorded to teaching. The conclusion is derived that an increase in the monetary return of teaching always yields higher teaching output, whereas the effect of a technological innovation is positive only when research and teaching are assumed to be substitute activities.

In his series of papers, Faria is also concerned with the allocation of a professor's time.[4] All of his models employ intertemporal optimization models with varying utility functions and constraints. Based on the models, Faria gives policy recommendations aimed at alleviating the problem identified in his papers. His first paper, Faria (2001), focuses the balance between academic work and consulting activities. It is assumed that faculty derives utility from both academic work (research and teaching) as well as external work (consulting) and that they have a high degree of freedom concerning the allocation of their time between the two activities. A professor maximizes his utility subject to the investment into academic work. Utility is discounted with faculty's subjective rate of time preference.

---

[4] When talking about professors in his papers, Faria considers them to be scholars of economics. Even though his results may not be generalizable to all sciences, they can be assumed to hold fairly well for the social sciences.

4.3 Economic Models on Universities

The model yields an equilibrium with "[...] a low level of academic work for a given level of external work." (p. 69). This phenomenon – referred to as the 'consultancy disease' – is especially likely to occur when the rate of time preference is larger than the depreciation rate of academic work.[5] The lower this depreciation rate, the smaller is the professor's preference for recent academic work. Faria concludes that policies designed to alleviate the consultancy disease should aim at increasing the rate of depreciation by setting high academic standards.

In his second paper, Faria (2002a) models a similar decision of faculty to allocate the time not spent with research or teaching between engagement in academic/scientific and business/political networks. The model illustrates that networks have direct and indirect effects on the production of academic and other professional output.

Faria (2005) and the earlier working paper, Faria (2002b), analyze the allocation of research effort between domestic versus international journal publications. In particular, the objective of the papers is to explain the apparent productivity gap between American and European economists as implied by the rankings of top journal publications.[6] Professors are assumed to be reputation maximizers in their home country. They have an incentive to both publish in top journals and to serve the domestic market. The top outlets are mainly Anglo-American journals, while European national academic markets have lower academic standards.[7] Top journal publications allow faculty to gain a high academic profile and reputation, a necessary condition for building a national reputation outside academia which can provide access to additional sources of income.

Faculty derives utility from the consumption of income. An equilibrium is derived where domestic and international publications respond inversely to changes in the parameters of the model, implying that there is a trade-off for international journal publications versus domestic journal publications. Faria deduces that the

---

[5] The rate of depreciation of academic work depicts the cost of a unit of academic work. The depreciation rate indicates the preference of faculty for recent academic work. The higher the rate of depreciation is, the higher is the preference for current academic work.
[6] See also the papers by Frey/Eichenberger (1992) and (1993) for detailed analyses of American vs. European economists.
[7] See for example the ranking of the "Verband der Hochschullehrer für Betriebswirtschaft" (Association of University Professors of Management), Hennig-Thurau et al. (2003)

top journal publication gap between European and American economists is not necessarily a sign that American economists are more productive than their European counterparts. The differences in (academic) labor markets and subsequently in the prevailing incentives lead to differing publication patterns of American and European economists.

In the fourth paper, Faria (2003) models economic faculty and their preferences toward quality and/or quantity of their publications and shows that there exists a trade-off that all economists face between the quality and the quantity of their publications.

All of these models focus on decision-making of an individual faculty member. The only constraint is the available amount of time for the different activities the professor may pursue. Faculty is modeled as an independent agent without references to the principal. Informational asymmetries do not play a role in these models.

In the next section, two models that focus on decision-making at the level of the academic department are presented.

4.3.3 Organizational Models

James/Neuberger (1981) present a model concerned with the decision structures in the university. An academic department is modeled as a multi-product, non-profit labor cooperative collectively run by its faculty members. The objective of the model is to predict the departmental behavior. The departmental utility function depends positively on the number and quality of its undergraduate and graduate students, and on the amount of research conducted.

In the model, department faculty maximizes its common team utility function subject to the available number of faculty by choosing the number of undergraduate and graduate students, and the teaching load. From the equilibrium conditions, the following key implications for departmental behavior are deduced:

- Faculty engages in both research and teaching, i.e. there is no complete specialization in either activity.

4.3 Economic Models on Universities

- Departments tend to expand student numbers because they can then employ additional faculty that will also contribute to research output.

- Teaching undergraduates is organized in larger classes and is therefore less costly than teaching graduate students.

- Undergraduate teaching is used to subsidize graduate teaching and research.

Apart from these formal conclusions, the paper also gives an insight into the problems of group decision-making, which have already been analyzed in chapter 3.

Borooah (1994) also focuses on the academic department. By illustrating the choices a department has to make in terms of the resource allocation between the two substitute activities of research and teaching, efficient combinations are derived. There are two types of faculty, researchers and lecturers. The departmental manager maximizes utility derived by research and teaching output. The parameters the manager can influence are the proportions of time spent in research and teaching by the two types of faculty.

The maximization problem faces four restraints. Firstly, the efficiency constraint implies that the combinations of time spent for research and teaching must lie on the highest possible production frontier. Secondly, the quality constraint guarantees that the quality of graduating students is equal to or exceeds a certain minimum quality level. Thirdly, the budget constraint ensures that revenue is equal to or exceeds costs. Fourthly, the credibility constraint indicates the minimum research and teaching output necessary to remain a credible academic department. As a result, the model derives specialization requirements and the inverse relationship between student number and student quality under certain assumptions. By extending the analysis to the level of the university, the model implies that resource allocation is driven by shadow prices which the university should aim at equalizing across the different departments.

These two institutional models generate an insight into the decisions at the level of the academic department. Similar to the faculty models, the departmental manager is assumed to be omniscient, i.e. there are no informational asymmetries.

In the next section, three tenure models are summarized that follow the logic of the principal-agent models.

4.3.4 Tenure Models

Ito/Kahn (1986) define tenure as "[...] a one-sided contract in which an employer gives up the right to dismiss an employee." (p. 1). Since tenure is prevalent in academia, there have been ample efforts by economists to explain its existence in the academic environment. This section will present three formal models dedicated to studying the effects of tenure in academia.[8]

Ito/Kahn (1986) illustrate with two related models that tenure can be regarded as a contract providing a guaranteed wage above spot wage levels. Their first model builds on a moral hazard situation between the university as the principal and faculty as the agent. Research effort and output are unobservable, and output is influenced by a random variable. Assuming a declining absolute risk aversion for faculty, the model shows that it is optimal for the university to pay the researcher a guaranteed flat wage because the higher a flat wage is, the more the researcher is induced to take on larger, riskier projects.[9]

In their second model, Ito/Kahn extend their analysis to include job mobility, renegotiation and a multi-period setting. In such a dynamic model, tenure also serves as an incentive device since it insures researchers from the downside risk of taking on large, risky research projects, yet does not rule out upward wage renegotiations. Offering the researcher a guaranteed flat wage contract is profitable for the university because the higher investment by the researcher offsets the costs of potentially retaining an unproductive researcher.

---

[8] For less formal accounts on tenure, see papers by Bess (1998), Brown (1997), Cater/Lew (2002), Ehrenberg/Pieper (1995), McKenzie (1996), McPherson/Schapiro (1999), McPherson/Winston (1983), Siow (1998), Stuchtey (1999) and Weigel (2003). For formal accounts on tenure-related issues see papers by Harris/Holmström (1982), Harris/Weiss (1984), Holmström (1983), Kahn/Hubermann (1988), Lazear (1979), and Waldman (1990).

[9] One measure for risk aversion is the Arrow-Pratt coefficient, calculated as $r_A(x) = -u''(x)/u'(x)$. If r_A is a decreasing function of x, then the utility function exhibits decreasing absolute risk aversion. Individuals with such a utility function take more risks the wealthier they are. See Mas-Colell et al. (1995), p. 190-194 for further detail.

4.3 Economic Models on Universities

Carmicheal (1988) proposes a different explanation for the existence of tenure. He asserts that tenure is a necessary condition for the functioning of the academic labor market since faculty plays a crucial role in hiring new candidates. In a setting of informational asymmetry, the university cannot observe the ability of the applying candidates, whereas incumbents can evaluate the research capabilities of the potential new hires, albeit imperfectly. This information is solicited from them at the beginning of each hiring period. The university maximizes the expected value of research output subject to the constraint that the incumbent professors reveal their true information about the potential hires. In the equilibrium of this signaling game, the incumbents will only tell the truth - and help the university achieve its objective of hiring the candidates with the best research abilities - if they are indifferent about the outcome of the revelation game. Consequently, incumbents must be given tenure to provide an incentive for hiring the best candidates available.

Richardson (1999) analyzes tenure under a two-period moral hazard situation. Tenure is modeled "[...] as a guaranteed minimum income above reservation utility in the second period, awarded to those achieving success in the first period." (p. 3). Only output is observable so that there exists a moral hazard problem of ex-post shirking once tenure has been granted. The principal can choose between offering spot contracts at the beginning of each period, and offering a tenure contract for both periods before period one. Through a utility maximizing model it can be shown that under certain conditions, the university will prefer to offer a tenure contract.

By extending the analysis to include agent heterogeneity, an adverse selection problem is introduced. There exist two types of professors, productive types and less productive types. It is assumed that the productivity of the professor cannot be observed by the university. In a situation where the principal employs a mixture of both types in the first period, those achieving tenure in the second period can be of either high or low type. It can then be shown that it is less costly for the university to induce high effort only from the more productive types that have tenure and let the less productive types shirk in the second period. This provides an explanation for the casually observed fact that some tenured faculty shirk while others show high effort. It also gives a rationale for the observed up- or-out tenure policy in many American universities where faculty not achieving tenure is dismissed. This practice may result from the belief of the principal that a professor who does not make tenure has a higher probability of being a less productive type than the proportion of low performance types in the pool of potential new hires. Therefore, it is more efficient to hire new faculty.

These models provide three different rationales for tenure. They have a common basis in adopting a principal-agent perspective where faculty is regarded as the agent and the university manager is considered to be the principal. In all three models, tenure is a solution for the problems resulting from the informational asymmetries inherent in those principal-agent relationships.

4.4 Conclusion

The university is a complex organization with many peculiarities, such as its non-profit status, the lack of a clearly defined objective function, and output that is complicated to observe and to evaluate. They make the application of standard modeling approaches of the microeconomic mainstream difficult. The previous subsection has shown how economists have approached the university from a formal modeling perspective. These models are valuable in making otherwise vague objective functions and preferences explicit and traceable. They yield deductive insights that go beyond those of more descriptive accounts of the functioning of the university. Naturally, they inherently tend toward a certain degree of abstraction, which is necessary to single out the relevant effects and to allow clear conclusions.

A number of explorative, theoretical papers have been written about university decision-making and the role of faculty. [10] Still, there does not exist a theoretical model that analyzes the effects of faculty participation in university decision-

---

[10] See for example McCormick/Meiners (1988), Brown (1997 and 2001). For further references, see also chapter 3.

4.4 Conclusion

making. Such a model is developed in the next chapter on the basis of strategic delegation models developed in the context of the firm.

5 Modeling Faculty Participation in University Decision-Making

5.1 Motivation and Overview

As already pointed out in chapter 3, faculty enjoys certain decision rights in many university systems: In Germany, the traditional public university grants faculty majority voting rights on many issues through the Academic Senate (Mittelstraß (2003)). In the UK, faculty plays an important role in the managing and governing bodies of the traditional universities, which include such institutions as Oxford, Cambridge and the University of London (Ackroyd/Ackryod (1999), p. 172-175). An empirical study among American colleges and universities confirmed that on average, 47,5% of all university decisions are either made by faculty or faculty has a veto over them (McCormick/Meiners (1988), p. 430).

There are a number of practically oriented accounts on the functioning of university decision-making, mostly by university managers, administrators, and presidents.[1] Based on organizational theory and the principal-agent framework, some more theoretically oriented analyses of decision-making structures and the rationale for strategic delegation in the university have been conducted.[2]

This dissertation follows an even more rigorous approach by applying a formal theoretical model of strategic delegation to the decision-making structures in the university. The objective is to come to a conclusion under which assumptions and conditions centralized decision-making by the university management is more efficient than decision-making delegated to faculty.

The model is the first economic model to address the question of who should hold decision power in the university - the university manager or the faculty - from a formal perspective. By introducing a mathematical framework, the model provides a first bridge between formal empirical research and the more explorative accounts on university governance. One important achievement of the model is the explicit discussion of the exogenous and endogenous variables that influence the efficiency of participative and centralized decision-making. The novelty about

---

[1] See for example papers by Birnbaum (1989a, 1989b, 1992) De Boer (1998), Dearlove (1998, 2002), Ehrenberg (1999), Pfnister (1970).

[2] Examples can be found in Brown (2001), Kovac/Ledic/Rafajac (2003), McCormick/Meiners (1988), Masten (2000), Ortmann (1997) and Waugh (2003).

this formal approach is not only its methodology, but also the fact that it is the first model to regard faculty participation in university decision-making as the delegation of authority from the principal to the agent, rather than treating it as a natural right of faculty. This approach opens university governance to an economic discussion that hopefully will evolve as fruitfully as the literature on corporate governance.

To give a short overview of the chapter, section 5.2 illustrates the problem of strategic delegation within the firm and presents three reference models. On the basis of these accounts, section 5.3 then presents a base case of strategic delegation in the university. Section 5.4 extends the base case to reflect some of the peculiarities of the university. Section 5.5 concludes the analysis and gives an outlook for future modeling effort in the university context.

5.2 Reference Models on Strategic Delegation

5.2.1 *Introduction*

Many interactions in the real world take place on the basis of delegated authority (Kockesen/Ok (2004), p. 397). A situation where the agent has significant decision powers is called strategic delegation, implying that the agent is entitled by a principal to make a decision over the course of action and to carry out a project in his own responsibility. The principal uses the agent for decision-making because he possesses some relevant information (Holmström (1980), p. 1).

As pointed out in the introduction above, faculty can be regarded as the agent of university management. Since there are a number of decisions over which faculty has formal or real authority, the insight from the accounts on strategic delegation in the firm can serve as a starting point for formally analyzing decision-making structures in the university.

Strategic delegation is discussed in the context of organizational economics, industrial organization, and political economy (Englmaier (2005), pp. 57-64). Since the focus of the dissertation lies on the internal organization of the university,

5.2 Reference Models on Strategic Delegation

this survey of strategic delegation only discusses the intra-firm effects of strategic delegation, i.e. between the principals and agents of one firm.[3]

Two general routes have been pursued in the study of strategic delegation: The principal-agent-based and the game-theoretic approach. Although principal-agent theory and game-theory are related and draw on the same equilibrium concepts, the difference between the two strands of theory is that game theory assumes the form of the interaction to be exogenously given while principal-agent theory endogenously derives the optimal form of interaction between principal and agent (Schmidt (1995), p. 11). In the following, the focus lies on the principal-agent approach to strategic delegation since principal-agent theory is applied in the economic analysis of the university in chapter 3.[4]

The central problem in principal-agent intra-firm delegation is that the agent may have a different objective in decision-making than the principal (Holmström (1980), p. 1). The greater the divergence of interests between principal and agent, the higher is the risk that the agent may implement a project that is beneficial to the agent but detrimental to the principal (Burkart et al. (1997), p. 693).

This gives rise to a situation called the commitment problem, referring to the difficulty of the principal to refrain from withdrawing the delegated authority from the agent. If the principal observes that the agent is taking decisions biased in favor of his personal interest, she is tempted to overrule the agent because this would make her better off in the given situation. Overruling the agent is thus ex-post efficient, yielding the principal a higher return than if the agent had taken his choice.

From an ex-ante perspective, however, it may be better for the principal not to overrule since this gives the agent higher ex-ante incentives to come up with the relevant information in the first place. Delegation may strengthen the incentives of the agent to show a higher level of search effort, which is favorable for his own benefit and that of the principal (Baker et al. (1999), p. 61).

---

[3] Fershtman (1985), Fershtman/Judd (1987), Schmidt (1997), Sklivas (1987), Vickers (1985), Rogoff (1985), Persson/Tabellini (1994), and Walsh (1995) apply strategic delegation in the context of political economy.

[4] See e.g. Fershtman et al. (1991) and Li et al. (2001) for game-theoretic accounts on strategic delegation.

One of the key implications of intra-firm strategic delegation is the trade-off of the benefit the principal derives from monitoring the agent and overruling him if he makes a bad decision and providing sufficient incentives to search for alternative decision proposals. Several mechanisms (e.g. financial instruments, organization structures) have been discussed to decrease the incentive of the principal to renege on her authority delegation to the agent, simultaneously strengthening the incentives of the agent to show high search effort (Aghion/Bolton (1992), pp. 490-492; (Aghion/Tirole (1997), p. 18-27).

The following three sections give a brief overview of the rationale and the key modeling assumptions of three important papers on intra-firm strategic delegation. These three models provide a starting point for applying a formal framework of strategic delegation to university decision-making.

5.2.2 Aghion/Tirole (1997)

The focus of Aghion/Tirole (1997) lies on real versus formal authority. The risk-neutral principal can give up his right to decide (formal authority) by delegating real authority, i.e. effective control over the project implementation decision, to the risk-averse agent.[5] Only projects that yield non-negative payoffs to both principal and agent are considered. The agent's task is to screen for the best project. The principal chooses how much to learn about the payoff distribution and then decides upon the recommendation of the agent. Principal and agent are assumed to have diverging interest over the best project.

Two authority settings are distinguished. Formal authority naturally lies with the principal (P-formal authority), but can also be contractually delegated to the agent (A-formal authority), who then acts independently and cannot be overruled by the principal. When formal authority lies with the principal, she can either rubber-stamp the project proposed by the agent, or she can implement her own preferred project when the agent's project provides her with a lower payoff. She will only make a decision when she is informed about the payoffs. The probability

---

[5] The agent is assumed to be so risk-averse that he does not respond to monetary incentives. This simplifying assumption is relaxed later on in the model.

5.2 Reference Models on Strategic Delegation

of being informed increases with her effort. In the case where the agent has formal authority, the principal effectively loses control over the decision and must accept the project the agent decides to implement.

The key point in their analysis of P-formal authority is the trade-off between the loss of control of the principal and the initiative of the agent. The less informed the principal is, the less likely she will overturn the agent's proposal. This lack of control creates incentives for the agent to implement projects that are suboptimal from the principal's point of view . On the other hand, low monitoring effort and consequently less ex-post agent control lead the agent to increase his search effort to come up with a good project in the first place. In comparing the two authority settings, it can be shown that delegation increases the agent's initiative: if "[...] the principal cannot overrule the agent, the agent has more incentives to become informed." (p. 12). Incentive compatibility is higher under A-formal than under P-formal authority.

Aghion/Tirole also analyze the question when authority should be allocated with the principal and when it should be formally delegated to the agent. Abstracting from incentives, delegation decisions are driven by the importance of the decision. For decisions that matter relatively little to the principal, and that are relatively important to the agent, delegation is more likely. Decisions of little importance to the principal are those yielding low possible payoff, or decisions that involve only a small conflict of interest between the agent and herself. Decisions that matter a lot to the agent are characterized by high private benefit to the agent, or by a great likelihood of being overruled due to a strong conflict of interests between agent and principal.

In a series of extensions to the base model, Aghion/Tirole also address the situation where formal delegation to the agent is not feasible through a contract. Under such a setting the question arises how the principal can credibly commit not to overrule the agent's project choice since the principal does not want to diminish the initiative of the agent. Organizational mechanisms such as a wide span of control, a high urgency of decision-making, the introduction of pay-for-performance schemes, and the existence of multiple principals increase the agent's real authority, and thus help to alleviate the commitment problem of the principal: A wide span of control hinders the principal in effectively gathering the information needed to overrule the agent; under situations of high urgency she does not have the time for an extensive project search. The introduction of pay for performance increases the agent's initiative for exerting high effort while decreasing the principal's monitoring incentives. Under feasible assumptions, multiple principals induce principal free-riding on the monitoring effort of the other principal(s), resulting in less monitoring and loss of control.

5.2.3 Baker/Gibbons/Murphy (1999)

The starting point of the paper by Baker/Gibbons/Murphy (1999) is that they assume that authority cannot be delegated formally, but only informally through self-enforcing contracts. They model the principal-agent interaction as an infinitely repeated game where the agent searches for projects and proposes them to the principal, who either approves or rejects them. Project payoff is either positive or negative.

The model distinguishes between an informed boss (she) who observes her payoffs from the projects prior to the decision whether to accept or refuse them, and an uninformed boss, who only observes the payoffs as they materialize after the implementation of the projects. Similar to the results obtained by Aghion/Tirole (1997), incentives are strengthened by delegation, i.e. the agent (he) exerts higher search effort when he has authority over the decision.

Due to the informal nature of this authority delegation, the principal can only promise to delegate the decision to his subordinate. In the informed boss model, the principal is tempted to renege on this promise by vetoing all proposed projects that do not yield her a positive payoff. The crucial restraint on the principal is her reputation: Once she has vetoed a proposal despite promising to rubber-stamp all projects, the agent will not trust her again. The behavior of principal and agent is thus characterized by a trigger strategy with a subgame-perfect, self-enforcing Nash equilibrium.[6] Baker et al. show that under certain conditions, informal delegation is efficient and feasible. The conditions depend on the principal's temptation to renege on her promise, which is driven by the congruence of interests between agent and principal, and the extreme values of the realized payoffs.

When the principal is uninformed, she must - blindly - rubber-stamp or approve all projects the agent proposes. She has no possibility to verify the payoffs ex-ante. To alleviate her lack of information, she could propose to the agent to ratify all projects as long as all previous projects yielded positive payoffs but threaten to withdraw this authority if a negative payoff is realized ex-post. In this case it is the agent who is tempted to break the agreement by proposing a project that is beneficial for himself but detrimental for his principal. Again following a trigger strategy, once the agent's reputation is tarnished, informal delegation will not take place anymore and the interaction is reduced to a series of one-shot games. The feasibility and efficiency of informal delegation now depends on the rate with which the agent discounts future payoffs as well as on the extreme values of the realized payoffs.

Aghion/Tirole (1997) model the trade-off between initiative and control under situations without formal authority delegation as a commitment problem of the principal. The model by Baker et al. generates the additional insight that in a dynamic framework, both parties can be tempted to renege on their commitment, depending on the informational structure.

---

[6] According to Gibbons (1992), a trigger strategy is a strategy where "[...] player i cooperates until someone fails to cooperate, which triggers a switch to noncooperation forever." (p. 91). For an explanation of a subgame-perfect Nash equilibrium, see Gibbons (1992), p. 88-89 and 122-125.

5.2.4 Burkart/Gromb/Panunzi (1997)

The primary focus of the paper by Burkart/Gromb/Panunzi (1997) lies on the analysis of the effects of block ownership vs. dispersed ownership of the firm on the incentives of the manager to show initiative. Block ownership is modeled to induce a high degree of management monitoring, whereas a dispersed ownership structure implies a higher degree of managerial discretion.

The model considers a firm run by a risk-neutral manager (he) and owned by an outside investor (she), holding a significant share of equity. The remainder of the shares are dispersed among small minority shareholders. Shareholders have formal authority, i.e. the right to decide over the projects the manager is supposed to implement. The task of the manager is to source projects and recommend them to the shareholders. By choosing to monitor, the shareholders can also become informed about the distributions of the payoffs and identify their preferred project. Searching and monitoring effort are exerted simultaneously, but monitoring is contingent on the manager becoming informed. Due to free-riding, only the block owner is assumed to engage in monitoring activities.

Shareholders have formal authority, but many decisions are delegated to the manager, who then enjoys effective control over the decision. This happens when the block owner chooses low monitoring effort and is thus not informed about the payoffs of the projects while the manager has the information necessary to make this decision. In maximizing firm value, the model constitutes the trade-off between control and initiative also identified in Aghion/Tirole (1997): Managerial initiative increases firm value but leaves room for managerial enrichment. Monitoring through shareholders ensures that only those projects are implemented that are in the best interest of the firm, but decreases the incentives for managers to show high effort in the first place. "[E]ven if managerial discretion is ex-post detrimental to shareholders, it can be beneficial ex-ante as it favors firm specific investment, like searching for new investment projects." (p. 694).

Thus, a dispersed ownership structure can help to solve the commitment problem by allowing the shareholder to credibly constrain their own interference with the manager's decision-making. This still holds when monetary incentives for the agent are introduced.

5.2.5 *Synopsis*

The three models above analyze intra-firm decision-making hierarchies as delegation problems of decision-making rights from the principal to the agent in different contexts. In the university, there also exists a certain decision-making structure, where decision and control rights are allocated to either university management or to faculty, depending on the decision. The similarities of the decision-making set-ups are the starting point for modeling the participation of faculty in university decision-making as a delegation problem. The base model presented in the next section closely follows the set-up of the reference models. The extension of this base model is presented in section 5.4.

5.3 An Initiative Model - Base Case

The mathematical notation of the base model draws on the reference papers by Aghion/Tirole (1997), Baker/Gibbons/Murphy (1999) and Burkart/Gromb/Panunzi (1997), discussed in section 5.2. The model outlined in the next section mirrors the modeling approach of the discussed reference models and applies it to the university.

5.3.1 *Set-up*

5.3.1.1 The University Context

A university is considered to be run by a university manager (she) as the principal employing one faculty member (he) as her agent.[7] Faculty is hired to carry out two primary tasks: To do research, and to offer teaching. The university regularly has to make strategic and operational decisions on topics such as governance structures, degrees offered, research and teaching specializations, resource allocation,

---
[7] Principal and agent are also referred to as the actors, the players, or the parties.

internationalization policy, etc. Decisions can have benefits for the university and for faculty, which makes decision-making important to both of them.

In addition to performing research and teaching, faculty as the agent is also able to search for information concerning the available alternatives for any decision the university faces. Since this model focuses on decision structures, only this activity of faculty is relevant in the following analysis. Neither the moral-hazard agency problem that university management and faculty face over effort provision in research and teaching nor the problem of allocating time between teaching and research will be addressed.[8]

The quality of decision-making depends on the information the decision-maker possesses about the payoffs the alternatives will generate for the university and for faculty. Information about the decision alternatives is not available without cost, so that the party exerting information search effort wants to profit from it in the decision-making process. Decision-making structures must therefore provide incentives for searching for relevant information. Information searching activities can be considered as university-specific investments that are only valuable in the specific context of the university.

Following the search of information, the decision to implement a certain alternative is taken by the party with decision authority. A priori, decision control is usually allocated to the principal. The principal may choose to delegate authority to the agent. Two concepts of authority can be distinguished: Formal authority refers to the right to decide on specified matters. It results from an explicit or implicit contract allocating this right to a certain actor or a group of actors. Formal authority does not always translate into real authority, i.e. the effective control over decisions. There may be instances where one party has formal authority but

---

[8] Instead, it is assumed that faculty has been offered an incentive contract by university management that optimally mitigates the standard agency shirking problem as far as this is possible through an incomplete contract. Compare for example contract specified in the model developed by Holmström/Milgrom (1991), which can be applied to the multi-tasking nature of faculty contracts. The model derives an optimal linear contract for an agent who handles two tasks, for one of which performance is very hard to measure. Taking into account that both research and teaching are typically considered hard to measure (Dilger (2001, pp. 138-139), an incentive contract for faculty could involve paying a fixed wage without providing any performance-based monetary incentive.

prefers to let the other party make the decision, thus delegating real authority to this party.

In the context of authority delegation, Baker et al. (1999) raise the point that formal authority always resides with the principal at the top of the hierarchy. They maintain that authority can never be delegated formally through a contract. Their key argument is that any agent can be fired except for the ultimate principal of the firm. This may be a valid point for the firm, but the university lacks a clearly defined owner who pools all decision rights in the organization. The wide-spread institution of tenure and the principle of academic freedom further question the validity of this assumption for the university. Without the applicability of an ownership concept and without the possibility of firing agents, this dissertation is based on the assumption that formal authority can be delegated from the principal to the agent in the university. Casual evidence indeed suggests that many university systems delegate formal decision authority to bodies dominated by faculty (the agent), such as the Academic Senate, either through legal regulation or through university charters. In the following model, formal authority is allocated either to the university manager or to faculty, and real authority depends on the information the parties possess.

5.3.1.2 The Decision-Making Process

Analog to the modeling framework in Aghion/Tirole (1997) and Burkart et al. (1997), it is assumed that the university faces n different decision alternatives, S_i, $i \in [1, 2, \ldots, n]$ and S_0, the retention of the status quo, for every decision it has to take. The alternatives S_i yield verifiable benefit R^i to the university, such as reputational gain, or additional financial resources. Alternatives also yield private, non-verifiable benefits b^i to faculty, such as academic reputation, perks on the job, etc., minus any disutility of implementing the alternative once it is decided. These net private benefits to faculty cannot be observed nor verified. Both R^i and b^i are treated as exogenous parameters in the following analysis. For simplicity reasons, they are standardized to the interval $[0, 1]$

The payoffs of S_0 are known: $R^0 = b^0 = 0$. The payoffs of A_i are not known ex-ante and the alternatives cannot be distinguished from each other without further investigation. The n alternatives therefore appear to be similar a priori. For simplicity reasons, only two of the n alternatives are 'relevant' in the sense that they yield positive payoffs to both university management and faculty (see Aghion/Tirole (1997) and Burkart et al. (1997) for a similar practice). The payoff structure of the two remaining alternatives is depicted in table 5.1, with $R, b, \lambda in [0, 1]$.

Table 5.1 The Project Payoff Structure in the Initiative Model

Alternative S_1	Alternative S_2	Probability
$\{R, b\}$	$\{0, 0\}$	λ
$\{R, 0\}$	$\{0, b\}$	$(1 - \lambda)$

λ is the exogenous parameter that measures the congruence of the benefits between university management and faculty. It can be regarded as the intensity of the conflict of interest between the university and faculty. The conflict of interest becomes clearer when the payoff matrix is manipulated to depict the expected payoff for the two alternatives (see table 5.2).

Table 5.2 The Adapted Project Payoff Structure

Alternative S_1	Alternative S_2
$\{\lambda R + (1-\lambda)R, \lambda b + (1-\lambda)0\}$	$\{\lambda 0 + (1-\lambda)0, \lambda 0 + (1-\lambda)b\}$
$=$	$=$
$\{R, \lambda b\}$	$\{0, (1-\lambda)b\}$

To illustrate the meaning of λ in table 5.2, its extreme values are considered: When $\lambda = 1$, there is perfect congruence of interests since both university management and faculty prefer alternative S_1, and the decision-making structure becomes irrelevant because both players always choose S_1. On the other hand, if $\lambda = 0$, university management and faculty prefer exactly opposite alternatives.

5.3 An Initiative Model - Base Case

The preferred alternative of university management is S_1, whereas faculty would prefer S_2.

It can be concluded that the principal always prefers S_1, whereas the favored alternative of faculty depends on the choice of λ. As $\lambda \to 0$ and congruence thus decreases, the conflict of interests between university management and faculty becomes more and more severe since faculty increasingly prefers alternative S_2. As $\lambda \to 1$, the conflict of interest disappears.

In order to focus on situations where agency problems persist, it is assumed that $\lambda \in (0, 1)$ in the following. This excludes the possibility of perfect congruence of interests as well as total conflict of interests.

Assumption 1: $\lambda \in (0, 1)$

The payoff distribution among the alternatives is initially unknown and information needs to be acquired before a decision can be taken. At date 1, faculty chooses to exert a non-verifiable effort $e \in (0, 1)$ at a cost $c(e) = \frac{e^2}{2}$.[9] This effort enables faculty to learn the payoffs of all alternatives at date 2 with probability e. With probability $(1-e)$, faculty learns nothing and still cannot distinguish the alternatives at date 2.[10]

The university manager wants to ensure a high project payoff for the university. At date 1, she chooses to exert a search effort $E \in (0, 1)$ at a cost $c(E) = \frac{E^2}{2}$, enabling her to also learn the payoffs of all alternatives at date 2 with probability E. The effort of the university manager is not contemporaneous on faculty effort,

---

[9] The cost function used here is a strictly convex function with $c(0) = 0$ and $c(1) = 0.5$. This reflects the diminishing marginal product of effort: The higher the effort already exerted, the lower is the value of an additional increase in effort and the higher is the cost of searching. Marginal cost of effort is therefore strictly increasing. See Mas-Colell et al. (1995), pp. 143-145, and Mankiw (2001), pp. 278-281 for more detail on cost functions.

[10] Linking the level of effort to the probability of achieving a high payoff implies that there exists a maximum and a minimum effort level that are standardized to the interval $[0, 1]$. Effort can be chosen continuously in this interval.

i.e. the university manager can learn the payoffs of the alternatives even if faculty does not.[11]

The decision over which alternative to implement in the two organizational settings is taken by the party with authority according to the following decision-making process:

1. University manager has formal authority

    In this setting, the principal has the right to decide at date 2. She will do so when she is informed (probability E) and will pick her preferred alternative. When she is not informed (probability $1 - E$), she will rely on the recommendation of her informed agent and rubber-stamp the alternative faculty proposes. When the university manager is not informed, faculty thus has real authority.

2. Faculty has formal authority

    In this setting, faculty has received the irrevocable right to make the decision over the alternative to be implemented. Acting as an 'independent' agent, faculty will pick his preferred alternative if he is informed (probability e) and otherwise accept the university manager's recommendation (probability $1 - e$), thus granting the university manager effective control, or real authority over the decision.

The set-up implies that under both authority settings formal and real authority can be collocated if the party holding formal authority is informed about the payoffs. Since this is not necessarily the case, formal and real authority can also lie with distinct players.

---

[11] This last notion is analog to the approach seen in Aghion/Tirole (1997) and Baker et al. (1999), but differs from Burkart et al. (1997). The reason for choosing the former over the latter is because it represents more closely the situation in the university. Burkart et al. (1997) give the principal only a monitoring function, whereas Aghion/Tirole as well as Baker et al. see principal and agent as potential decision makers in their own right. This implies that the decision will fall back to the principal if the agent is incapable of making it or unwilling to do so. Burkart et al. instead assume that the principal, in this case the block shareholder, only engages in (passive) monitoring, rather than in the (active) search for information as the principals do in the other two papers. Since the principal in this model is the university manager who is responsible for running the university, the latter initiative perspective is deemed to be more adequate.

5.3 An Initiative Model - Base Case

When neither of the two parties is informed (probability $(1-e)(1-E)$), the status quo will be retained since the two relevant alternatives that yield non-negative benefits for both parties cannot be determined with certainty without additional information. The possibility of selecting one of the 'irrelevant' alternatives generating a very bad outcome would lead to negative expected payoffs. In comparison, receiving a payoff of 0 by retaining the status quo is always preferred.

5.3.2 The Model

5.3.2.1 Introduction

The focus of the following model lies on the analysis of the incentives that induce the agent (faculty) and the principal (university manager) to exert search effort. The differences of the incentives under the two organizational settings are examined and authority delegation is evaluated from a total welfare perspective. For demonstration purposes and reasons of simplicity, the model abstracts from monetary incentives for faculty by assuming that faculty is risk-averse and does not respond to monetary incentives.[12]

5.3.2.2 University Management Authority

In the first setting, formal authority lies with the principal, i.e. the university manager. This setting is therefore also referred to as P-formal authority, or university control. In order to distinguish effort levels, $e \equiv p$ and $E \equiv P$ for all settings under P-formal authority. Payoffs for university manager U and faculty F are:[13]

$$(5.1) \qquad U = RP + (1-P)\lambda Rp - \frac{P^2}{2}$$

$$(5.2) \qquad F = \lambda bP + (1-P)bp - \frac{p^2}{2}.$$

---

[12] Since faculty in general is considered to be motivated intrinsically and not only through monetary payments, this assumption seems justified for the university context. See also the discussion in section 3.3.2.
[13] The payoff functions are only defined for the domains of $p, P \in [0,1]$.

The payoff function of the university is interpreted as follows: With probability P, the university manager is informed about the payoffs, exercises her formal authority, and chooses her preferred alternative with payoff R. With probability $(1-P)p$, the university manager is uninformed and faculty is informed. The latter then suggests his preferred alternative, yielding λR to the university management. Since $\lambda R > 0$, the university manager optimally rubber-stamps the proposed alternative, giving faculty real authority over the decision. $c(P) = \frac{P^2}{2}$ denotes the cost of university management effort.

The payoff function of faculty is set up along similar lines. If the university manager is informed (probability P), she chooses her preferred alternative, yielding λb to faculty. In the case where the university manager is not informed and faculty is informed (probability $(1-P)p$), faculty proposes his preferred alternative and gains benefit b. $c(p) = \frac{p^2}{2}$ denotes the cost of effort for faculty.

Both payoff functions are strictly concave, which can be derived from the algebraic signs of the second derivatives (Chiang (1984), pp. 242-243). Since $\frac{\partial^2 U}{\partial P^2} < 0$, the payoff function of the university manager, U, is concave in effort P. For faculty, $\frac{\partial^2 F}{\partial p^2} < 0$, so that the payoff function of faculty, F, is concave in effort p.[14] This condition is necessary to ensure that the first-order conditions generate maximum values.

To find her optimal effort level, the university manager maximizes her payoff function with respect to her effort level P. Her best response function (BRF) is defined by setting the first-order derivative of the payoff function with respect to P equal to 0, and solving for P:

(5.3)
$$\frac{\partial U}{\partial P} = 0$$
$$P = (1 - \lambda p)R.$$

The best response function shows that the more effort the agent shows, the less searching effort the principal puts forth. Principal and agent effort therefore compensate each other, which can be formally inferred from the downward slope of the curve with regard to p ($\frac{\partial P}{\partial p} < 0$).

---

[14] The notation for the second derivative follows Chiang (1984), pp. 239-240.

5.3 An Initiative Model - Base Case

The agent maximizes his payoff function F with respect to his effort p. His best response function is determined by the first-order condition (FOC)

$$\frac{\partial F}{\partial p} = 0$$

(5.4)
$$p = (1-P)b.$$

The lower the interference by the principal, i.e. the lower P is, the higher will be the effort of the agent ($\frac{\partial p}{\partial P} < 0$). This is the decisive characteristic of any initiative model (Aghion/Tirole (1997), p. 10). Lower effort implies a loss of effective control for the principal and increases the likelihood that the agent has real authority. This gives the agent the opportunity to implement a project that is favorable for him but not necessarily for the university. This prospect raises the incentives of the agent to show a high search effort to learn the payoffs of the different alternatives.

A trade-off between control and initiative is implied in the two best response functions: If the searching effort of the principal, P, increases due to an exogenous reason, e.g. a rise in R, the effect on the expected payoff to the university manager is unclear. On the one hand, she increases effort and is more likely to be informed ($P \uparrow$). Thus, the university manager gains more control, or real authority, over the choice of the alternative. This raises expected payoff since $\frac{\partial U}{\partial P} > 0$. On the other hand, when monitoring effort increases, faculty effort will decrease ($p \downarrow$) since rising intervention through the principal lowers the influence of the agent's effort on the outcome of the decision. Less faculty effort will have a negative effect on the expected payoff of the university manager since $\frac{\partial U}{\partial p} > 0$. In order to examine these effects that arise from changes in the exogenous parameters in greater detail, the equilibrium values have to be determined.

By solving the best response functions, equations (5.3) and (5.4), for the values of P and p, the effort equilibrium values P^* and p^* are established.

(5.5)
$$P^* = \frac{(1-\lambda b)R}{1-\lambda bR}$$

and

(5.6) $$p^* = \frac{(1-R)b}{1-\lambda bR}.$$

The equilibrium can also be derived graphically by plotting the two BRFs into one graph (see figure 5.1). For this, the BRF of the agent (equation (5.4)) has to be adjusted to the format of the BRF of the principal (equation (5.3)).

$$\begin{aligned} p &= (1-P)b \\ \Leftrightarrow P &= 1 - \frac{1}{b}p. \end{aligned}$$

To depict the graphs, the following random values are assumed for λ, b, and R: $\lambda = 0.5$, $b = 0.5$, and $R = 0.7$. The downward slope of the two best response functions becomes evident, implying that a decrease (increase) in P results in an increase (decrease) of p.

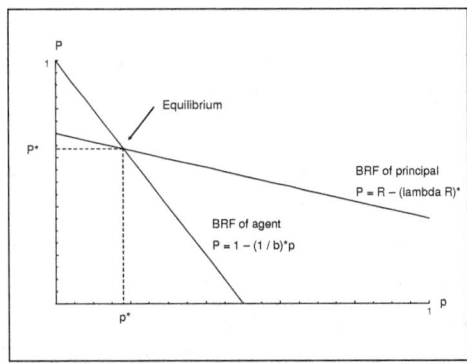

Fig. 5.1 The Best Response Functions of University Management and Faculty Under University Management Authority

As pointed out above in the discussion of the trade-off implied in the BRFs, two questions arise from the equilibrium. The first addresses the change of the equilibrium effort values when an exogenous parameter changes due to an external shock. The second, related, question refers to the change in the payoff levels of the players following the subsequent shift in equilibrium effort values. Contrasting the new equilibrium after the change in the exogenous parameter with the old equilibrium before the shock is called comparative statics analysis. In the following, the comparative statics are shown graphically in order to visualize the relevant effects (see section 5.6.2 in the appendix for a numerical treatment). While the graphs are derived on the basis of the values used for the graph above, the numerical treatment shows that the conclusions drawn below for a particular set of graphs are valid for all values of the parameters within their respective domain.

Three types of external shocks can arise: An increase or decrease in λ, in b, and in R. For simplicity reasons, and without loss of generality, the following analysis will only be concerned with increases in the exogenous parameters. Each of these effects is considered separately in the following analysis of the equilibria in order to be able to distinguish the impact of each exogenous parameter on the payoff functions on an individual basis. A joint treatment does not allow conclusive insights as the effects of the different exogenous parameters would be confused. The approach of holding all variables or parameters, except the one that is being studied, constant is referred to as the 'ceteris paribus' principle (Mankiw (2001), p. 70).

1. The effects of an increase in λ

    As illustrated by figure 5.2, an increase in the congruence parameter λ steepens the slope of the best response function of the principal. Since λ does not directly affect the BRF of the agent, this graph remains stable. For every level of p, the principal will now exert less effort P.

    The economic intuition behind this effect is the following: When λ increases, the interests between the principal and the agent become more congruent. Therefore, the principal can trust the agent to a greater degree to make a good decision on her behalf. She can therefore reduce her effort, knowing that faculty will increase his effort to compensate for the reduction in P. When P declines, faculty's likelihood of gaining real authority over the decision increases, which strengthens his incentive to show high effort. Therefore, the change in λ affects the equilibrium level of the agent indirectly via the shift of the BRF of the principal. The new equilibrium is located below and to the right of the old equilibrium as university manager effort P^* decreases and faculty effort p^* increases.

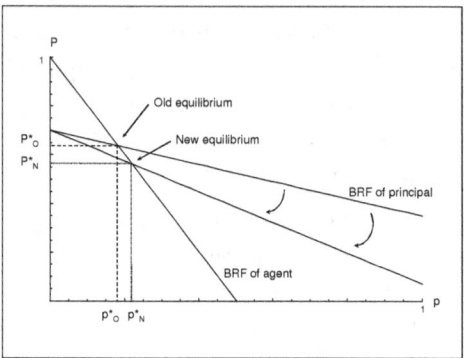

Fig. 5.2 New Equilibrium after an Exogenous Change in λ

The second question in comparative statics examines how the change in λ affects the payoff levels U and F (equations (5.1) and (5.2)). The mathematical method used for this analysis is the concept of the total derivative (Chiang (1984), pp. 198-203). The total derivative of U captures five effects: Firstly, the effect λ has on U directly; secondly, the effect λ has on P; thirdly, the effect P has on U directly, fourthly, the effect that a change in P has on p, and lastly, the effect the resulting change in p has on the objective function U. Figure 5.3 shows this chain of direct and indirect effects.

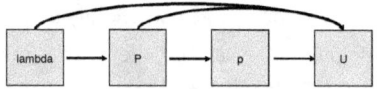

Fig. 5.3 Direct and Indirect Effects of λ

Following the notation of Chiang (1984), the total derivative $\frac{dU}{d\lambda}$ reads:

$$\frac{dU}{d\lambda} = \frac{\partial U}{\partial p} \cdot \frac{dp}{d\lambda} + \frac{\partial U}{\partial P} \cdot \frac{dP}{d\lambda} + \frac{\partial U}{\partial \lambda}$$

5.3 An Initiative Model - Base Case

$\frac{dp}{d\lambda}$ is not directly defined through the BRF of the agent since λ is not included in the BRF of the agent.[15] Therefore, the indirect effect that the BRF of the principal, which depends on λ, has on the BRF of the agent needs to be taken into account. The total derivative then yields:

$$\begin{aligned}\frac{dU}{d\lambda} &= \frac{\partial U}{\partial p} \cdot \frac{\partial p}{\partial P} \cdot \frac{\partial P}{\partial \lambda} + \frac{\partial U}{\partial P} \cdot \frac{dP}{d\lambda} + \frac{\partial U}{\partial \lambda} \\ &= ((1-P)R\lambda) \cdot (-b) \cdot (-Rp) + (R - pR\lambda - P)cdot(-Rp) + \\ &\quad ((1-P)Rp) \\ &= (1 + R((b(1-P) + p)\lambda) - 1)pR > 0\end{aligned}$$

for all $p, P, b, R, \lambda \in (0,1)$. The total effect of an increase in λ on the payoff of the university manager, U, is positive. The decrease in the effort of the university manager is offset by the decrease in effort cost and the increases in p and λ.

The same analysis has to be conducted for F in order to analyze the direct and indirect effects of a change in λ on the payoff of faculty. The total derivative reads

$$\begin{aligned}\frac{dF}{d\lambda} &= \frac{\partial F}{\partial p} \cdot \frac{\partial p}{\partial P} \cdot \frac{\partial P}{\partial \lambda} + \frac{\partial F}{\partial P} \cdot \frac{dP}{d\lambda} + \frac{\partial F}{\partial \lambda} \\ &= ((1-P)b - p) \cdot (-b) \cdot (-pR) + (\lambda b - bp) \cdot (-pR) + bP \\ &= b((1 - bRp)P + (b - \lambda)Rp).\end{aligned}$$

The effect of λ on F cannot be determined precisely as the sign of the total derivative is ambiguous. While the first term of the total derivative is positive, the sign of the second term and thus the sign of the total derivative depends on the relationship between b and λ. Thus, it is unclear whether the increases in p and λ can compensate for the decrease in P in the payoff function of faculty.

---

[15] This can also be concluded from the fact that the BRF of the agent does not shift as a result of a change in λ, as figure 5.2 shows.

2. The effects of an increase in R

A change in the level of the project payoff of the principal, R, only applies to the best response function of the university manager while the BRF of faculty remains stable. The slope of her BRF steepens, and the axis intercept on the P-axis increases, as figure 5.4 shows. For every level of p, the university manager now exerts higher effort since her incentives are strengthened by the increase in benefit. When R increases, more is at stake for the university manager, so that she becomes reluctant to give real authority to faculty. The higher her own effort P is, the higher is the probability that she retains both real and formal authority.

From the BRF of faculty, it is evident that an increase in monitoring through an increase in P diminishes the probability of faculty having real control over the decision. The incentives to exert high effort are therefore lower, and faculty reduces his effort level p. The new equilibrium is located above and to the left of the old equilibrium as principal effort increases and agent effort decreases as a result. The effect of R on the optimal effort level p^* of the agent works indirectly through the best response function of the agent, which is influenced by the effort level of the principal.

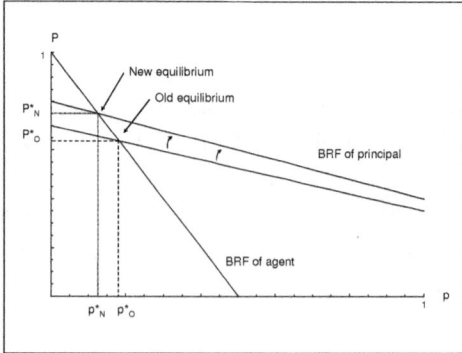

Fig. 5.4 New Equilibrium after an Exogenous Change in R

5.3 An Initiative Model - Base Case

In order to assess the effect a change in R has on the payoff levels U and F, the total derivatives $\frac{dU}{dR}$ and $\frac{dF}{dR}$ have to be evaluated (see section 5.6.2.1 in the appendix of this chapter for a numerical treatment). The total derivative of U with respect to R is positive for all $p, P, b, R, \lambda \in (0,1)$. An increase in project payoff increases the total payoff of the principal. The total derivative of F with respect to R, on the other hand, is ambiguous. Its algebraic sign depends on the relationship between b, λ and P.

3. The effects of an increase in b

   Contrary to λ and R, the exogenous variable b only affects the best response function of faculty. Figure 5.5 shows that an increase in b flattens the slope of the best response function of faculty while leaving the BRF of the university manager unchanged. For every P, the agent will now show a higher level of effort since the increase in private benefit strengthens his incentives to show high search effort. The BRF of the principal, on the other side, decreases in p. The university manager will exert less effort when p increases as a result of the increase in b. Through the increase in p, the increase in b leads the principal to reduce her effort. This enhances the likelihood that faculty will have real authority and will implement his preferred project. The new equilibrium is located slightly below and clearly to the right of the old equilibrium as a result of the increase in p^* and the small decrease in P^*.

   The total derivatives of U and F with respect to b yield an insight into the effects of a change of b on the payoff levels U and F (see section 5.6.2.1 in the appendix for a numerical treatment). Both $\frac{dU}{db}$ and $\frac{dF}{db}$ are positive, implying that a positive change in b increases the payoffs of both university manager and faculty because the subsequent increase in p more than offsets the decrease in P.

Comparative statics help to understand the structure of the equilibrium under university management authority. The effort of the principal, P, rises in response to an increase in R, while it decreases with both λ and b. For faculty, the opposite

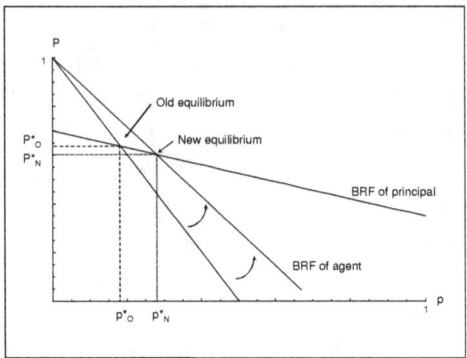

Fig. 5.5 New Equilibrium after an Exogenous Change in b

applies, as p increases in λ and b while declining in R. In terms of the total utility levels, the direct and indirect effects of the changes in the exogenous variables are clear for the payoff of the university manager: For an increase in any of the three exogenous parameters, the payoff of the university manager increases. For the case of faculty payoff, the sum of direct and indirect effects are clearly positive for increases in b while the impact of increases in λ and R depends on the relationships between b, λ and P. This closes the discussion of the equilibrium under university management authority. The next section analyzes the payoffs, the effort equilibrium, and the comparative statics results when faculty has formal authority.

5.3.2.3 Faculty Authority

For this subsection it is assumed that control rights have been formally delegated to faculty. Effort levels are represented by $e \equiv a$ and $E \equiv A$. Payoffs for university manager U and faculty F are as follows:

$$(5.7) \qquad U = \lambda R a + (1-a) R A - \frac{A^2}{2}$$

$$(5.8) \qquad F = ba + (1-a)\lambda b A - \frac{a^2}{2}.$$

5.3 An Initiative Model - Base Case

The payoff function of university management consists of the following elements: If faculty is informed (probability a), he chooses his preferred alternative, yielding λR to the university manager. If faculty is not informed and the university manager is informed (probability $(1-a)A$), the latter proposes her preferred alternative and receives benefit R. $\frac{A^2}{2}$ denotes the costs of university management effort.

The faculty payoff function is interpreted accordingly: If the agent is informed (probability a), he exercises his formal authority and chooses his preferred alternative, yielding him payoff b. If faculty is not informed and the university manager is informed (probability $(1-a)A$), the latter suggests her preferred alternative, yielding λb to faculty. Since $\lambda b > 0$, faculty optimally rubber-stamps the proposed alternative of the university manager, thus giving the university manager real authority over the decision. $\frac{a^2}{2}$ denotes the costs of faculty effort.

The concavity of the payoff functions can be derived from the algebraic signs of the second derivatives. Since $\frac{\partial^2 U}{\partial A^2} < 0$, the payoff function of the university manager is concave in effort A. For faculty, $\frac{\partial^2 F}{\partial a^2} < 0$, so that the payoff function of faculty is concave in effort a.

To determine the optimal level of A, the university manager maximizes her payoff function with respect to A. Her best response function is defined by setting the first-order derivative of U with respect to A equal to 0, and solving for A:

(5.9)
$$\frac{\partial U}{\partial A} = 0$$
$$A = (1-a)R.$$

Higher faculty effort induces lower effort by the university manager because the likelihood of the university manager having real authority decreases with increasing faculty effort a. This can be inferred from the negative slope of the reaction curve of the principal.

Faculty maximizes his payoff function with respect to a to find his optimal effort level. His best response function is defined by the FOC

$$\frac{\partial F}{\partial a} = 0$$
(5.10) $$a = (1 - \lambda A)b.$$

The agent's best response function is downward sloping in the effort of the principal ($\frac{\partial a}{\partial A} < 0$). Less searching effort from the university manager induces faculty to exert more effort to ensure his preferred project is undertaken.

The fundamental trade-off between control and initiative is exactly opposite to the setting under P-formal authority: Higher effort by the agent (i.e. higher a) induces lower initiative (lower A) by the principal because she is unlikely to have real authority when faculty increases his effort. The prospect of real authority delegation implied by a lower a, on the other hand, strengthens the incentives of the principal to show high effort.

From the two best response functions, the equilibrium values for the effort levels A and a are derived:

(5.11) $$A^* = \frac{(1-b)R}{1 - \lambda b R}$$

and

(5.12) $$a^* = \frac{(1 - R\lambda)b}{1 - \lambda b R}.$$

To show the equilibrium graphically, the two best response functions are plotted into one graph. Equation (5.9) depicts the BRF of the principal; the BRF of the agent is converted to the same format:

$$a = (1 - \lambda A)b$$
$$\Leftrightarrow A = \frac{1}{\lambda} - \frac{1}{b\lambda}p.$$

In figure 5.6, the following random values are assumed for λ, b, and R: $\lambda = 0.5$, $b = 0.5$, and $R = 0.7$. From the graphs, the downward slope of the two

5.3 An Initiative Model - Base Case

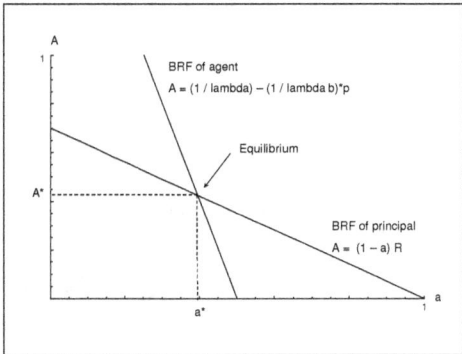

Fig. 5.6 The Best Response Functions of University Management and Faculty Under Faculty Authority

best response function becomes evident, implying that a decrease (increase) in a triggers an increase (decrease) of A.

The following discussion turns to the graphical investigation of the structure of the equilibrium. Comparative statics analyses of the equilibrium values show the impact of a change in one of the exogenous parameters λ, R and b on the equilibrium effort values. The direct effects on the equilibrium effort levels as well as the resulting changes in the payoff levels of the university manager and faculty are examined. Without loss of generality, the external shocks are assumed to increase the respective exogenous parameter.

1. The effects of an increase in λ

    As illustrated by figure 5.7, an increase in the congruence parameter λ flattens the slope of the best response function of faculty and increases the axis intercept on the A-axis. Since λ does not directly affect the BRF of the principal, this graph remains stable. For every level of A, the agent will now exert less effort a. In a setting of faculty authority, it is faculty who profits from an increase in congruity of interests since the university manager can be trusted to a greater degree not to exploit the real authority faculty might delegate to her. Therefore, faculty can reduce his effort.

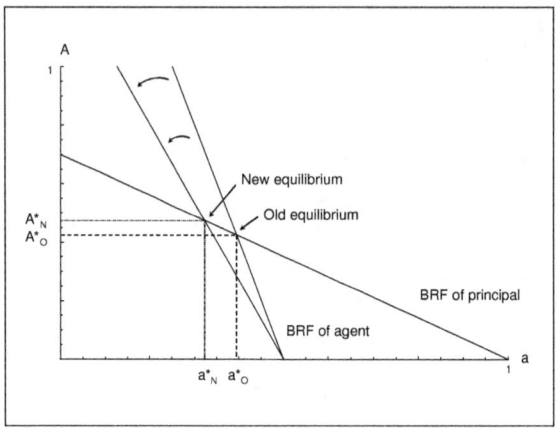

Fig. 5.7 New Equilibrium after an Exogenous Change in λ

The principal responds to a decrease in a with an increase in effort A since the likelihood of having real authority increases with lower a. Indirectly, via the shift of the BRF of the agent, the change in λ thus affects the equilibrium effort level of the principal. The new equilibrium is located above and to the left of the old equilibrium as university manager effort A^* increases and faculty effort a^* decreases.

The second step of comparative statics analysis involves determining how the change in λ affects the payoff levels U and F. In order to derive the direct and indirect effects of λ on the payoff levels, the total derivatives $\frac{dU}{d\lambda}$ and $\frac{dF}{d\lambda}$ are calculated.

Beginning with F, the total derivative $\frac{dF}{d\lambda}$ reads:

$$\frac{dF}{d\lambda} = \frac{\partial F}{\partial a} \cdot \frac{da}{d\lambda} + \frac{\partial F}{\partial A} \cdot \frac{dA}{d\lambda} + \frac{\partial F}{\partial \lambda}$$

$\frac{dA}{d\lambda}$ is not directly defined through the BRF of the principal. Instead, the indirect effect that the BRF of the agent (equation 5.10) has on the BRF of the principal (equation 5.9) needs to be taken into account. The total derivative then yields:

$$\begin{aligned}\frac{dF}{d\lambda} &= \frac{\partial F}{\partial a}\cdot\frac{da}{d\lambda} + \frac{\partial F}{\partial A}\cdot\frac{\partial A}{\partial a}\cdot\frac{\partial a}{\partial \lambda} + \frac{\partial F}{\partial \lambda} \\ &= (b(1-\lambda A) - a)\cdot(-bA) + ((1-a)b\lambda)\cdot(-R)\cdot(-bA) + \\ &\quad ((1-a)Ab) \\ &= (b((A-aR+R)\lambda - 1) + 1)bA > 0\end{aligned}$$

for all $a, A, b, R, \lambda \in (0,1)$. The total effect of an increase in λ on the payoff of faculty is positive. Faculty profits from an increase in λ because the increases in A and λ compensates for the decrease in a.

The total derivative for U with respect to λ illustrates the direct and indirect effects a change in λ has on the payoff of the university manager.

The total derivative reads

$$\begin{aligned}\frac{dU}{d\lambda} &= \frac{\partial U}{\partial a}\cdot\frac{\partial a}{\partial \lambda} + \frac{\partial U}{\partial A}\cdot\frac{\partial A}{\partial a}\cdot\frac{\partial a}{\partial \lambda} + \frac{\partial U}{\partial \lambda} \\ &= (R(\lambda - A))\cdot(-bA) + (R(1-a) - A)\cdot(-R)\cdot(-bA) + Ra \\ &= R((1-bRA)a + (R-\lambda)bA).\end{aligned}$$

The effect of λ on U is ambiguous. The first term of the total derivative is always positive. The sign of the second term depends on the relationship between R and λ. Therefore, it is unclear whether the principal profits from an increase in interest congruence.

2. The effects of an increase in R

   A change in the project payoff to the principal, R, only applies to the best response function of the university manager. The slope of the BRF steepens, and the axis intercept on the A-axis increases, as figure 5.8 shows. For every level of a, the university manager will now exert higher effort A. When the benefit of implementing the preferred project for the university increases, so does her information searching effort.

From the BRF of faculty, it is evident that an increase in university management effort diminishes his incentives to exert high effort. The more effort the university manager exercises, the more faculty will rely on university management having real authority and making the decision. Faculty will consequently lower his own effort a. The new equilibrium is thus located above and to the left of the old equilibrium as principal effort increases and agent effort decreases as a result. The effect of R on the optimal effort level a^* works indirectly through the best response function of the agent, which is negatively influenced by the increased effort level of the principal.

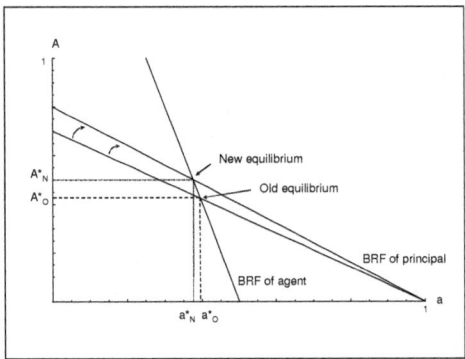

Fig. 5.8 New Equilibrium after an Exogenous Change in R

In order to assess the effect that a change in R has on the payoff levels U and F, the total derivatives $\frac{dU}{dR}$ and $\frac{dF}{dR}$ have to be evaluated (see appendix section 5.6.2.2). Both the total derivative of U with respect to R and the total derivative of F with respect to R are positive for all $a, A, b, R, \lambda \in (0,1)$. This implies that the sum of the direct and indirect effects of a change in R on the payoffs of the principal and the agent is always positive. Both faculty and university management profit from an increase in R since the additional effort of the principal compensates for the reduction of the effort level of the agent.

5.3 An Initiative Model - Base Case

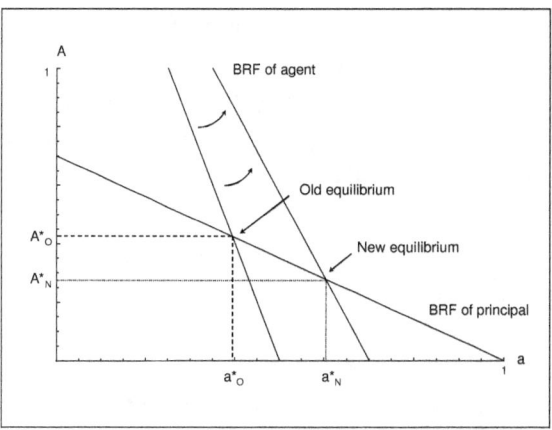

Fig. 5.9 New Equilibrium after an Exogenous Change in b

3. The effects of an increase in b

   The exogenous variable b only affects the best response function of faculty, the agent. As becomes evident from figure 5.9, an increase in b flattens the slope of the best response function of faculty while leaving the BRF of the university manager unchanged. For every A, the agent will now show a higher level of effort since an increase in private benefit strengthens the incentives of the agent to show high search effort in order to implement his preferred project. The BRF of the principal, on the other hand, decreases in a, so that the university manager will exert less effort when the effort of faculty increases as a result of the increase in b. Thus, an increase in b indirectly, via the increase in a, leads the principal to reduce her effort. The new equilibrium is located below and to the right of the old equilibrium as a result of the increase in a^* and the decrease in A^*.

   The total derivatives yield an insight into the effects of a change of b on the payoff levels U and F (see appendix section 5.6.2.2). The total derivative of $\frac{dF}{db}$ is positive, implying that an increase in b leads to an increase in the total payoff level of faculty. Faculty benefits from an increase in b since the positive effects from higher a and b more than compensate the reduction in A. This effect depends on the positive direct impact of b on F and on the indirect positive effects of a and A on F. No clear conclusion can be drawn for the total derivate of U with respect to b. Its sign depends on the relationship between R, λ and a.

The structure of the equilibrium can be summarized as follows: When the level of interest congruence between principal and agent raises, i.e. λ increases, the principal reduces her effort level while the agent increases effort. The total effect on the payoff levels is positive for the agent. The change in the payoff level of the principals depends on the relationship between the endogenous and exogenous variables. When the benefit R increases, the principal will increase her effort level because she gains more when her preferred project is implemented. The total effects of the exogenous changes on the payoffs U and F is positive since the subsequent rise in effort level A compensates the reduction of the agent's effort. When b rises, the agent increases his effort a. With regard to the payoff, the agent's payoff rises, while the payoff of the principal increases only under specific variable constellations.

Despite giving an important insight into the structure of the equilibrium, comparative statics analyses cannot give an indication which authority setting is more beneficial for the players in terms of the payoff levels. The next section addresses this issue by comparing absolute equilibrium effort and payoff values under the two different allocations of control.

5.3.2.4 Comparative Analysis

This section compares the absolute equilibrium values of effort and payoffs under the different authority scenarios. The objective of this analysis of the equilibrium outcomes is to establish the conditions under which contractible delegation, i.e. A-formal authority, is more efficient than centralization, i.e. P-formal authority, and vice versa.

5.3 An Initiative Model - Base Case

First, the equilibrium effort levels of the agent, p^* and a^*, are compared.

$$p^* = \frac{(1-R)b}{1-\lambda bR}$$

$$a^* = \frac{(1-\lambda R)b}{1-\lambda bR}.$$

With $\lambda \in (0,1)$, $a^* > p^*$. This implies that under formally delegated authority, faculty effort in equilibrium is higher than under principal control. Equivalently, with equations (5.5) and (5.11), it can be shown that $P^* > A^*$. The university manager exerts more searching effort when she has formal control over the decision than when she delegates authority to faculty.

Result 1 Formal delegation of authority from the principal to the agent strengthens the search incentives of the agent. The effort made by faculty under A-formal authority is higher than the effort exerted under P-formal authority. The effort of the university manager is higher under P-formal authority than under A-formal authority.

The comparison of the effort levels in the two scenarios does not allow for a direct conclusion about the relation of the payoffs of the parties or about total social benefit in the two settings. It is unclear whether a higher P compensates a lower p in the P-formal setting and whether a lower A is compensated by a higher a under A-formal authority. In the following, the payoff levels of both parties, U and F as well as total welfare, defined as $T = U + F$, are compared. Superscripts distinguish the organizational setting, P for P-formal and A for A-formal authority.

In order to compare equilibrium values, the values of P^*, p^*, A^* and a^* are inserted into the payoff functions (5.1), (5.2), (5.7) and (5.8).

$$F^P = \frac{b(2b^2B^2\lambda^3 + 2B\lambda + b((B-1)^2 - 2B(B+1)\lambda^2))}{2(bB\lambda - 1)^2}$$

$$F^A = \frac{1}{2}(\frac{(b-1)^2}{(bB\lambda-1)^2} + 2b - 1)$$

For faculty, delegation would be efficient if $F^A > F^P$. It can be shown that there exist values for λ, R and b so that this efficiency condition is satisfied. For all $b, R \in (0, 1)$, if congruence is low ($\lambda \leq \frac{1}{3}$), faculty prefers having formal authority. Under the same conditions, the equilibrium values of the university manager's payoff exhibit the opposite relationship: $U^P > U^A$. If $\lambda > \frac{1}{3}$, the preference of faculty depends on the values of R and b (see appendix 5.6.1 for the conditions under which $F^A < F^P$ and $U^P < U^A$).

Result 2 Preferences for the organizational settings are opposed to each other with regard to equilibrium payoff levels. Both parties prefer to have formal authority for themselves as long as $\lambda \leq \frac{1}{3}$.

To derive the optimal authority setting from a total welfare perspective as proposed by Baker et al. (1999), the payoff of university management and faculty are added for the two settings. Total welfare T^A, T^P are defined as the sum of the payoffs under the respective authority constellation. Inserting the equilibrium values P^*, p^*, A^*, and a^* into the payoff functions yields their respective equilibrium values.

$$\begin{aligned} T^P &= U^P + F^P \\ &= \frac{2b^3 R^2 \lambda^3 - 4b(R-1)R\lambda + R^2 + b^2\left((R-2)R\left((2R+1)\lambda^2 + 1\right) + 1\right)}{2(bR\lambda - 1)^2} \end{aligned}$$

$$\begin{aligned} T^A &= U^P + F^A \\ &= \frac{R^2 + b\left(2bR^3\lambda^3 + (b-2)(2b+1)R^2\lambda^2 - 4(b-1)R\lambda + bR^2 - 2R^2 + b\right)}{2(bR\lambda - 1)^2}. \end{aligned}$$

For delegation (A-formal authority) to be more efficient than centralized decision-making (P-formal authority), there must exist a region where $T^A - T^P > 0$. It can be shown that this is the case for $b > R$. For high levels of b compared to R, total welfare is higher under A-formal authority. In contrast, for $b < R$, the opposite applies, i.e. total welfare is then higher under P-formal authority.

5.3 An Initiative Model - Base Case

Result 3 There are economic environments where delegation of authority is efficient from a total welfare point of view. They depend on the relative importance of the decision for the university manager and for the faculty member.

These results may provide a rationale for delegating authority to faculty over decisions that affect and benefit mostly faculty. On the other hand, decisions that are more critical to the university than to faculty should be made by university management.

5.3.3 Synopsis from the Initiative Model

The adaptation of a strategic delegation model to the university context provides a first insight into the inner workings of university decision-making. In general, faculty exerts higher effort in the decision-making process when the decision is important to him, either because his private benefits are high, or because the potential damage the university manager can inflict on him by taking an unfavorable decision is significant (e.g. when the conflict of interests is strong). The effort of the university manager negatively influences faculty effort. Therefore, faculty has stronger incentives to put in high effort when formal authority over decision-making has been delegated to faculty because authority comes with the possibility of achieving higher private benefit. In terms of total welfare, this delegation is efficient for those decisions that matter more to faculty than to the university.

With regard to the university, this model has two main shortcomings:[16]

- The model does not take into account that university manager and faculty may have different perceptions of what the relevant decision alternatives may be. Therefore, the idea that both players are searching for the payoff structure of the same alternatives can be questioned.

- No reference is made to the inherent information advantages the players are assumed to possess. Section 3.5.3 points out that faculty has superior knowledge concerning the academic affairs of the university, whereas the

---

[16] General limitations to the modeling approach are discussed in the conclusion of this chapter (see section 5.5).

university manager is better informed with regard to operational, financial, and other managerial decisions.

In the next section, the base case is extended to address these issues and to yield a more conclusive insight into faculty participation in university decision-making.

5.4 A Proposal Model - Extension

5.4.1 *Modeling Idea*

Building on the basic structure outlined in the initiative model in section 5.3, the model presented in this section will alter the set-up by incorporating stylized characteristics about the university, the university manager, and the faculty member. The objective is to allow conclusions that are more specific for the university context.

Two main differences distinguish the extension model from the base case.

1. The set-up of the proposal model reflects the notion that due to their different preferences, university management and faculty tend to perceive different alternatives as preferable for any given decision. This is included in the model by letting university management and faculty each propose their preferred alternative.

2. Depending on the type of decision, it is assumed that either university management or faculty is the decision 'specialist'. For some decisions, faculty is less able to source information, whereas in other areas, faculty possesses superior knowledge. The model introduces an efficiency factor into the cost function of faculty to capture this effect on the efforts of the players and on the optimal allocation of decision rights.

In particular, the introduction of an efficiency parameter changes the focus of the model: The focus no longer lies on the incentive effect of delegation like in the base case, but on the impact of the cost efficiency parameter on optimal effort provisions and on optimal total welfare levels.

5.4.2 Set-up

5.4.2.1 The University Context

Similar to the base model, this model considers a university as an organization run by a university manager (she) employing one risk-averse faculty (he) member who does not respond to monetary incentives. Faculty primarily engages in research and teaching. In addition to performing research and teaching, faculty is also able to search for information concerning the available alternatives for the decision problems the university faces. Decision-making requires costly information about the available alternatives and their payoffs.

Formal authority over a specific decision resides with the university manager or the faculty member. The distinction between formal and real authority will become evident from the set-up of the payoff functions and the decision-making process outlined in the next section.

5.4.2.2 The Decision-Making Process

For any given decision problem the university faces, each of the two parties, university management and the faculty member, can propose their preferred alternative. Alternatives yield benefit R to the university (e.g. reputational gain, financial resources) and private benefits b to faculty (e.g. reputation, perks on the job, or the acquisition of human capital). Benefits are regarded as net benefits, i.e. the disutility of implementing the alternative has been taken into account. It is assumed that the benefits are soft information that cannot be verified.[17] The payoffs of the alternative the university manager prefers and proposes are R^U, b^U, the payoffs of the preferred alternative of faculty are R^F, b^F.

The two players do not know their preferred alternative ex-ante. Searching effort needs to be exerted in order to gain the relevant information about the payoffs. At date 1, faculty therefore chooses to put forth a non-verifiable effort

---

[17] The concept of soft information is borrowed from Aghion/Tirole: "Soft information cannot be verified by the other party, and therefore its communication must be interpreted as a pure suggestion for project choice" (Aghion/Tirole (1997), p. 7).

5.4 A Proposal Model - Extension

$e \in (0,1)$ at a cost $c(e) = \alpha \frac{e^2}{2}$, allowing him to find and propose his preferred alternative at date 2.[18]

$\alpha \in [1, \infty)$ is a parameter that shows how efficient faculty is in the provision of his effort in relation to the university manager. Setting $\alpha \geq 1$ implies that in the decisions analyzed in the following, faculty has a disadvantage in the searching technology since his costs are equal to or greater than the university manager's costs for any given level of effort. Such decisions are for example financial, purely organizational, or operational decisions.

Also at date 1, the university manager chooses to exert effort $E \in (0,1)$ at a cost $c(E) = \frac{E^2}{2}$, enabling her to propose her preferred alternative at date 2. The fact that the university manager is more efficient for the decisions studied in the following model is implied by incorporating α into the cost function of the faculty member, so that no additional factor must be introduced into the cost function $c(E)$.

For simplicity reasons, in the following model, the payoffs R and b will take only two values, 0 or 1. The payoffs are dependent on the effort exerted in the search for alternatives, i.e. each party "[...] can take actions that affect the probability of discovering a project he likes, such as searching across more potential projects and considering alternative ways to implement a given project" (Baker et al. (1999), p. 59). The higher the search intensity, i.e. the higher the effort levels e and E, the higher the probability of discovering a 'good' project with high payoff. Effort can thus be defined as the probability of finding a project with high payoff.

Table 5.3 gives an overview of the probability distribution over the project payoffs

Conditional probabilities are applied accordingly for the payoff of the other player: Given $R_U = 1$, the conditional probability that the payoff for faculty is high ($b_U = 1$) is λ. When $R_U = 0$, the conditional probability for $b_U = 0$ is μ. The same applies for the proposal of faculty: Given $b_F = 1$, the conditional probability

---

[18] The cost function applied here has the same characteristics as the cost function in the base model (see section 5.3.1.2). It is a strictly convex function with $c(0) = 0$ and $c(1) = 0.5$. This reflects the diminishing marginal product of effort: The higher the effort already exerted, the lower is the value of an additional increase in effort and the higher is the cost of searching. Marginal cost of effort is therefore strictly increasing.

Table 5.3 The Project Payoff Structure in the Proposal Model

University management proposal	Faculty proposal
$Prob(1) = E$	$Prob(1) = e$
$Prob(0) = 1 - E$	$Prob(0) = 1 - e$

that the payoff for university management is high ($R_F = 1$) is λ. When $b_F = 0$, the conditional probability for $R_F = 0$ is μ, with $\lambda, \mu \in (0,1)$.

Analog to the base model, λ and μ are interpreted as congruence parameters. The higher λ, the greater is the probability that a good project for one party will also yield a good project for the other one. The higher μ, the more likely is it that a bad project for one party will also lead to a bad project for the other party. Therefore, the higher the values are, the higher is the congruence of project payoffs between the university manager and faculty. The probabilities for each of the four different states are depicted by tables 5.4 and 5.5.

Table 5.4 The Conditional Probabilities of the Payoffs (Management Proposal)

University management proposal	
Prob(R,b)	Prob(R,b)
$Prob(1,1) = E\lambda$	$Prob(0,1) = (1-E)(1-\mu)$
$Prob(1,0) = E(1-\lambda)$	$Prob(0,0) = (1-E)\mu$

Table 5.5 The Conditional Probabilities of the Payoffs (Faculty Proposal)

Faculty proposal	
Prob(R,b)	Prob(R,b)
$Prob(1,1) = e\lambda$	$Prob(1,0) = (1-e)(1-\mu)$
$Prob(0,1) = e(1-\lambda)$	$Prob(0,0) = (1-e)\mu$

The timing of the decision-making process is as follows: At date 1, university management and faculty choose to exert effort E and e. At date 2, they discover their preferred alternative and their payoffs, and disclose them to the other party. The party with formal authority then takes the decision over which alternative to implement. Like in the base model, there exist two distinct settings:

5.4 A Proposal Model - Extension

1. **University manager has formal authority**

   In this setting, the university manager has the formal right to decide at date 2. She will pick her alternative when it yields her a payoff of 1, which happens with probability E. In case her own alternative yields her a low payoff of 0, which happens with probability $(1-E)$, she picks the alternative proposed by faculty, yielding her an expected value (EV) greater than 0. In case the university manager does not find a 'good' project through her own effort, faculty has real authority over the decision.

2. **Faculty has formal authority**

   In this setting, faculty has received the irrevocable right to make the decision over the alternative to be implemented. Acting independently, faculty will pick his alternative if it yields him a high private benefit of 1 (probability e), and will pick university management's alternative with $EV > 0$ when his own alternative yields a low payoff of 0 (probability $1-e$). If faculty does not discover a project with a high payoff, real authority over the decision lies with the university manager.

In the next section, the proposal model is developed under the two different authority settings.

5.4.3 The Model

5.4.3.1 University Management Authority

This section considers the case when the university manager has the right to make the decision at date 2. For all settings under university control, $e \equiv p$ and $E \equiv P$. Payoffs for university manager U and faculty F then are as follows:

$$(5.13) \qquad U = P + (1-P)(p\lambda + (1-p)(1-\mu)) - \frac{P^2}{2}$$

$$(5.14) \qquad F = P\lambda + (1-P)p - \alpha\frac{p^2}{2}.$$

These payoff functions are interpreted as follows: The university manager exerts effort P and with probability P, she finds her preferred alternative with payoff $R^U = 1$. In this case, she will choose her own alternative, yielding her a payoff of 1. If, on the other hand, she observes her payoff to be $R^U = 0$ (probability $1 - P$), she will then pick the alternative faculty proposes. She does this because the expected payoff of choosing faculty's preferred alternative, $(p\lambda + (1-p)(1-\mu))$, is greater than the payoff from choosing her own alternative, which is 0.[19] It is rational of the university manager to choose faculty's project, thus giving faculty real authority over the decision. $c(P) = \frac{P^2}{2}$ denotes the cost function of effort.[20]

For faculty, payoff depends on the conditional probability of $b^U = 1$ given the fact that $R^U = 1$, which is $P\lambda$. In case $R^U = 0$ (probability $1-P$), faculty's project is chosen, where the payoff then only depends on faculty effort p. $c(p) = \alpha \frac{p^2}{2}$ is the cost function of faculty effort with the efficiency parameter $\alpha \geq 1$.[21]

As in the base model, payoff functions are strictly concave in effort, ensuring that the first-order conditions yield maximum values. Since $\frac{\partial^2 U}{\partial P^2} < 0$, the payoff function of the university manager is concave in effort P. The payoff function of faculty is concave with respect to effort p since $\frac{\partial^2 F}{\partial p^2} < 0$.

In order to find the optimal level of effort P, the university manager maximizes his payoff function with respect to P. Her best response function is defined by setting the first-order derivative with respect to P equal to 0 and solving for P:

$$\frac{\partial U}{\partial P} = 0$$

(5.15) $$P = (1 - \mu - \lambda)p + \mu.$$

---

[19] The expected value of the payoffs from the preferred alternative of faculty is calculated due to the fact that information is soft and cannot be verified. Even though faculty discloses the information about his preferred alternative, the university manager does not know these payoffs with certainty.

[20] To illustrate the logical steps for deriving equation (5.13), the following equation shows the extensive form:

$$U = P \cdot 1 + (1 - P)(p\lambda \cdot 1 + p(1 - \lambda) \cdot 0 + (1 - p)\mu \cdot 0 + (1 - p)(1 - \mu) \cdot 1) - \frac{P^2}{2}.$$

[21] The extensive form of equation (5.14) reads:

$$F = P\lambda \cdot 1 + P(1 - \lambda) \cdot 0 + (1 - P)p \cdot 1 + (1 - P)(1 - p) \cdot 0 - \alpha \frac{p^2}{2}.$$

5.4 A Proposal Model - Extension

Faculty maximizes his payoff function with respect to p. His best response function in information gathering is defined by the FOC:

$$\frac{\partial F}{\partial p} = 0$$

(5.16) $$p = \frac{1}{\alpha}(1 - P).$$

The two reaction functions show the interdependencies between the effort levels of the two players. Differentiating the two best response functions with respect to the other player's effort gives an insight into the relation of the two efforts.

Differentiating the BRF of the university manager with respect to p yields:

$$\frac{\partial P}{\partial p} = 1 - \lambda - \mu.$$

The magnitude and the algebraic sign of the change of P resulting from a change in p depend on the exogenous parameters λ and μ, and on their relation to each other. Two cases can be distinguished:

1. $(\lambda + \mu) > 1$

    This condition implies that the sum of the congruence parameters for good and bad projects is relatively high. It follows that $(1 - \mu - \lambda) < 0$, and thus the derivative $\frac{\partial P}{\partial p} < 0$. With high congruence, an increase in p leads to a decrease in P because the university manager - as the holder of formal authority - can trust faculty not to misuse his real authority in case she does not find a good project. P and p can be regarded as substitutive efforts.

2. $(\lambda + \mu) < 1$

    This condition implies that the combined congruence for good and bad projects is relatively low. Consequently, $1 - \mu - \lambda > 0$, and thus $\frac{\partial P}{\partial p} > 0$. An increase in p results in an increased effort level P. University management demonstrates higher effort with increasing effort of faculty because the latter cannot be trusted sufficiently. P and p are thus complementary efforts.

For the remainder of this model, only case 1 is analyzed since this makes the results comparable to the base model and the reference models. In the following, it is assumed that $\lambda, \mu \in (\frac{1}{2}, 1)$, which ensures $\lambda + \mu > 1$.

Assumption 1: $\lambda, \mu \in (\frac{1}{2}, 1)$

This implies that the situation where both players gain either high or low payoffs is more likely than a state where one player is better off than the other, i.e. payoffs $1, 1$ and $0, 0$ are more likely than $1, 0$ and $0, 1$.

Differentiating the BRF of faculty with respect to P yields:

$$\frac{\partial p}{\partial P} = -\frac{1}{\alpha}.$$

The change in p resulting from a change in P depends on α. The best response function of faculty decreases in the effort of the university manager as $\frac{\partial p}{\partial P} < 0$. The higher P, the less likely is it that faculty has real authority. Thus, faculty has less incentive to exert high effort. P and p are substitutive efforts because faculty demonstrates lower effort the higher the effort of the university manager is.

In order to establish the equilibrium effort values, P^* and p^*, the BRFs from equations (5.15) and (5.16) are solved for P and p.

$$(5.17) \qquad P^* = \frac{1 - \lambda - (1 - \alpha)\mu}{1 + \alpha - \lambda - \mu}$$

and

$$(5.18) \qquad p^* = \frac{1 - \mu}{1 + \alpha - \lambda - \mu}.$$

For all $\lambda, \mu \in (\frac{1}{2}, 1)$, and $\alpha \geq 1$, the equations yields solutions $P^*, p^* \in (0, 1)$.

To show the equilibrium graphically, the two BRFs are plotted into one graph. For this, the BRF of the agent has to be adjusted to the format of the principal's BRF:

$$p = \frac{1}{\alpha}(1 - P)$$
$$\Leftrightarrow P = 1 - \alpha p.$$

5.4 A Proposal Model - Extension

In figure 5.10, the following random values are assumed for λ, μ, and α: $\lambda = 0.6$, $\mu = 0.7$, and $\alpha = 1.2$. The downward slope of the two best response functions becomes evident, implying that a decrease in P results in an increase of p.

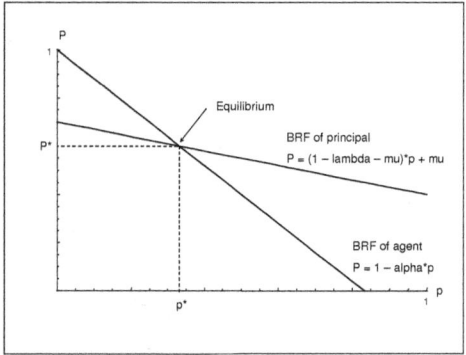

Fig. 5.10 The Best Response Functions of University Management and Faculty Under University Management Authority

Two questions arise concerning the structure of the equilibrium. The first addresses the change of the equilibrium values when the exogenous parameters vary due to an external shock. The second, related, question refers to the change in the payoff levels of principal and agent from the subsequent shift in equilibrium effort values. The results from the comparative statics analyses of the equilibrium are illustrated in section 5.4.3.3. The next section first derives the equilibrium in the organizational setting where faculty has formal authority over the decision.

5.4.3.2 Faculty Authority

In the following setting, faculty has been given authority over decision-making.[22] To distinguish the effort levels from the setting under university control, $e \equiv a$ and $E \equiv A$. Payoffs for university manager U and faculty F are represented by the following functions:

$$(5.19) \qquad U = a\lambda + (1-a)A - \frac{A^2}{2}$$

$$(5.20) \qquad F = a + (1-a)(A\lambda + (1-A)(1-\mu)) - \alpha\frac{a^2}{2}.$$

For university management, payoff depends on the probability for $R^F = 1$ given $b^F = 1$, which is $a\lambda$. In case $b^F = 0$ (probability $1-a$), the university manager's project is chosen, where the payoff then only depends on university management effort A. The cost function of the university manager is represented by $c(A) = \frac{A^2}{2}$.

Faculty chooses his own alternative if it yields payoff 1 (probability a). In case it generates only payoff 0 (probability $1-a$), he chooses university management's alternative, yielding a payoff of $A\lambda + (1-A)(1-\mu)) > 0$. The logic for this choice is similar to the setting where the university manager has formal authority: If faculty does not find a project with a high payoff, he chooses the project university management has proposed since the expected payoff of the university manager's alternative is greater than 0, the payoff guaranteed by his own alternative. In such a situation, effective decision control is delegated to the university manager. The cost function is represented by $c(a) = \alpha\frac{a^2}{2}$, where α is a cost efficiency parameter with $\alpha \geq 1$.

The payoff functions are concave in their respective efforts, as the derivatives show: $\frac{\partial^2 U}{\partial A^2} < 0$, and $\frac{\partial^2 F}{\partial a^2} < 0$. These are sufficient conditions for obtaining maximum values of the payoff functions with respect to the effort levels.

---

[22] The expression "faculty control" is used synonymously.

5.4 A Proposal Model - Extension

To determine the optimal effort level, the university manager maximizes U with respect to A. Her best response function is defined by setting the first-order derivative with respect to A equal to 0 and solving for A:

(5.21)
$$\frac{\partial U}{\partial A} = 0$$
$$A = 1 - a.$$

Faculty maximizes his payoff function with respect to a. His best response function is defined by the FOC:

(5.22)
$$\frac{\partial F}{\partial a} = 0$$
$$a = \frac{1}{\alpha}(A(1 - \lambda - \mu) + \mu).$$

The derivatives of the reaction functions with respect to the other player's effort show how the effort levels of the two players are related. Differentiating the university manager's BRF with respect to a shows that the derivative is constant:

$$\frac{\partial A}{\partial a} = -1.$$

A marginal increase in a will always result in an identical marginal decrease in A. The best response function of the university manager decreases in faculty effort because the likelihood of having real authority is smaller when a increases. The smaller the chance of effectively controlling the decision is, the lower are the incentives for the university manager to exert high effort. A and a are substitutive efforts because the university manager demonstrates lower effort the higher the effort of the faculty member is.

Differentiating the best response function of faculty with respect to A yields:

$$\frac{\partial a}{\partial A} = \frac{1}{\alpha}(1 - \lambda - \mu).$$

The magnitude and the sign of the change in the effort level a resulting from a change in effort A depend on the relation between λ and μ. Due to assumption 1, $(\lambda + \mu) > 1$. Therefore, $\frac{\partial a}{\partial A} < 0$. An increase in A leads to a decrease in a because the faculty member can trust the university manager not to misuse the real authority delegated to her if he himself is not informed. A and a can be regarded as substitutive efforts.

From the two reaction functions, equations (5.21) and (5.22), the equilibrium values for A^* and a^* are derived:

(5.23) $$A^* = \frac{\alpha - \mu}{1 + \alpha - \lambda - \mu}$$

and

(5.24) $$a^* = \frac{1 - \lambda}{1 + \alpha - \lambda - \mu}.$$

Assuming $\lambda, \mu \in (\frac{1}{2}, 1)$ and $\alpha \geq 1$ ensures equilibrium values $A^*, a^* \in (0, 1)$.

To show the equilibrium graphically, the two BRFs are plotted into one graph. The BRF of the agent (equation (5.22)) has to be adjusted to the same format of the BRF of the principal:

$$a = \frac{1}{\alpha}(1 - \lambda - \mu)A)$$
$$\Leftrightarrow A = \frac{\mu - \alpha a}{1 - \lambda - \mu}.$$

In figure 5.11, the following random values are assumed for λ, μ, and α: $\lambda = 0.6$, $\mu = 0.7$, and $\alpha = 1.2$. From the graphs in figure 5.11, the downward slope of the two best response function becomes evident, implying that a decrease in A results in an increase of a.

The next section discusses the comparative statics effects of the equilibria under university control and faculty control settings. Comparative statics analyze the change in the endogenous variables following a change in one of the exogenous parameters and thus give an insight into the structure of the equilibria.

5.4 A Proposal Model - Extension

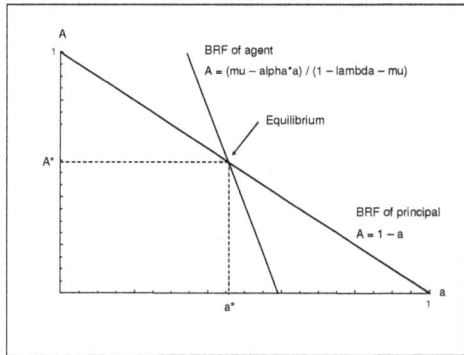

Fig. 5.11 The Best Response Functions of University Management and Faculty Under Faculty Authority

5.4.3.3 Comparative Statics

5.4.3.3.1 Introduction

In order to understand the structure of the equilibrium, the effects of a change in the exogenous parameters on the equilibrium efforts and payoffs have to be examined. In the following, the comparative statics are shown graphically in order to illustrate the relevant effects on the equilibrium effort levels (see section 5.6.2 in the appendix for a numerical treatment).[23] The effects on the payoff functions of the players are illustrated with the help of total derivatives.

Three types of external shocks can arise: An increase or decrease in λ, in μ, and in α. For simplicity reasons, and without loss of generality, the following analysis will only be concerned with increases in the exogenous parameters. Each of these effects is considered separately in the following analysis of the equilibria. A joint treatment does not allow conclusive insights since the effects of the different exogenous parameters could not be differentiated.

---

[23] The graphs in this section are derived on the basis of the values used for the graphs in sections 5.4.3.1 and 5.4.3.2 above. $\lambda = 0.6$, $\mu = 0.7$, and $\alpha = 1.2$ serve as the reference point of this analysis. The numerical treatment shows that the conclusions drawn for this particular set of graphs are valid for all values of the parameters within their respective domain.

138   5 Modeling Faculty Participation in University Decision-Making

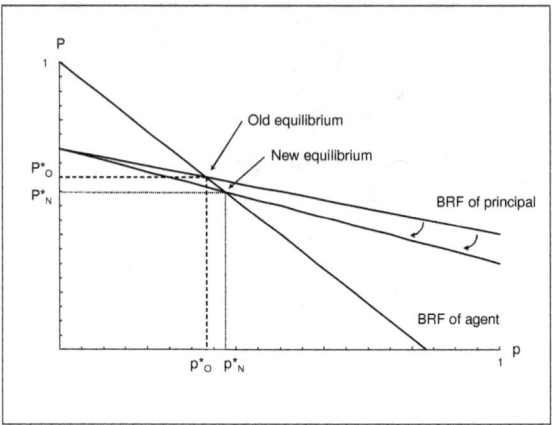

Fig. 5.12 New Equilibrium after an Exogenous Change in λ

The next two sections illustrate the structure of the equilibria and the underlying economic rationale for the settings of university control and faculty control. The detailed calculations are shown only for changes in λ. Sections 5.6.3.1 and 5.6.3.2 in the appendix of this chapter present the numerical treatments of changes in μ and α under university control and faculty control, respectively.

5.4.3.3.2 University Control

1. The effects of an increase in λ.

    An increase in λ, the parameter of the congruence of interests for high payoffs between the university and faculty, leads to a decrease in the optimal value of the effort of university management. Figure 5.12 shows that the slope of the BRF of the principal steepens while the BRF of the agent remains stable. For every value of p, the university manager now exerts less effort than before the change in the exogenous parameter.

    The economic intuition behind this effect is the following: When λ increases, the interests between the principal and the agent become more congruent. Therefore, the principal can trust the agent to a greater degree to make a

5.4 A Proposal Model - Extension

decision that is in the best interest of both players. She can reduce her effort, knowing that faculty will increase his effort to compensate for it. When P declines, faculty's likelihood of gaining real authority over the decision increases, which strengthens his incentive to show high effort. Therefore, the change in λ affects the equilibrium level of the agent indirectly via the shift of the BRF of the principal. The new equilibrium is located below and to the right of the old equilibrium as university manager effort P^* decreases and faculty effort p^* increases.

Through the changes in the equilibrium values, a change in λ has an indirect effect on the payoff levels U and F (equations (5.13) and (5.14)). In order to illustrate the direct and indirect effects of λ on the payoff levels, the total derivatives $\frac{dU}{d\lambda}$ and $\frac{dF}{d\lambda}$ are calculated.

The total derivative $\frac{dU}{d\lambda}$ reads:

$$\frac{dU}{d\lambda} = \frac{\partial U}{\partial p} \cdot \frac{dp}{d\lambda} + \frac{\partial U}{\partial P} \cdot \frac{dP}{d\lambda} + \frac{\partial U}{\partial \lambda}$$

$\frac{dp}{d\lambda}$ is not directly defined through the BRF of the agent.[24] Therefore, the indirect effect of the BRF of the principal on the BRF of the agent needs to be taken into account. The total derivative then yields:

$$\begin{aligned}
\frac{dU}{d\lambda} &= \frac{\partial U}{\partial p} \cdot \frac{\partial p}{\partial P} \cdot \frac{\partial P}{\partial \lambda} + \frac{\partial U}{\partial P} \cdot \frac{dP}{d\lambda} + \frac{\partial U}{\partial \lambda} \\
&= ((1-P)(\lambda + \mu - 1)) \cdot (-\frac{1}{\alpha}) \cdot (-p) + \\
&\quad (\mu - P - p(\lambda + \mu - 1)) \cdot (-p) + (p - pP) \\
&= \frac{1}{\alpha}(p(\lambda + \mu - P(\lambda + \mu - 1) + \alpha(1 - \mu + p(\lambda + \mu - 1)) - 1)) > 0
\end{aligned}$$

for $p, P \in (0,1)$, $\lambda, \mu \in (\frac{1}{2}, 1)$, and $\alpha \geq 1$. The total effect of an increase in λ on the payoff of the university manager is positive. The university manager decreases her effort P (and thus her costs of effort), but the subsequent increases in p and λ more than offset this in the payoff function.

---

[24] This can also be concluded from the fact that the BRF of the agent does not shift as a result of a change in λ, as figure 5.12 shows.

The next step involves setting up the total derivative for F in order to analyze the direct and indirect effects a change in λ has on the payoff of faculty. The total derivative reads

$$\begin{aligned} \frac{dF}{d\lambda} &= \frac{\partial F}{\partial p} \cdot \frac{\partial p}{\partial P} \cdot \frac{\partial P}{\partial \lambda} + \frac{\partial F}{\partial P} \cdot \frac{dP}{d\lambda} + \frac{\partial F}{\partial \lambda} \\ &= (1 - P - p\alpha) \cdot (-\frac{1}{\alpha}) \cdot (-p) + (\lambda - p) \cdot (-p) + P \\ &= \frac{1}{\alpha}(P(\alpha - p) + (1 - \alpha\lambda)p). \end{aligned}$$

The effect of λ on F is ambiguous. The first term of the total derivative is positive, while the sign of the second term depends on the relationship between λ and α.[25] The total derivative $\frac{dF}{d\lambda}$ thus can be either positive or negative since it is unclear whether the increases in p and λ can compensate for the decrease in P in the payoff function of faculty.

2. The effects of an increase in μ.

   Contrary to an increase in λ, an increase in μ induces the principal to exert higher effort. The axis intercept on the P-axis increases and the slope of the BRF of the principal steepens. The best response function of the agent remains unchanged. Higher congruence for bad projects implies that for a given a, the alternative proposed by faculty yields lower expected payoff to the university. Ceteris paribus, the expected payoff of the university manager would decrease with increasing μ.

   In order to increase the likelihood of having both formal and real authority herself, the university manager increases her effort in μ. Due to the downward slope of his best response function, faculty reacts to the increase in university management effort with a decrease in p. His incentives are weakened by the increase in management effort which reduces the likelihood that faculty has real authority over the decision.

---

[25] For $\alpha < 2$, the sign of the second term is positive if $\lambda < \frac{1}{\alpha}$. For all $\alpha \geq 2$, the term will always be negative since $\lambda > \frac{1}{2}$. The sign of the total derivative then depends on the magnitude of the two terms.

5.4 A Proposal Model - Extension

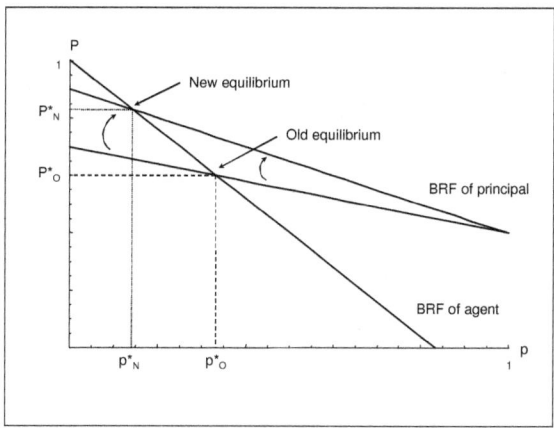

Fig. 5.13 New Equilibrium after an Exogenous Change in μ

In order to assess the effect a change in μ has on the payoff levels U and F, the total derivatives $\frac{dU}{d\mu}$ and $\frac{dF}{d\mu}$ have to be evaluated. The total derivative of U with respect to μ is negative for $p, P, \in (0,1)$, $\lambda, \mu \in (\frac{1}{2}, 1)$, and $\alpha \geq 1$. An increase in the congruence for bad projects decreases the total payoff of the principal as the increase in P compensates for the decrease in p and the negative impact of the rise of μ on the profit function ($\frac{\partial U}{\partial \mu} < 0$).

The total derivative of F with respect to μ, on the other hand, is ambiguous. Its algebraic sign depends on the relationship between α, λ and P. No conclusive statement can be made regarding the sum of effects of an increase in μ on F.

3. The effects of an increase in α.

  An increase in α only affects the best response function of the agent, while the BRF of the principal remains stable. Figure 5.14 shows that the slope of the BRF of faculty steepens, implying that p decreases when the cost factor of faculty increases. The economic intuition behind this effect is straightforward: The higher α, the more costly it is for faculty to exert effort. He will therefore respond to the increase in searching costs by reducing

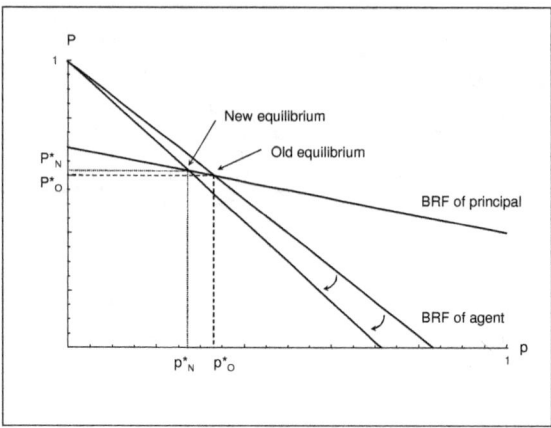

Fig. 5.14 New Equilibrium after an Exogenous Change in α

his optimal level of effort. As the best response function of the university manager is downward sloping in the effort of faculty, she will react with an increase in P to compensate the reduction in her agent's effort. Indirectly, via the impact p has on P, an increase in α induces the university manager to increase her optimal effort level.

The total derivatives of U and F with respect to α yield an insight into the effects of a change of α on the payoff levels U and F. The total derivative of U with respect to α is negative, so that any increase in the cost of faculty effort reduces the payoff to the university manager. The increase in P does not compensate for the subsequent increase in effort costs and for the decrease in p. For the case of faculty payoff, the sign of the total derivative $\frac{dF}{d\alpha}$ depends on the relationships between λ, μ, α, P and p. No conclusive statement can be inferred on the impact of an increase in α on the payoff of faculty.

5.4 A Proposal Model - Extension

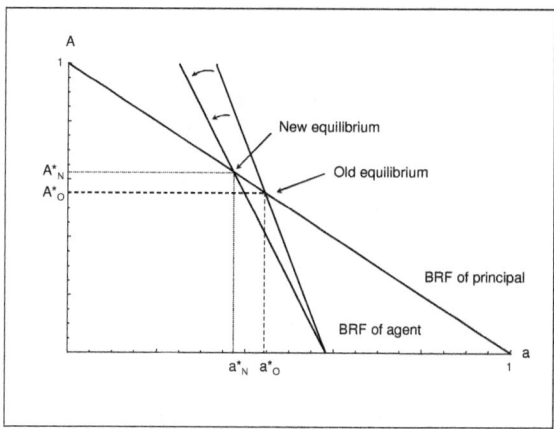

Fig. 5.15 New Equilibrium after an Exogenous Change in λ

5.4.3.3.3 *Faculty Control*

This section analyzes the effort equilibrium as illustrated by figure 5.11 for the setting when faculty has formal authority over the decision. Three types of external shocks and their effect on equilibrium effort and payoffs are considered:

1. The effects of an increase in λ

    An increase in λ, the congruence of interests for high payoffs between the university and faculty, induces a decrease in the optimal value of the effort of faculty. Figure 5.15 shows that the slope of the BRF of the agent flattens and the axis intercept on the A-axis decreases. The BRF of the principal remains stable. For every value of A, faculty now exerts less effort than before the change in the exogenous parameter.

    The economic intuition behind this effect is the following: When λ increases, the interests between the principal and the agent become more congruent. Therefore, the agent, who has formal authority in this setting, can trust the principal to a greater degree to make a good decision. He can reduce his effort, knowing that the university manager will increase her effort to compensate for the reduced effort of faculty. When a decreases, the likelihood that the university manager gains real authority over the decision increases, which strengthens her incentive to show high effort. Therefore, the change in λ affects the equilibrium level of the principal indirectly via the shift of the BRF of the agent. The new equilibrium is located above and to the left of the old equilibrium as faculty effort a^* decreases and university management effort A^* increases.

To find out how the change in λ affects the payoff levels U and F (equations (5.19) and (5.20)), the total derivatives $\frac{dU}{d\lambda}$ and $\frac{dF}{d\lambda}$ are calculated.

Beginning with F, the total derivative $\frac{dF}{d\lambda}$ reads:

$$\frac{dF}{d\lambda} = \frac{\partial F}{\partial a}\cdot\frac{da}{d\lambda} + \frac{\partial F}{\partial A}\cdot\frac{dA}{d\lambda} + \frac{\partial F}{\partial \lambda}$$

$\frac{dA}{d\lambda}$ is not directly defined through the BRF of the principal. Instead, the indirect effect that the BRF of the agent has on the BRF of the principal needs to be taken into account. The total derivative then yields:

$$\begin{aligned}\frac{dF}{d\lambda} &= \frac{\partial F}{\partial a}\cdot\frac{da}{d\lambda} + \frac{\partial F}{\partial A}\cdot\frac{\partial A}{\partial a}\cdot\frac{\partial a}{\partial \lambda} + \frac{\partial F}{\partial \lambda} \\ &= (\mu - \alpha a - (\lambda + \mu - 1)A)\cdot(-\frac{A}{\alpha}) + \\ & \quad ((1-a)(\lambda+\mu-1))\cdot(-1)\cdot(-\frac{A}{\alpha}) + (1-a)A \\ &= \frac{1}{\alpha}(A(\alpha + \lambda - a(\lambda + \mu - 1) + A(\lambda + \mu - 1) - 1)) > 0\end{aligned}$$

for all $a, A, \in (0,1)$, $\lambda, \mu \in (\frac{1}{2}, 1)$, and $\alpha \geq 1$. The total effect of an increase in λ on the payoff of faculty, F, is positive. Faculty profits from an increase in λ because the increases in A and λ compensate for the decrease in a.

The next step involves setting up the total derivative for U in order to analyze the direct and indirect effects a change in λ has on the payoff of the university manager.

5.4 A Proposal Model - Extension

The total derivative reads

$$\begin{aligned}\frac{dU}{d\lambda} &= \frac{\partial U}{\partial a}\cdot\frac{\partial a}{\partial \lambda}+\frac{\partial U}{\partial A}\cdot\frac{\partial A}{\partial a}\cdot\frac{\partial a}{\partial \lambda}+\frac{\partial U}{\partial \lambda}\\ &= (\lambda - A)\cdot(-\frac{A}{\alpha})+(1-a-A)\cdot(-1)\cdot(-\frac{A}{\alpha})+a\\ &= \frac{1}{\alpha}(a\alpha-(a+\lambda-1)A) > 0\end{aligned}$$

for $a, A, \in (0,1)$, $\lambda \in (\frac{1}{2}, 1)$, and $\alpha \geq 1$. The effect of λ on U is also positive. With an increase in congruity for good projects, the university manager exerts higher effort A. Together with the increase in λ this compensates for the decrease in faculty effort a in the payoff function of the university manager.

2. The effects of an increase in μ

    Similar to the increase in λ, an increase in μ flattens the slope of the BRF of the agent and decreases the axis intercept on the A-axis. From figure 5.16 it becomes evident that a flattening of the slope implies that the agent exerts a higher effort. The best response function of the principal remains unchanged. Higher μ, i.e. higher congruence for bad projects, implies that for a given A, the alternative proposed by the university manager yields lower expected payoff to faculty. Ceteris paribus, the expected payoff of faculty would decrease with increasing μ.

    In order to increase the likelihood of having both formal and real authority to himself, faculty increases her effort in μ. Due to the downward slope of his best response function, the university manager reacts to the increase in university management effort with a decrease in A. Her incentives are weakened by the increase in management effort which reduces the likelihood that faculty has real authority over the decision. The new equilibrium is characterized by a lower A^* and a higher a^*. The increase of μ affects the optimal level of A indirectly via the BRF of the university manager, which is negatively affected by the increase in a.

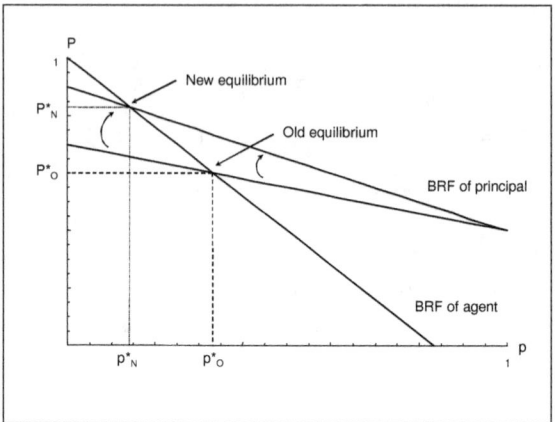

Fig. 5.16 New Equilibrium after an Exogenous Change in μ

In order to assess the effect a change in μ has on the payoff levels U and F, the total derivatives $\frac{dU}{d\mu}$ and $\frac{dF}{d\mu}$ have to be evaluated. The total derivative of F with respect to μ is negative for $a, A \in (0,1)$, $\lambda, \mu \in (\frac{1}{2}, 1)$, and $\alpha \geq 1$. An increase in the congruence for bad projects decreases the total payoff of faculty because the positive effect from additional a is compensated by the cost of effort and the decrease in A. The total derivative of U with respect to μ, on the other hand, is ambiguous. Its algebraic sign depends on the relationship between λ and a.[26] No conclusive statement can be made regarding the sum of effects of an increase in μ on U.

3. The effects of an increase in α

   An increase in α only affects the best response function of the agent, while the BRF of the principal remains stable. Figure 5.17 shows that the slope of the BRF of faculty steepens, implying that a decreases when the cost factor of faculty increases. The economic intuition behind this effect is straightforward: The higher α, the more costly it is for faculty to exert effort.

---

[26] If $a > (1 - \lambda)$, then the total derivative is positive and an increase in μ would have a positive overall effect on the payoff of the university manager. If $a < (1 - \lambda)$, then the total derivative is negative.

5.4 A Proposal Model - Extension

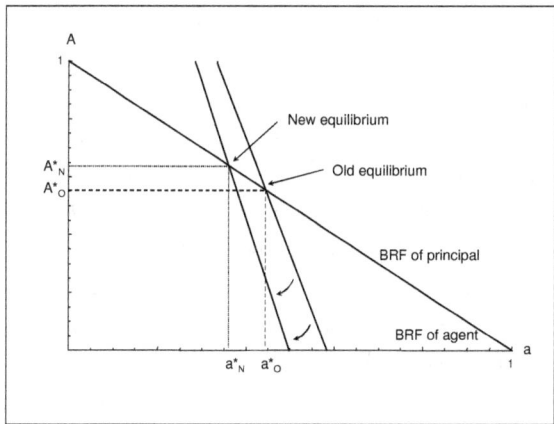

Fig. 5.17 New Equilibrium after an Exogenous Change in α

Faculty will therefore respond to the increase in searching costs by reducing his optimal level of effort. As the best response function of the university manager is downward sloping in the effort of faculty, she will react with an increase in A to compensate the reduction in the agent's effort. Indirectly, via the impact a has on A, an increase in α induces the university manager to increase her optimal effort level.

The total derivatives of U and F with respect to α depict the influence a change in α has on the payoffs. The total derivatives of U and F with respect to α are ambiguous. If $a > (1 - \lambda)$, then the total derivative $\frac{dU}{d\alpha}$ is positive and an increase in α would have a positive overall effect on the payoff of the university manager. If $a < (1 - \lambda)$, then the total derivative is negative. For the case of faculty payoff, the sign of the total derivative $\frac{dF}{d\alpha}$ depends on the relationships between λ, μ, α, A and a. No conclusive statement can be inferred on the impact of an increase in α on the payoff of faculty.

In regard to the effort equilibria, the two organizational settings show identical comparative static results for an increase in α. An increase in the costs of faculty effort leads to a reduction of the effort of the agent. Consequently, the principal increases her effort because the likelihood of having real authority increases when faculty reduces effort.

Concerning increase of λ and μ, the changes in the equilibrium effort levels under university control and faculty control show opposite signs. An increase in λ leads to a decrease (increase) in P^* (A^*) and consequently, an increase (decrease) in p^* (a^*). An increase in μ causes an increase (decrease) in P^* (A^*) and induces a decrease (increase) in p^* (a^*). The economic intuition behind this is straightforward: The party with formal control is interested in delegating authority by decreasing his own effort whenever the congruence for good project payoff, λ, increases. When the congruence for bad projects, μ, increases, then the party in control wants to ensure that he has both formal and real authority and will thus increase his effort.

Despite giving an important insight into the structure of the equilibrium, comparative statics analyses cannot give an indication which authority setting is more beneficial for the players in terms of the payoff levels. The next section addresses this issue by comparing absolute equilibrium payoff values under the two different allocations of control.

5.4.3.4 Comparative Analysis

In order to derive which authoritative setting is more efficient, the equilibrium total welfare levels under university and faculty control have to be compared. In the following, it will be analyzed whether there are regions where total welfare of faculty authority exceeds total welfare of university control. The objective is to illustrate which indications α can give for the optimal allocation of decision rights.

Equilibrium total welfare is defined as the sum of university manager and faculty payoffs in equilibrium, dependent on α: $T(\alpha) = U(\alpha) + F(\alpha)$.[27] Super-

---

[27] Equilibrium payoffs are obtained by inserting P^*, p^*, A^* and a^* into equations (5.13), (5.14), (5.21), and (5.22) respectively.

5.4 A Proposal Model - Extension

scripts distinguish the organizational setting, P for principal-formal authority (or university control) and A for agent-formal authority (or faculty control).

$$
\begin{aligned}
T^P(\alpha) &= U^P + F^P \\
&= \frac{1}{2(\lambda+\mu-\alpha-1)^2}\left[(\mu(2\lambda+\mu-2)+2)\alpha^2 - \right. \\
&\quad \left. (2(\mu+1)\lambda^2 - 2\mu^2\lambda + \mu^2 - 4\mu + 3)\alpha + (2\lambda+1)(\lambda+\mu-1)^2\right] \\
T^A(\alpha) &= U^A + F^A \\
&= \frac{1}{2}\left(\frac{(\alpha+1)(\lambda-1)^2}{(\lambda+\mu-\alpha-1)^2} - \frac{2(\alpha-\lambda+1)(\lambda-1)}{\lambda+\mu-\alpha-1} + 3\right).
\end{aligned}
$$

For delegation (faculty authority) to be more efficient than centralized decision-making (university authority), there must exist a region where $(T^P < T^A)$, i.e. where $(T^P - T^A) < 0$. To find this region, the points of intersection of $(T^P - T^A)$ with the abscissa (α-axis), i.e. the points where $(T^P - T^A) = 0$, are analyzed. Define

$$
\begin{aligned}
D(\alpha) &\equiv T^P(\alpha) - T^A(\alpha) \\
&= \frac{1}{2(\lambda+\mu-\alpha-1)^2}\left[(\alpha-1)(\alpha(\mu-1)(2\lambda+\mu-1) + \right. \\
&\quad \left. (1-\lambda)(-\lambda(1-2\mu) + 2(\mu-1)\mu + 1))\right]
\end{aligned}
$$

The roots of $D(\alpha)$ are:

$$\alpha_1 = 1$$

and

$$\alpha_2 = \frac{(\lambda-1)(2(\mu-1)\mu + \lambda(2\mu-1)+1)}{(1-\mu)(1-2\lambda-\mu)}$$

Since α is defined in the domain $[1, \infty)$, α_2 should be greater than 1. Therefore, some restrictions apply to λ. Given assumption 1, $\lambda, \mu \in [\frac{1}{2}, 1)$, $\alpha_2 > 1$ if

$$\lambda < \frac{(\mu-2)(\mu-1)}{1-2\mu} + \sqrt{\frac{\mu(\mu^3+2\mu-4)+2}{(1-2\mu)^2}}$$

Assumption 2: $\lambda < \frac{(\mu-2)(\mu-1)}{1-2\mu} + \sqrt{\frac{\mu(\mu^3+2\mu-4)+2}{(1-2\mu)^2}}$

By analyzing the derivative of $\frac{\partial D}{\partial \alpha}$ at the two roots α_1 and α_2, a conclusion on the algebraic sign of D between the two roots can be drawn.

$$\frac{\partial D}{\partial \alpha} = \frac{1}{2(\alpha - \lambda - \mu + 1)^3} \big[(\mu(4\mu - 9) + 3)\lambda^2 - (1 - 2\mu)\lambda^3 + \\ ((\mu - 2)\mu(2\mu - 5) - 4)\lambda + (4 - \mu)(\mu - 1)\mu + \\ \alpha \left((3 - 2\mu)\lambda^2 + 2(1 - \mu)(2\mu - 3)\lambda + \mu((5 - 2\mu)\mu - 6) + 2\right) + 2 \big]$$

At α_1, the value of $\frac{\partial D}{\partial \alpha}$ is

$$\frac{\partial D}{\partial \alpha}(\alpha_1) = \frac{(\mu - 1)^2(2\lambda + \mu - 1)^2 \left((2\mu - 1)\lambda^2 + 2(\mu - 2)(\mu - 1)\lambda + (4 - 3\mu)\mu - 2\right)}{2(\lambda + \mu)^2(+\mu + \lambda - \mu^2 - 1)^2}$$

At α_2, the value of $\frac{\partial D}{\partial \alpha}$ is

$$\frac{\partial D}{\partial \alpha}(\alpha_2) = \frac{(1 - 2\mu)\lambda^2 - 2(\mu - 2)(\mu - 1)\lambda + \mu(3\mu - 4) + 2}{2(\lambda + \mu - 2)^2}$$

Given assumptions 1 and 2, it can be shown that

$$\frac{\partial D}{\partial \alpha}(\alpha_1) > 0$$
$$\frac{\partial D}{\partial \alpha}(\alpha_2) < 0$$

This implies that between α_1 and α_2, $D > 0$. For all α larger than α_2, $D < 0$. To show this graphically, figure 5.18 plots D with two random values for λ and μ that satisfy assumptions 1 and 2, e.g. $\lambda = 0.6$ and $\mu = 0.7$.[28]

Independent of the particular values chosen for λ and μ in figure 5.18, for all $1 < \alpha < \alpha_2$, it is efficient from a total welfare perspective to allocate the decision right to the university manager. For all $\alpha > \alpha_2$, it is more efficient to allocate the formal decision rights to faculty. Despite allocating formal authority to faculty, the likelihood that real decision control will be delegated back to the university manager due to low faculty effort a increases with higher α.

---

[28] For all λ and μ satisfying assumptions 1 and 2, the graph of D follows a similar course, i.e. always exhibits two roots and a global maximum.

5.4 A Proposal Model - Extension

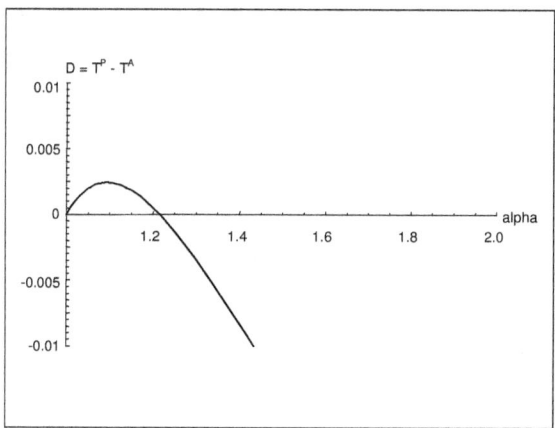

Fig. 5.18 The Difference between Total Welfare under University Control and under Faculty Control in Equilibrium dependent on α

This is the decisive result of the comparative analysis. It shows that it is not only the allocation of formal authority rights, but also the prospect of the delegation of real authority that provides incentives to exert effort. As α increases significantly above 1, the incentive of faculty to show high effort decreases as a result of the rising costs of effort. In this situation, university management increases her effort in order to obtain real authority and to implement her preferred project.

In order to explain the particular course of $D = T^P - T^A$ as shown in figure 5.18, the graphs of the two components of D, T^P and T^A, are analyzed.

1. $T^P(\alpha)$ represents the total welfare function at the effort equilibrium under university control. It is defined by the sum of the equilibrium payoff values U^P and F^P. Its graph is presented in figure 5.19 for $\lambda = 0.6$ and $\mu = 0.7$.

   To explain the decreasing slope of $T^P(\alpha)$, the following brief analysis draws on the insights from the total derivatives of U^P and F^P with respect to α. As becomes clear from section 5.4.3.3.2, the equilibrium value of U decreases as α increases. The impact on the equilibrium value of F is less clear as

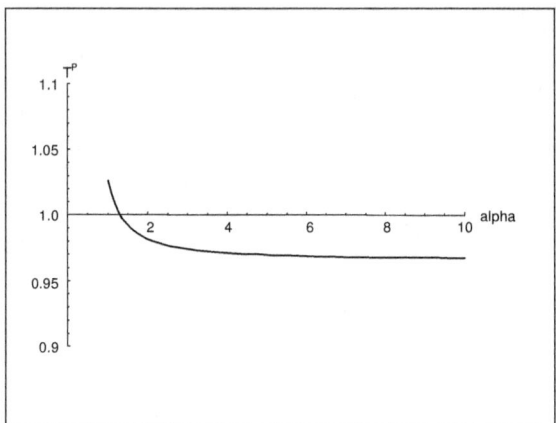

Fig. 5.19 Equilibrium University Welfare dependent on α

it depends on the relationship between the endogenous variables and the exogenous parameters. For the particular values chosen here, $\frac{dF}{d\alpha}$ is at first negative. For large α, it turns positive since faculty then reduces effort in order to economize on the increasing searching costs. The sum of the two total derivatives is negative for all $\alpha \leq 1$ as the decrease in U^P is always larger than the increase of F^P for large α. This explains the downward slope of the function $T^P(\alpha)$ in figure 5.19.

2. $T^A(\alpha)$ is the total welfare function at the equilibrium of effort provision for the setting where faculty has authority over decision-making. In order to explain the course of the graph depicted in figure 5.20, the total derivatives of its two components, U^A and F^A are analyzed.

As set out in section 5.4.3.3.3, $\frac{dU}{d\alpha}$ and $\frac{dF}{d\alpha}$ are generally ambiguous in terms of their sign. For the particular values chosen for the graph, the total derivatives are negative for small α slightly above 1. As α increases, however, the resulting changes in the effort levels A and a reverse the signs of the total derivatives. Above certain levels of α, any additional increase in α has a positive effect on the payoffs of the university manager and faculty as the

5.4 A Proposal Model - Extension

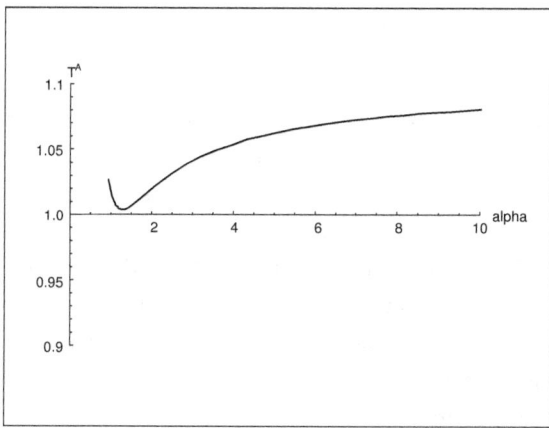

Fig. 5.20 Equilibrium Faculty Welfare dependent on α

increase in A compensates for the decrease in a. This explains the switch in the sign of the derivative $\frac{\partial T^A(\alpha)}{\partial \alpha}$ as shown in figure 5.20.

To summarize the implications above: Given assumptions 1 and 2, university authority is more efficient for low levels of faculty inefficiency ($1 < \alpha < \alpha_2$) because T^P decreases slower than T^A for small α at the same time. Thus, $T^P > T^A$ for small α. For larger α, T^A increases while T^P continues to decrease, so that $T^A > T^P$. It is therefore more efficient to delegate formal authority to faculty for higher levels of faculty inefficiency, i.e. $\alpha > \alpha_2$.

The next section summarizes the results of the proposal model and illustrates some possibilities for further development of a decision-making model for the university.

5.4.4 Synopsis from the Proposal Model

The key message from the proposal model is that for high degrees of faculty inefficiency, i.e. for large α, formal authority should be delegated to faculty. The explanation of this result lies in the fact that real authority is more and more likely to be allocated with the university manager as α increases. Centralizing decision rights with the university is therefore not always the optimal solution even when faculty's decision technology is more costly than that of the university manager. Leaving formal control with faculty as faculty grows more and more inefficient implies that faculty will reduce his effort as it becomes too costly. Consequently, the university manager increasingly gains effective control and thus has an incentive to exert more effort.

The proposal model can serve as an explanation of the fact that members in practice often have far-reaching decision rights even in areas where they do not necessarily possess superior expertise.[29] In such situations, proposal model suggests that the writing of decision memos and agenda setting is performed increasingly by the university manager, who exerts more effort (more cheaply) than faculty.

The proposal model gives strategic delegation a double twist beyond the trade-off illustrated in the base model in section 5.3. In the proposal model, decision rights are only formally delegated to faculty because it is clear that the likelihood of informal delegation back to the university manager increases with increasing faculty inefficiency. When the costs of searching information rise for faculty, he has little incentives to increase his effort. However, the university manager overcompensates this by exerting higher effort and exercising real authority.

Due to the simplified set-up, the results of the model naturally have some limitations. By including some of the following aspects, the model could be developed further to generate more insight into the allocation of decision rights:

---

[29] See e.g. McCormick/Meiners (1988) and Brown (2001) for evidence from the US. In Germany, many State Acts on Higher Education grant faculty-dominated bodies such as the senate the right to decide a multitude of matters that do not all fall in the realm of research or teaching. Refer to chapter 7 for further insight into decision-making at German universities.

- In order to generalize the conclusions, the model could be calculated with general payoffs instead of 0 and 1. For the set-up of this particular model, incorporating general payoffs would have been too complex mathematically.

- Payoff could be modeled as a vector of the different aspects that influence the payoff of a project. This would make the different perceptions of what constitutes a 'good' project and the conflict of interests between university management and faculty more evident.

The next section summarizes the insights gained from the study of economic modeling in the university context and from the two models developed to examine faculty participation in university decision-making.

5.5 Conclusion

This chapter demonstrates how formal economic modeling can be applied to analyze the decision-making structure in universities. In the context of other modeling accounts concerned with the university and the reference models on strategic delegation of the firm, the motivation is to show how a formal model can help to analyze the role of faculty participation in university decision-making.

For this purpose, two related models – the initiative and the proposal model – are developed. The main conclusion from the initiative model is that formal delegation of authority to faculty increases faculty's incentive to exert more search effort, thus enabling him to make better decisions. In terms of total welfare, the initiative model established a criterion for delegation: Formal decision control should be delegated contingent on the relation of the payoffs which an alternative yields to the university and to faculty. When private benefits to faculty are higher than the benefit for the university, the decision right should be allocated to faculty, and vice versa.

The proposal model is set in a slightly different context where university management and faculty propose competing alternatives for any given decision. The university manager is assumed to be the decision specialist in the variant of the model studied since he possesses a cheaper information searching technology. The key insight that is derived from this approach is that delegation of authority to the faculty member does not necessarily increase the incentives of faculty to exert more effort, but rather enhances the incentives of the university manager to exert higher effort. By introducing a cost efficiency factor into the faculty's cost function, the effects of higher costs of effort compared to the university manager are captured.

The higher this efficiency factor, i.e. the more costly it is for faculty to provide effort, the lower will be the optimal effort level for faculty and the higher the effort level for the university manager. The total welfare analysis shows that it is initially efficient for the university manager to retain the control rights when faculty is slightly less efficient than the university manager in providing effort. As faculty becomes more and more inefficient in effort provision, it is favorable from a total welfare perspective for the university manager to formally delegate authority to faculty, knowing that the likelihood of obtaining real authority of the decision herself increases as well.

While the results of this first model concerned with the formal study of faculty participation in university decision-making provide a first step to discovering the underlying mechanisms of university governance, further modeling efforts could address some of the following issues not incorporated into the models developed in this dissertation:

- Only one member of university management and faculty is considered in the model, which assumes homogeneous preferences among the group. Extending the framework to allow multiple faculty members would allow to capture the effects of group decision-making.

- A future model could incorporate the time the players spend in the decision process. For university management, searching for information, evaluating alternatives, and ultimately making decisions can be considered part of the job description. Faculty's main tasks, on the other hand, are research and teaching, so that the proposition could be put forward that involvement in decision-making distracts their attention from fulfilling their actual tasks. The role of influence activities could also be analyzed in this context.

- Despite the fact that monetary incentives do not play a very important role in universities to date, the effects of introducing performance-based compensation could be addressed. Incentives would have to differentiate between the primary tasks of faculty, i.e. research and teaching, and involvement in university governance.

- The modeling of the payoff structure could be further refined to incorporate the notion that faculty payoff not only depends on his private benefit but also on the overall prestige of the university. This should produce a higher degree of interest congruity between university management and faculty.

Mathematical models provide theoretical insight and understanding of the basic mechanisms of a certain phenomenon. They necessarily reduce the complexity of the real world by making simplified assumptions. Therefore, the problem arises of how to make implementable recommendations for practice from the mathematical discussions. In order to provide a richer perspective on university decision-making and to be able to derive meaningful policy implications, the next two chapters consequently focus on universities in reality. The purpose is to analyze the role of faculty participation in German university decision-making and to explain the effects this organizational structure is observed to have in reality.

5.6 Appendix

5.6.1 Conditions for the Initiative Model

Section 5.3.2.4 showed the conditions under which $F^A > F^P$ and $U^P > U^A$. There are, however, regions where $F^A < F^P$ and $U^P < U^A$.

- When $\frac{1}{3} < \lambda \leq \frac{1}{2}$, then $F^A < F^P$ and $U^P < U^A$ if $0 < b < \frac{3\lambda-1}{2\lambda^2}$ and $0 < B < \frac{2\lambda-2}{2b\lambda^2-\lambda-1}$, or if $\frac{3\lambda-1}{2\lambda^2} \leq b < 1$ and $0 < B < 1$.

- When $\frac{1}{2} < \lambda < 1$, then $F^A < F^P$ and $U^P < U^A$ if $0 < b < 1$ and $0 < B < \frac{2\lambda-2}{2b\lambda^2-\lambda-1}$.

5.6.2 Comparative Statics for the Initiative Model

This section presents the numerical treatment of the comparative statics for the initiative model. For the economic rationale, see sections 5.3.2.2 and 5.3.2.3.

5.6.2.1 University Control

Comparative statics analysis of the equilibrium values yields insights into the reaction of the equilibrium values P^* and p^* to exogenous changes in the parameters λ, R and b given $\lambda, b, R \in (0,1)$.

1. P^* decreases with λ.

   The higher the congruence of interests between the university and faculty, the less the university manager exerts search effort.
   $$\frac{\partial P^*}{\partial \lambda} = \frac{(R-1)bR}{(\lambda bR - 1)^2} < 0.$$

2. P^* increases with R.

   The higher the benefit of implementing the preferred project for the university manager, the higher will be her information searching effort.
   $$\frac{\partial P^*}{\partial R} = \frac{1-\lambda b}{(\lambda bR - 1)^2} > 0.$$

3. P^* decreases with b.

   The higher the private benefit of the agent, the more effort he will exert and consequently, the lower will be the effort of the principal.
   $$\frac{\partial P^*}{\partial b} = \frac{(R-1)\lambda R}{(\lambda bR - 1)^2} < 0.$$

The same analysis can be conducted for the equilibrium effort value of faculty, p^*. It can be noted that the reaction in p^* to changes in the parameters λ, R and b are exactly opposite to those in P^*.

1. p^* increases with λ.

   A higher λ leads the principal to exert less effort because the congruence of

5.6 Appendix

interests between principal and agent increases. Thus, the incentives of the agent are strengthened and he shows a higher effort.

$$\frac{\partial p^*}{\partial \lambda} = \frac{(1-R)b^2 R}{(\lambda b R - 1)^2} > 0.$$

2. p^* decreases with R.

    A higher R implies a higher searching effort from the principal, which diminishes the agent's incentives for effort.

$$\frac{\partial p^*}{\partial R} = \frac{(b\lambda - 1)b}{(\lambda b R - 1)^2} < 0.$$

3. p^* increases with b.

    The higher the potential private benefit of the agent, the higher his searching effort.

$$\frac{\partial p^*}{\partial b} = \frac{1-R}{(\lambda b R - 1)^2} > 0.$$

In the following, the total derivatives of U and F are shown with respect to R and b.

1. Total derivatives with respect to R

    The total derivative $\frac{dU}{dR}$ reads:

$$\begin{aligned}\frac{dU}{dR} &= \frac{\partial U}{\partial p} \cdot \frac{dp}{dP} \cdot \frac{dP}{dR} + \frac{\partial U}{\partial P} \cdot \frac{dP}{dR} + \frac{\partial U}{\partial R} \\ &= ((1-P)R\lambda) \cdot (-b) \cdot (1-\lambda p) + (R - P - R\lambda p) \cdot (1-\lambda p) + \\ &\quad (P + \lambda p - \lambda p P) \\ &= \lambda p + R(\lambda p - 1)((b + p - bP)\lambda - 1) > 0\end{aligned}$$

    for $p, P, b, R, \lambda \in (0,1)$.

The total derivative $\frac{dF}{dR}$ reads:

$$\begin{aligned}
\frac{dF}{dR} &= \frac{\partial F}{\partial p} \cdot \frac{dp}{dP} \cdot \frac{dP}{dR} + \frac{\partial F}{\partial P} \cdot \frac{dP}{dR} + \frac{\partial F}{\partial R} \\
&= ((1-P)b - p) \cdot (-b) \cdot (1 - \lambda p) + (b(\lambda - p)) \cdot (1 - \lambda p) + 0 \\
&= b(b(P-1) + \lambda)(1 - p\lambda).
\end{aligned}$$

The sign of the total derivative $\frac{dF}{dR}$ is ambiguous and depends on the relationships between p, P, b, R and λ.

2. Total derivatives with respect to b

The total derivative $\frac{dU}{db}$ reads:

$$\begin{aligned}
\frac{dU}{db} &= \frac{\partial U}{\partial p} \cdot \frac{dp}{db} + \frac{\partial U}{\partial P} \cdot \frac{dP}{dp} \cdot \frac{dp}{db} + \frac{\partial U}{\partial b} \\
&= ((1-P)R\lambda) \cdot (1-P) + \\
&\quad (R - P - R\lambda p) \cdot ((1-P)R\lambda) \cdot (1-P) + 0 \\
&= -(P-1)^2 R\lambda (P + R(\lambda p - 1) - 1) > 0
\end{aligned}$$

for $p, P, b, R, \lambda \in (0,1)$.

The total derivative $\frac{dF}{db}$ reads:

$$\begin{aligned}
\frac{dF}{db} &= \frac{\partial F}{\partial p} \cdot \frac{dp}{db} + \frac{\partial F}{\partial P} \cdot \frac{dP}{dp} \cdot \frac{dp}{db} + \frac{\partial F}{\partial b} \\
&= (b(1-P) - p) \cdot (1-P) + (b\lambda - bp) \cdot (-R\lambda) \cdot (1-P) + \\
&\quad (\lambda P + (1-P)p) \\
&= \lambda P + b(P-1)(P + R\lambda(\lambda - p) - 1) > 0
\end{aligned}$$

for $p, P, b, R, \lambda \in (0,1)$.

5.6 Appendix

5.6.2.2 Faculty Control

Comparative statics analysis of the equilibrium values yields insights into the reaction of the equilibrium values A^* and a^* to exogenous changes in the parameters λ, R and b given $\lambda, b, R \in (0,1)$.

1. A^* increases with λ.

    The higher λ, the lower is faculty's effort, and thus the higher the university manager's effort.
    $$\frac{\partial A^*}{\partial \lambda} = \frac{(R-bR)bR}{(\lambda bR - 1)^2} > 0.$$

2. A^* increases with R.

    The higher the benefit of implementing the preferred project for the university, the higher will be her information searching effort.
    $$\frac{\partial A^*}{\partial R} = \frac{1-b\lambda}{(\lambda bR - 1)^2} > 0.$$

3. A^* decreases with b.

    The higher the private benefit of the agent is, the more effort the agent exerts. This has a negative effect on the incentives of the principal, who consequently reduces her effort.
    $$\frac{\partial A^*}{\partial b} = \frac{(\lambda R - 1)R}{(\lambda bR - 1)^2} < 0.$$

The same analysis can be conducted for the equilibrium value of the agent's effort a^*. The reaction in a^* to changes in the parameters λ, R and b are exactly opposite to those in A^*.

1. a^* decreases with λ.

    The higher the congruence of interests between the university and faculty, the less effort faculty exerts.
    $$\frac{\partial a^*}{\partial \lambda} = \frac{(R-1)bR}{(\lambda bR - 1)^2} < 0.$$

2. a^* decreases with R.

   Higher benefit R to the university induces the university manager to exert higher effort. This in turn negatively influences the optimal effort level of the agent.

   $$\frac{\partial a^*}{\partial R} = \frac{(b-1)\lambda b}{(\lambda bR - 1)^2} > 0.$$

3. a^* increases with b.

   The higher the private benefit of implementing his preferred project, the higher will be the search effort of the agent.

   $$\frac{\partial a^*}{\partial b} = \frac{1 - \lambda R}{(\lambda bR - 1)^2} > 0.$$

In the following, the total derivatives of U and F are shown with respect to R and b.

1. Total derivatives with respect to R

   The total derivative $\frac{dU}{dR}$ reads:

   $$\begin{aligned} \frac{dU}{dR} &= \frac{\partial U}{\partial a} \cdot \frac{da}{dP} \cdot \frac{dA}{dR} + \frac{\partial U}{\partial A} \cdot \frac{dA}{dR} + \frac{\partial U}{\partial R} \\ &= (R(\lambda - A)) \cdot (-b\lambda) \cdot (1-a) + (R - A - aR) \cdot (1-a) + \\ & \quad ((1-a)A + \lambda a) \\ &= \lambda a + (a-1)R(a + b\lambda(\lambda - A) - 1) > 0. \end{aligned}$$

   for $a, A, b, R, \lambda \in (0, 1)$.

   The total derivative $\frac{dF}{dR}$ reads:

   $$\begin{aligned} \frac{dF}{dR} &= \frac{\partial F}{\partial a} \cdot \frac{da}{dA} \cdot \frac{dA}{dR} + \frac{\partial F}{\partial A} \cdot \frac{dA}{dR} + \frac{\partial F}{\partial R} \\ &= (b - a - b\lambda A) \cdot (-b\lambda) \cdot (1-a) + ((1-a)b\lambda) \cdot (1-a) + 0 \\ &= (1-a)b\lambda(b(A\lambda - 1) + 1) > 0. \end{aligned}$$

   for $a, A, b, R, \lambda \in (0, 1)$.

5.6 Appendix

2. Total derivatives with respect to b

   The total derivative $\frac{dU}{db}$ reads:

   $$\begin{aligned}
   \frac{dU}{db} &= \frac{\partial U}{\partial a} \cdot \frac{da}{db} + \frac{\partial U}{\partial A} \cdot \frac{dA}{da} \cdot \frac{da}{db} + \frac{\partial U}{\partial b} \\
   &= (R(\lambda - A)) \cdot (1 - \lambda A) + (R - A - aR) \cdot (-R) \cdot (1 - \lambda A) + 0 \\
   &= R((a-1)R + \lambda)(1 - \lambda A).
   \end{aligned}$$

   The sign of the total derivative $\frac{dU}{db}$ is ambiguous and depends on the relationships between a, A, b, R and λ.

   The total derivative $\frac{dF}{db}$ reads:

   $$\begin{aligned}
   \frac{dF}{db} &= \frac{\partial F}{\partial a} \cdot \frac{da}{db} + \frac{\partial F}{\partial A} \cdot \frac{dA}{da} \cdot \frac{da}{db} + \frac{\partial F}{\partial b} \\
   &= (b(1 - \lambda A) - a) \cdot (1 - \lambda A) + ((1-a)b\lambda) \cdot (-R) \cdot (1 - \lambda A) + \\
   &\quad (a + (1-a)\lambda A) \\
   &= \lambda A + b(\lambda A - 1)((A - Ra + R)\lambda - 1) > 0.
   \end{aligned}$$

   for $a, A, b, R, \lambda \in (0, 1)$.

5.6.3 Comparative Statics for the Proposal Model

This section presents the numerical treatment of the comparative statics for the proposal model. For the economic rationale, see section 5.4.3.3.

5.6.3.1 University Control

Comparative statics analysis of the equilibrium values yields insights into the reaction of the equilibrium values P^* and p^* to exogenous changes in the parameters λ, μ and α given $\lambda, \mu \in (\frac{1}{2})$ and $\alpha \geq 1$.

1. P^* decreases with λ.

   The higher the congruence of interests for high payoffs between the university and faculty, the less search effort the university manager exerts.

   $$\frac{\partial P^*}{\partial \lambda} = \frac{\alpha(\mu - 1)}{(\lambda + \mu - \alpha - 1)^2} < 0.$$

2. P^* increases with μ.

   The higher the congruence of interests for low project payoffs is, the more effort the university manager exerts.
   $$\frac{\partial P^*}{\partial \mu} = \frac{(\alpha - \lambda)\alpha}{(\lambda + \mu - \alpha - 1)^2} > 0.$$

3. P^* increases in α.

   The higher α is, the lower faculty effort is, and thus the higher the university manager's effort is.
   $$\frac{\partial P^*}{\partial \alpha} = \frac{(1 - \mu)(\lambda + \mu - 1)}{(\lambda + \mu - \alpha - 1)^2} > 0.$$

The same analysis can be conducted for the equilibrium effort value of faculty, p^*. The reaction of p^* to changes in the parameters λ, μ and α are exactly opposite to those in P^*.

1. p^* increases with λ.

   A higher congruence of interests for good projects between the university and faculty induces the university manager to exert less effort. An increase in λ thus strengthens the incentives for faculty to show high search effort.
   $$\frac{\partial p^*}{\partial \lambda} = \frac{1 - \mu}{(\lambda + \mu - \alpha - 1)^2} > 0.$$

2. p^* decreases with μ.

   The higher the congruence of bad projects is between university management and faculty, the more effort the university manager exerts. Faculty reacts to the increased effort of the university manager by reducing his own effort.
   $$\frac{\partial p^*}{\partial \mu} = \frac{\lambda - \alpha}{(\lambda + \mu - \alpha - 1)^2} < 0.$$

3. p^* decreases with α.

   The higher α, the lower the efficiency of faculty and the more costly is faculty

5.6 Appendix

effort. Since the cost of effort affects the payoff function negatively, effort decreases with increasing α.

$$\frac{\partial p^*}{\partial \alpha} = \frac{\mu - 1}{(\lambda + \mu - \alpha - 1)^2} < 0.$$

In the following, the total derivatives of U and F are shown with respect to μ and α.

1. Total derivatives with respect to μ

   The total derivative $\frac{dU}{d\mu}$ reads:

   $$\begin{aligned}
   \frac{dU}{d\mu} &= \frac{\partial U}{\partial p} \cdot \frac{dp}{dP} \cdot \frac{dP}{d\mu} + \frac{\partial U}{\partial P} \cdot \frac{dP}{d\mu} + \frac{\partial U}{\partial \mu} \\
   &= (P-1)(\lambda + \mu - 1) \cdot (-\frac{1}{\alpha}) \cdot (1-p) + \\
   &\quad (\mu - P(\lambda + \mu - 1)p) \cdot (1-p) - 1 + p + P - pP \\
   &= \frac{1}{\alpha}[(p-1)(\lambda + \mu - 1 - (\lambda + \mu - 1)P + \\
   &\quad \alpha(1 - \mu + p(\lambda + \mu - 1))] < 0.
   \end{aligned}$$

   for $p, P, \in (0,1)$, $\lambda, \mu \in (\frac{1}{2}, 1)$, and $\alpha \geq 1$.

   The total derivative $\frac{dF}{d\mu}$ reads:

   $$\begin{aligned}
   \frac{dF}{d\mu} &= \frac{\partial F}{\partial p} \cdot \frac{dp}{dP} \cdot \frac{dP}{d\mu} + \frac{\partial F}{\partial P} \cdot \frac{dP}{d\mu} + \frac{\partial F}{\partial \mu} \\
   &= (1 - P - \alpha p) \cdot (-\frac{1}{\alpha}) \cdot (1-p) + (\lambda - p) \cdot (1-p) + 0 \\
   &= \frac{1}{\alpha}[(1-p)(P + \alpha\lambda - 1)] < 0.
   \end{aligned}$$

   The sign of the total derivative $\frac{dF}{d\mu}$ is ambiguous and depends on the relationships between p, P, λ, μ and α.

2. Total derivatives with respect to α

   The total derivative $\frac{dU}{d\alpha}$ reads:

   $$\begin{aligned}
   \frac{dU}{d\alpha} &= \frac{\partial U}{\partial p} \cdot \frac{dp}{d\alpha} + \frac{\partial U}{\partial P} \cdot \frac{dP}{dp} \cdot \frac{dp}{d\alpha} + \frac{\partial U}{\partial \alpha} \\
   &= (1-P)(\lambda+\mu-1) \cdot \left(\frac{P-1}{\alpha^2}\right) + \\
   &\quad (\mu - P - (\lambda+\mu-1)p) \cdot (1-\lambda-\mu) \cdot \left(\frac{P-1}{\alpha^2}\right) + 0 \\
   &= \frac{1}{\alpha^2}[(P-1)(\lambda+\mu-1)(1-\mu+(\lambda+\mu-1)p)] < 0.
   \end{aligned}$$

   for $p, P, \in (0,1)$, $\lambda, \mu \in (\frac{1}{2}, 1)$, and $\alpha \geq 1$.

   The total derivative $\frac{dF}{d\alpha}$ reads:

   $$\begin{aligned}
   \frac{dF}{d\alpha} &= \frac{\partial F}{\partial p} \cdot \frac{dp}{d\alpha} + \frac{\partial F}{\partial P} \cdot \frac{dP}{dp} \cdot \frac{dp}{d\alpha} + \frac{\partial F}{\partial \alpha} \\
   &= (1 - P - \alpha p) \cdot \left(\frac{P-1}{\alpha^2}\right) + (\lambda - p) \cdot (1-\lambda-\mu) \cdot \left(\frac{P-1}{\alpha^2}\right) - \frac{p^2}{2} \\
   &= \frac{(P-1)(1-P-\alpha p + (p-\lambda)(\lambda+\mu-1))}{\alpha^2} - \frac{p^2}{2}.
   \end{aligned}$$

   The sign of the total derivative $\frac{dF}{d\alpha}$ is ambiguous and depends on the relationships between p, P, λ, μ and α.

5.6.3.2 Faculty Control

Comparative statics analysis of the equilibrium values yields insights into the reaction of the equilibrium values A^* and a^* to exogenous changes in the parameters λ, μ and α given $\lambda, \mu \in (\frac{1}{2})$ and $\alpha \geq 1$.

1. A^* increases with λ.

   A higher congruence of interests for good projects between the university and faculty induces faculty to exert less effort. An increase in λ thus strengthens the incentives for the university manager to show high search effort.

   $$\frac{\partial A^*}{\partial \lambda} = \frac{\alpha - \mu}{(\lambda + \mu - \alpha - 1)^2} > 0.$$

5.6 Appendix

2. A^* decreases with μ.

   The higher the congruence of interests for low project payoffs is, the more effort faculty exerts and the university manager consequently lowers her effort.
   $$\frac{\partial A^*}{\partial \mu} = \frac{\lambda - 1}{(\lambda + \mu - \alpha - 1)^2} < 0.$$

3. A^* increases in α.

   The higher α is, the lower faculty effort is, and thus the higher the university manager's effort is.
   $$\frac{\partial A^*}{\partial \alpha} = \frac{1 - \lambda}{(\lambda + \mu - \alpha - 1)^2} > 0.$$

The same analysis can be conducted for the equilibrium effort value of faculty, a^*. The reaction of a^* to changes in the parameters λ, μ and α are exactly opposite to those in A^*.

1. a^* decreases with λ.

   The higher the congruence of interests is between a good project of the university and faculty, the less effort faculty exerts.
   $$\frac{\partial a^*}{\partial \lambda} = \frac{\mu - \alpha}{(\lambda + \mu - \alpha - 1)^2} < 0.$$

2. a^* increases with μ.

   The higher the congruence of interests for low project payoffs is, the more effort faculty exerts.
   $$\frac{\partial a^*}{\partial \mu} = \frac{1 - \lambda}{(\lambda + \mu - \alpha - 1)^2} > 0.$$

3. a^* decreases with α.

   The higher α, the lower the efficiency of faculty and the more costly is faculty effort. Since the cost of effort affects the payoff function negatively, effort decreases with increasing α.

$$\frac{\partial a^*}{\partial \alpha} = \frac{\lambda - 1}{(\lambda + \mu - \alpha - 1)^2} < 0.$$

In the following, the total derivatives of U and F are shown with respect to μ and α.

1. Total derivatives with respect to μ

   The total derivative $\frac{dU}{d\mu}$ reads:

   $$\begin{aligned}
   \frac{dU}{d\mu} &= \frac{\partial U}{\partial a} \cdot \frac{da}{d\mu} + \frac{\partial U}{\partial A} \cdot \frac{dA}{da} \cdot \frac{da}{d\mu} + \frac{\partial U}{\partial \mu} \\
   &= (\lambda - A) \cdot \left(\frac{1-A}{\alpha}\right) + (1 - a - A) \cdot \left(\frac{1-A}{\alpha}\right) \cdot (-1) + 0 \\
   &= -\frac{(A-1)(a+\lambda-1)}{\alpha}.
   \end{aligned}$$

   The sign of the total derivative $\frac{dU}{d\mu}$ is ambiguous and depends on the relationships between a, A, λ, μ and α.

   The total derivative $\frac{dF}{d\mu}$ reads:

   $$\begin{aligned}
   \frac{dF}{d\mu} &= \frac{\partial F}{\partial a} \cdot \frac{da}{d\mu} + \frac{\partial F}{\partial A} \cdot \frac{dA}{da} \cdot \frac{da}{d\mu} + \frac{\partial F}{\partial \mu} \\
   &= (\mu - \alpha a - (\lambda + \mu - 1)A) \cdot \left(\frac{1-A}{\alpha}\right) + \\
   &\quad ((1-a)(\lambda + \mu - 1)) \cdot (-1) \cdot \left(\frac{1-A}{\alpha}\right) + (a + A - aA - 1) \\
   &= \frac{1}{\alpha}(A-1)(\alpha + \lambda - (\lambda + \mu - 1)a + A(\lambda + \mu - 1) - 1) \langle 0.
   \end{aligned}$$

   for $a, A, \in (0, 1)$, $\lambda, \mu \in (\frac{1}{2}, 1)$, and $\alpha \geq 1$.

5.6 Appendix

2. Total derivatives with respect to α

The total derivative $\frac{dU}{d\alpha}$ reads:

$$\begin{aligned}
\frac{dU}{d\alpha} &= \frac{\partial U}{\partial a} \cdot \frac{da}{d\alpha} + \frac{\partial U}{\partial A} \cdot \frac{dA}{da} \cdot \frac{da}{d\alpha} + \frac{\partial U}{\partial \alpha} \\
&= (\lambda - A) \cdot \left(\frac{(\lambda + \mu - 1)A - \mu}{\alpha^2} \right) + \\
&\quad (1 - a - A) \cdot (-1) \cdot \left(\frac{(\lambda + \mu - 1)A - \mu}{\alpha^2} \right) + 0 \\
&= \frac{1}{\alpha^2} \left(a + \lambda - 1 \right) \left((\lambda + \mu - 1)A - \mu \right).
\end{aligned}$$

The sign of the total derivative $\frac{dU}{d\alpha}$ is ambiguous and depends on the relationships between a, A, λ, μ and α.

The total derivative $\frac{dF}{d\alpha}$ reads:

$$\begin{aligned}
\frac{dF}{d\alpha} &= \frac{\partial F}{\partial a} \cdot \frac{da}{d\alpha} + \frac{\partial F}{\partial A} \cdot \frac{dA}{da} \cdot \frac{da}{d\alpha} + \frac{\partial F}{\partial \alpha} \\
&= (\mu - a\alpha - (\lambda + \mu - 1)A) \cdot \left(\frac{(A(\lambda + \mu - 1) - \mu)}{\alpha^2} \right) + \\
&\quad ((1-a)(\lambda + \mu - 1)) \cdot (-1) \cdot \left(\frac{(A(\lambda + \mu - 1) - \mu)}{\alpha^2} \right) - \frac{a^2}{2} \\
&= \frac{(a-1)(\lambda + \mu - 1)((\lambda + \mu - 1)A - \mu)}{\alpha^2} + \\
&\quad \frac{(\mu - a\alpha - (\lambda + \mu - 1)A)(A(\lambda + \mu - 1) - \mu)}{\alpha^2} - \frac{a^2}{2}.
\end{aligned}$$

The sign of the total derivative $\frac{dF}{d\alpha}$ is ambiguous and depends on the relationships between a, A, λ, μ and α.

Part III
Empirical Insights

6 The Methodology of the Empirical Study

6.1 Introduction

Parts I and II of this dissertation covered the theoretical steps of the research process outlined in section 1.3. This part turns to the validation of the theoretical hypotheses through empirical evidence by conducting the first qualitative empirical study on decision-making in universities in Germany based on thirteen expert interviews.

The primary objective of the empirical study is to provide an understanding of the practical dimension of faculty participation in university decision-making in Germany and of its effects on the university. Based on this practical understanding, implementable recommendations concerning possible reform measures for the organization of university governance and decision-making can be made.

Chapter 6 sets outs the research question and develops the empirical methods and instruments that are used in the analysis. The methodological choices are justified in the context of the available research methods.[1]

Chapter 7 presents the results from the analysis. The effects faculty participation in decision-making has on the university are illustrated and an explanation for their existence is offered.

The empirical study will progress along the following steps of an empirical research process: (1) the formulation of a research question and the selection of a suitable research methodology, (2) the design of a conceptual model and the development of key questions, (3) the selection of the data collection method, (4) the choice of an evaluation strategy and the evaluation of the data collected, and lastly (5), the interpretation and presentation of the results (Gläser/Laudel (2004), p. 60). The description of the different steps contributes to the objectivity, the reliability, and the validity of the empirical analysis.

Before turning to the research question, two empirical accounts that are concerned with university governance in the US are presented. They serve as a basis

---

[1] This dissertation cannot provide an in-depth treatment of empirical research in the social sciences as this lies outside its scope. For exhaustive presentations, see Bortz/Döring (2002), Brüsemeister (2000), Denzin/Lincoln (1998), Flick (2002), Lamnek (1995a, 1995b), Mayring (2002), Roth/Holling (1999), Schnell et al. (2005).

for developing the research question and the choice of methodology for the study conducted in Germany.

6.2 Empirical Background

McCormick/Meiners (1988) and Brown (2001) investigate the benefits and costs of faculty participation and the proposed trade-off of the positive and negative effects on university performance. The objective of these studies is to demonstrate the existence of such effects. Little emphasis is placed on discovering the underlying causes.

Based on a property-rights approach, McCormick/Meiners (1988) assert that collective decision-making is less efficient than centralized decision-making. According to their argumentation, faculty participation in governance yields worse decision-making results and negatively influences academic performance.

University performance is approximated with three different indicators: The output of economics departments, the publications by former graduate students, and the Scholastic Aptitude Test (SAT) scores of incoming freshmen. To determine the degree of faculty participation in university decision-making, the study draws on data from a 1970 AAUP survey of faculty governance which reveals the percentage of university decisions made by faculty. This measure is used as the independent variable in the regression analysis. The statistical results show that "[...] faculty who do research and teach graduate students do not govern much, and faculty who govern do not publish or educate graduate students much." (p. 437). McCormick/Meiners come to the conclusion that faculty participation in university decision-making is not beneficial for the university and they raise the question why universities still organize this way.

The apparent discrepancy between the predictions of McCormick/Meiners (1988) and the organizational structures of universities in reality serves as the starting point for Brown (2001). Based on agency theory, Brown argues that the optimal level of faculty participation should vary by decision type suggesting that stakeholder control over "[...] certain types of academic decisions may lead to improved performance." (p. 130).

Brown (2001) groups decisions into different categories and uses the data from the AAUP survey to determine the percentage of decisions controlled by faculty for each decision type. Thus, a more differentiated view on faculty participation in university decision-making is derived. The degree of faculty participation for each decision type serves as the independent variable in the regression analysis.

University performance is approximated with three separate measures: SAT scores of freshmen, a rating of universities, and faculty salaries. The main conclusion of the regression analyses is that university performance and faculty participation in decision-making are related, but that it depends on the type of decision whether this relationship is positive or negative. These results are not stable across the three performance proxies, so that causal relationships between faculty participation and university performance cannot be ascertained. Increased faculty participation may be good or bad and the effects vary by the type of decisions in which faculty participates. Brown (2001) confirms the existence of the trade-off effect of faculty participation that is proposed in chapter 3.

As a result of their quantitative approach, the studies by McCormick/Meiners (1988) have some shortcomings. Firstly, they fail to illustrate the conditions under which faculty participation has the respective effects. Secondly, they cannot indicate the causal relationships that exist between the degree of faculty participation and university performance. This is due to a lack of a conceptual model that shows the expected causes and effects. Thirdly, due to the difficulty of measuring university performance, it remains unclear whether the respective indicators validly depict the performance of the university. These shortfalls are addressed in the design of the empirical analysis of university decision-making in Germany.

6.3 The Set-up of the Empirical Study

6.3.1 *The Research Question*

The objective of the empirical study of German university governance firstly is to provide a practical review of the theoretical propositions concerning the effects of faculty participation and secondly, to attempt to derive their underlying causes.

In line with the research objective of this dissertation pointed out in chapter 1, the research question for this empirical study is:

What are the practical effects of faculty participation in university decision-making on the university and what are the reasons for their occurrence?

This question is both explorative as well as explanatory. On the one hand, the study seeks to describe the effects of faculty participation in university decision-making within the dynamics of the German university system. On the other hand, a first preliminary insight is given into the reasons that explain the existence of these effects. They provide an understanding of the key drivers of the effects of faculty participation in university-decision making and how they can be explained. The objective of this qualitative study is not to measure the effects of faculty participation, but to describe and explain them. This circumvents the difficulty of specifying a precise, measurable indicator of university performance. The research question of this study is therefore clearly distinguishable from the questions posed by McCormick/Meiners (1988) and Brown (2001) in their quantitative studies, and it fills a gap that these studies have left open.

Based on the research question, a methodological approach has to be selected and justified. The next section addresses the question of the suitable empirical research methodology.

6.3.2 Methodology

6.3.2.1 The Objective of Empirical Research

The objective of empirical research is to generate an insight into a special phenomenon by systematically evaluating empirical, experience-based evidence. Empirical research is concerned with the analysis and explanation of different factors and the influences they have on the phenomenon that is to be explained. These factors are constructs that represent the characteristics of reality. Figure 6.1

6.3 The Set-up of the Empirical Study

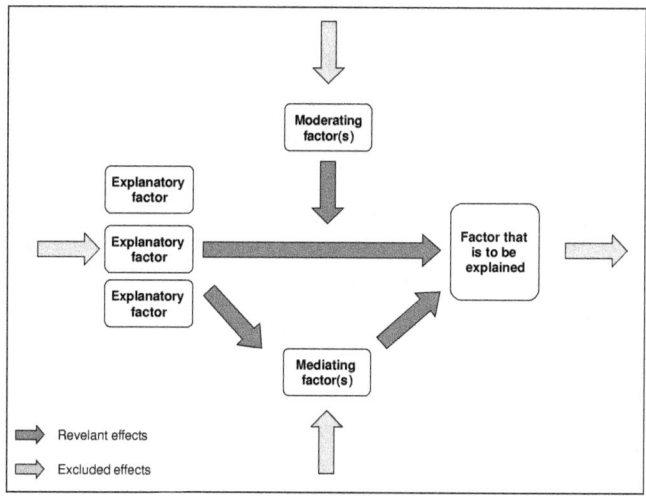

Fig. 6.1 Types of Variables in Empirical Research

gives an overview of the different types of influencing factors that are commonly assumed to exist. Factors are distinguished into explanatory factors and those factors that are to be explained.[2] Apart from these two key factors, there also exist moderating and mediating factors. Moderating factors influence the impact an explanatory factor has on the factor that is to be explained, and mediating factors represent an indirect effect of the explanatory factor on the factor that is to be explained (Bortz/Döring (2002), pp. 5-7; Gläser/Laudel (2004), pp. 78-80).

Propositions about the relationships between the factors lie at the core of empirical research. Depending on the design of the empirical study, these propositions serve as the starting point for the empirical analysis, or constitute the result of the analysis. In research fields with little theoretical background, empirical research can help to formulate hypotheses through inductive reasoning.[3]

---

[2] In quantitative empirical research, these would be referred to as independent and dependent variables. In qualitative research, influence factors are less narrowly defined and are rather regarded as summary categories for relevant information.

[3] See Chalmers (1999), pp. 40-44 for a discussion of the caveats of the method of induction.

On the other hand, empirical studies can be used to examine whether an existing theory and the hypotheses derived from it hold in reality. While empirical research can never verify theoretical proposition, it can provide a confirmation of the practical relevance of the theory (Popper (2002, 1935), pp. 50, 52). Deductive reasoning is applied to conclude that a general theory or hypothesis holds for a specific research subject (Bortz/Döring (2002), pp. 34-35). In summary, induction can be regarded as a concept that expands knowledge by applying a special case to the general case, whereas deductive reasoning preserves knowledge by finding a special case where general theory holds.

6.3.2.2 Quantitative vs. Qualitative Approaches

Empirical research can be divided into quantitative and qualitative research. The two methodologies can be distinguished by the nature of the data used. Data in quantitative research is numerical, whereas qualitative research operates with verbal data. The data collection and evaluation methods also differ: Quantitative data can be obtained by counting, measuring, testing, observing, and surveying events, actions, and behavior. Verbal data can only be obtained through open qualitative interviews, qualitative observation, and non-interactive qualitative methods (e.g. textual analysis). Thus, the data used in qualitative research is richer in terms of the information it conveys, whereas quantitative data has a higher degree of standardization, facilitating the comparison of the information. Concerning the evaluation methodology, quantitative research uses statistical techniques to process the numerical data that has been collected, whereas the verbal data is analyzed with various interpretative methods.

Another key difference between quantitative and qualitative empirical research is the type of research objective pursued: Quantitative analysis searches for statistically significant relationships, i.e. joint occurrence of certain characteristics that point to causal relations between independent and dependent variables. Qualitative empirical research, on the other hand, is concerned with directly investigating the underlying causal relationships and mechanisms. Due to small sample

6.3 The Set-up of the Empirical Study

sizes, however, qualitative research cannot claim to discover universal causal mechanisms and relationships. In general, quantitative and qualitative empirical research have complementary advantages and disadvantages, so the choice of the adequate research methodology depends on the research question (Gläser/Laudel (2004), pp. 23-24, see also Jick (1983), p. 135, Lamnek (1995a), pp. 218-244, and Spöhring (1989), pp. 98-102)).

6.3.2.3 The Rationale for a Qualitative Study

The empirical study carried out in the context of this dissertation constitutes the first empirical analysis of the decision structures in German universities. As pointed out in the section above, the methodological choice any empirical study has to make is between a quantitative and a qualitative approach. A quantitative analysis seeks to establish statistically significant relationships and yields generalizable results by studying a representative sample. This is clearly an advantage of such a quantitative empirical research.

In the context of the specific research question of this study, however, it also faces two serious drawbacks: The first results from the problem of identifying the relevant variables to test with quantitative methods. Secondly, the standardization of the data, which is a prerequisite for the collection of numerical data, is difficult in the university context due to its lack of objective performance measures. In order to conduct a quantitative study on university decision structures, a significant level of theoretical knowledge needs to be generated in order to interpret the statistical relationships derived by the quantitative analysis. Due to the lack of such a comprehensive theory on university governance, it may be difficult to answer the research question with a quantitative approach.

Qualitative research aims at empirically discovering relationships between the influence factors directly. The information generated is richer in content, thus providing a broader as well as a deeper insight into the possibly relevant information. This is especially important when little prior knowledge exists to guide the researcher in the design of the research process, as it is the case for university governance structures. Since the relevant data categories cannot be determined ex ante, the openness and flexibility inherent in qualitative research methodology have the advantage of generating more valid data. The setback of qualitative empirical research is the difficulty inherent in generalizing the results. Qualitative research focuses on fewer samples, so that representativeness is difficult to achieve.

The methodology proposed used in the empirical study in this dissertation is qualitative. It will enable a genuine first insight into the effects of faculty participation in university decision-making and the underlying reasons. The advantages of the qualitative approach are expected to outweigh its drawback when compared with a quantitative approach: The decisive argument is that qualitative research is able to explain the reasons underlying the phenomena of the real world, whereas a quantitative approach in the study of university governance is limited in its explanatory value of the underlying causalities (see Brown (2001), who encountered similar problems in his quantitative empirical study on university governance in the US).

Choosing a qualitative approach for this study can also be justified with the initial stage of empirical research on university governance in Germany. Once a sufficient level of knowledge has been generated by qualitative empirical research, quantitative methods may then be tested for their applicability. As such, this empirical study can be regarded as a preliminary study that will pave the way to more quantitatively oriented research.

The emphasis of this chapter and the analysis lies on the methods of qualitative empirical research and the results implied by the qualitative data. Qualitative empirical research is guided by overarching methodological principles that provide a common basis for carrying out research. The principles that define qualitative research are openness, a theory-based approach, and a rule-based research procedure.[4]

---

[4] For a more detailed overview of the methodological requirements of qualitative research, see Gläser/Laudel (2004) and Lamnek (1995a).

6.3 The Set-up of the Empirical Study

1. Openness

    Qualitative research postulates that the process of collecting data has to be open for unexpected information. Data should not be categorized prematurely, nor should the process of investigation be overly structured (Gläser/Laudel (2004), pp. 27-28).

2. Theory-based research

    In order to develop scientific knowledge, qualitative empirical research needs to incorporate existing theories, for example by deriving testable hypotheses from available theories that guide the design of the research process (Brüsemeister (2000), pp. 28-30). Without a theory-based insight into the scope and nature of the problem studied, it is difficult to determine the information relevant for answering the research question.[5]

3. Rule-based procedures

    In order to maintain objectivity in qualitative research, the research process has to follow explicit rules. These rules include a precise description of the design and the chronological progression of the research process so that the it can be verified whether a specific set-up follows academic standards (Gläser/Laudel (2004), p. 29).

The next step of the research process is to design a conceptual model of the influencing factors and their relationships, and to derive key questions that guide and structure the planning of the research process. The optimal method for collecting the relevant information can only be chosen with a clear understanding of the information needed to answer the research questions and to validate the conceptual model.

---
[5] See Chalmers (1999) for an insight into the discussion on the supremacy of theory versus facts which has taken place in the philosophy of science.

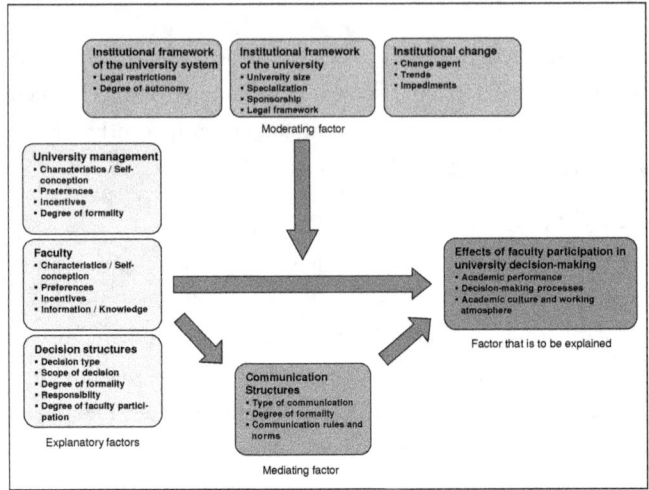

Fig. 6.2 A Conceptual Model of the Effects of Faculty Participation

6.3.3 *A Conceptual Model of Influencing Factors*

The conceptual model provides the structural backbone to the empirical research process (Gläser/Laudel (2004), pp. 82-84). It is based on the trade-off hypotheses generated in chapter 3. The positive effects of faculty participation in university decision-making result from faculty monitoring, management commitment, and a higher quality of information in the decision processes. The negative effects stem from the diverging interests and from the costs associated with collective decision making. The conceptual model proposed in figure 6.2 shows the expected relationships between certain influencing factors and the effects from faculty participation. These factors are based on the existence of the effects outlined in chapter 3.

Based on principal-agent theory, one important influence factor are the economic agents in university decision-making, i.e. faculty and university management. Their preferences, motives, and characteristics are assumed to contribute to the explanation of the effects from faculty participation. Faculty and the university manager operate within a framework of decision structures and routines.

6.3　The Set-up of the Empirical Study

These structures have an impact on how faculty participation is realized and are thus also considered as an explanatory factor. As outlined in section 6.3.2.1, explanatory factors are only studied with regards to their effects. The question why faculty and university management have certain preferences or motives is thus excluded since it lies beyond the scope of this study.

Explanatory factors are assumed to have a direct impact on the factors that are to be explained. In addition, they can also have an indirect effect through a mediating factor. In this model, communication structures and rules are regarded as such a mediating factor. The way communication functions in the university is influenced by faculty, the university manager, and the decision-structures of the university, and in turn it has an impact on the effects that faculty participation in decision-making have on the university.

Two factors account for the internal and external framework in which the university operates in order to understand their relevance for explaining the effects of faculty participation. The institutional framework of the university and the institutional framework of the university system are the two moderating factors that are assumed to modify the relationship between the independent variables and the dependent variables. As university systems and universities are subject to internally and externally induced change processes, the third moderating factor captures the influence of the reform and transformation process on faculty participation in university decision-making.

The factor that is to be explained are the effects of faculty participation in university decision-making. The effects can have a positive or a negative impact and can occur in different areas, e.g. academic quality and managerial professionalism. The focus lies on determining the nature of these effects within the conceptual framework this study proposes and to explain their occurrence.

The conceptual model fulfills two basic functions. Firstly, it integrates existing theoretical knowledge and propositions into a coherent overview. Secondly, it serves as a starting point for the design of the data collection process. The conceptual model indicates the information necessary for answering the research question and for validating the relationships proposed between the factors. The next section discusses the approach to data collection, and the methods and tools employed.

6.4 The Data Collection

In regard to the methodology of data collection, four questions have to be answered:

1. What is the relevant sample and what cases are selected from the sample?
2. What method is used to collect the qualitative data?
3. From who is the data collected?
4. What is the relevant tool for collecting data?

6.4.1 *Defining the Sample*

In order to study the effects of faculty participation in university decision-making, the relevant unit of analysis is the university. In Germany, the educational sector, including higher education, has traditionally been dominated by public institutions, financed through government funds. During the last two decades, a number of private universities have been founded. Of the 109 full universities with doctoral programs existing in Germany in the academic year 2005/2006, 80% are public institutions, 12% are state-accredited universities sponsored by the church, and 8% are private, state-accredited universities (Hochschulrektorenkonferenz (2005)).[6] The legal framework in Germany is determined through a federal law, the "Hochschulrahmengesetz" (Framework Act of Higher Education), and the respective state laws that impose basic regulations with regard to the functions of a university, its students, its personnel, the organizational structures, examination procedures, etc. Although recent reforms of the federal as well as the state acts

---

[6] These numbers only take into account the full universities offering all three types of degrees (undergraduate, graduate, and post-graduate) and conducting both research and teaching.

6.4 The Data Collection

have all pointed in the same direction, there still exist differences between the "Bundesländer" (federal states), especially in regard to the degree of autonomy granted to the individual university.

Based on a theoretical methodology developed by Glaser/Strauss (1967), two criteria can be identified for the selection of the relevant sample and the choice of cases within the sample that are studied in detail. The first criterion refers to holding the moderating and mediating variables of the conceptual model constant. This greatly facilitates the analysis of the underlying relationships. In this study, two of the three mediating variables are held constant by limiting the sample of universities to one "Bundesland". The institutional framework of the university is not held constant through this measure. Including universities that vary in size, scope and other institutional characteristics is important because this provides a better basis for generalizing the results of the study. Consequently, the effects of different state laws on the university governance systems are excluded from the analysis.

The second sampling criterion of Glaser/Strauss (1967) refers to the desired variation of the central independent variables of the conceptual model. In this study, the variation is achieved by selecting a number of universities from the sample as units of analysis. Within the selected "Bundesland", universities are chosen that differ in their institutional framework. Indicators such as size, public or private sponsorship, the degree of academic specialization, and the specific legal regulation applicable to this university can be used to distinguish the different environments in which universities operate. The objective of this extreme case sampling method is to include at least one public and one private university, one large and one small university, and a university with special legal regulation.[7]

---

[7] For a discussion of different sampling strategies, see Flick (2002), p. 109 and (Gläser/Laudel (2004), pp. 95-97.

On the basis of these guidelines, three universities are selected from the sample state:[8]

1. A small private university, focused on a small number of academic subjects to which state regulations apply only in certain areas (referred to as university PR (for private) in the following).

2. A large public university, offering the full spectrum of academic disciplines and without special legal clauses (referred to as university TP (for typical public)).

3. A large public university, with an academic focus on technical sciences but nonetheless a broad degree spectrum, to which a special legal clause applies (referred to as university SP (for special public)).

These three universities represent extreme cases in regard to their institutional framework and are therefore expected to differ in terms of their decision structures as well.

6.4.2 Expert Interviews as a Data Collection Method

The second question posed above refers to the method of data collection. Qualitative data can be generated through interviewing, observation, and non-interactive methods (e.g. textual analysis) (Bortz/Döring (2002), pp. 307-326). In general, the data collection process is of crucial importance to any empirical study because the quality of the data obtained predetermines the quality and credibility of the results and interpretations that can be obtained from them. In order to be scientifically viable, the process of data collection in general must satisfy three quality criteria: Objectivity, reliability, and validity (Bortz/Döring (2002), pp. 326-329. See Flick (2002), pp. 319-330 and Lamnek (1995), pp. 158-186 for discussions).

---

[8] Due to the fact that the data collected includes sensible information, neither the "Bundesland", nor the specific universities that are examined in detail will be named in the dissertation, nor will the names of the interview partners be given. All interview partners were assured anonymity.

6.4 The Data Collection

Objectivity and reliability are necessary conditions for the validity of a methodological tool. In addition to being objective and reliable, a valid method has to comprehensively grasp what it intends to grasp (Lamnek (1980), p. 111). Qualitative research seeks to fulfill all three quality criteria to the best degree possible, and also puts a large emphasis on other criteria such as plausibility, credibility, and applicability (Lamnek (1995a), pp. 184-185).

In order to obtain information about the variables that are identified within the conceptual model, conducting interviews appears to be the most plausible method. Since this study is the first empirical study of university decision-making structures, prior information is scarce and many of the existing accounts are based more on casual anecdotes than on scientific analysis. Only through interviews, the information the actors possess about their own preferences, incentives and behavior can be extracted.

Observation-based methods cannot achieve this since they can only extract the information that is visible from the communication processes and the behavior of the actors but cannot answer the question of the underlying motives. Furthermore, in terms of the practical feasibility, it would be difficult to persuade professors or university managers to allow a research to follow them in their natural working environment and to observe their actions, behavior, and confidential discussions. The time required for such an observation process also poses a serious impediment to such an approach.

Non-interactive methods such as the study of legal regulations and university charters can facilitate the preparation of interviews and can validate the information given. However, due to the fact that there exists little written information about university governance and university decision-making in practice, and only few of these documents are publicly accessible, a data collection strategy based exclusively on non-interactive methods cannot obtain the information needed to answer the research question. The data collection method that is used for this study is based on interviews, supported by document analysis of university charters and legal documents.

Interview types can be distinguished in terms of their degree of structure into structured or unstructured interviews. Structured interviews make use of a questionnaire, specifying the exact working and succession of questions that will be asked during the interview. In unstructured interviews, questions are asked freely both in terms of content and sequence. Semi-structured interviews use questionnaires but allow the interviewer to adapt the wording and the sequence of the questions to the specific interview situation. Most interviews conducted in qualitative empirical research employ a questionnaire since this improves the quality of the data collection process.

Expert interviews are a special form of structured or semi-structured, standardized interviews with mostly open questions. The objective of the expert interview is to gain an insight into a very specific problem by questioning individuals that are specialists in the relevant fields, i.e. who possess special knowledge, skills, or practical experiences. Contrary to other interview types in qualitative research in the social sciences, the interviewee in an expert interview is not primarily regarded as an individual with feelings and perceptions about his social environment. Instead, his expert status and the knowledge he is assumed to possess are the defining characteristics (Flick (2002), pp. 139-141).

The questionnaire-based semi-structured expert interview seems most suitable in this context since the study is interested in the reproduction of the effects of faculty participation on the university. The scope of the interviews can therefore be reduced to the knowledge the interview partners possess about the effects and their causes, one of the key requirements for conducting expert interviews.

In terms of the quality criteria of data collection pointed out above, expert interviews appear to yield sufficient degrees of objectivity, reliability, and validity. Objectivity is achieved through a detailed description of the set-up and the process of data collection. The use of a questionnaire also helps to ensure the objectivity of data collection. Furthermore, experts are often professionals, so that their answers are expected to be fairly stable and reliable over time. Concerning the validity of the information collected through expert interviews, it has been pointed out that the textual richness of the answers ensures a high level of validity. The problem of validity in qualitative research is more apparent in the stage of interpreting the data since standardized procedures are not available (Lamnek (1995a), p. 171).

6.4.3 Selecting Interview Partners

Experts are differentiated into two categories: Firstly, experts that possess the relevant contextual knowledge as a result of their professional activity. Potential interview partners in this category are members of the university. Three types of members are selected for the interviews: University managers as the internal principal of the university, senate faculty members as the agents participating in university decision-making, and university trustees as the overseer of university management. Three interviews are conducted per university, resulting in a total number of nine interviews with university members.

The second group of experts includes individuals that are not directly involved with a particular university, but have an indirect professional interest in the university system. This group includes consultants, policy advisers, and politicians. Two consultants, one policy adviser, and one politician from the respective State Ministry for Education are selected for this study, bringing the total number of interviews to thirteen. Figure 6.3 gives an overview of the thirteen interview partners.[9]

Since the objective is not to examine the effects of faculty participation in university governance from the viewpoint of one particular constituency, including a variety of interview partners from within the university as well as from without ensures that different perspectives enter into the study. The different backgrounds of the interview partners also enable the analysis of any differences in the perceptions of the constituencies, generating a fuller informational basis for the analysis of the relationships underlying the effects of faculty participation.

---

[9] The numbers assigned to the interviewees are used to reference their statements in the presentation of the results in chapter 7.

Interviewee No.	Institution	Position
I	Private university (PR)	Member of the university management board
II		Member of the academic senate
III		Chairman of the board of trustees
IV	Typical public university (TP)	Chairman of the university management board
V		Member of the academic senate
VI		Member of the board of trustees
VII	Public university with special legal clause (SP)	Chairman of the university management board
VIII		Member of the academic senate
IX		Chairman of the board of trustees
X	State Ministry for Higher Education	Department head for higher education and research
XI	University policy think tank	Director
XII	Management Consultancy	Senior consultant with experience in public sector and university consulting
XIII		Senior consultant with experience in public sector and university consulting

Fig. 6.3 An Overview of the Interview Partners

The experts who are assumed to possess the information, knowledge, and experience needed in order to answer the research questions belong to the educational elite. This fact provides another reason for conducting personal, qualitative interviews since structured written questionnaires with closed questions may not be able to grasp the degree of differentiation such elite interview partners are able to provide (Attelander/Kopp (1999), p. 149).

6.4.4 Questionnaires as a Data Collection Tool

Expert interviews are semi-structured interviews conducted with a questionnaire, specifying the questions that are asked during the interview. The questions can be reformulated in terms of their wording and their order may be changed as the interview progresses in order to react flexibly to the interview context. In order to allow the standardization of answers, it is important that all interviewers are asked

6.4 The Data Collection

similar questions in order to ensure the comparability and ability to aggregate the answers into standardized categories. Due to the fact that there exist different types of interview partners in this study, the questionnaires need to be slightly adapted to reflect the knowledge and insight the respective interview partner is expected to possess.

The questionnaire has to reflect the conceptual model that provides the basic structure of this qualitative analysis. Since the conceptual model provides only a stylized illustration of the hypothesized relationships, however, it is too abstract to directly translate it into interview questions. Gläser/Laudel (2004, pp. 88-90) therefore propose formulating key questions as an intermediary step between the design of the conceptual model, the selection of sample cases and interview partners, and the design of the questionnaire. Key questions mediate between the abstract, conceptual model and the pragmatic level of the actual interview and illustrate the information that is needed in order to validate the conceptual model and to answer the research question.

Based on the research question and the conceptual model, four key questions are derived for this empirical study:

1. What are the participative elements in university decision-making structures in regards to faculty?

2. What are the characteristics, the preferences, the motives and the self-conceptions of the actors involved in university decision-making?

3. Which effects from faculty participation in university decision-making can be observed in the university?

4. How could the institutional and organizational setting of the university be improved with regards to the decision-making system?

These questions constitute the scope of the information that is collected through the interview. Accordingly, the questionnaire is structured into four sections, each referring to one key question. For each section, a number of different interview questions are developed.

Questionnaires consist of different types of interview questions (Gläser/Laudel (2004), pp. 118-126).

1. With regard to the content, fact-based questions are differentiated from opinion-based questions. Fact-based questions relate to an actual event or an observation of the interviewee. Opinion-based questions ask the interviewee for an interpretation of a certain situation. The majority of the questions in an expert interview should be fact-based questions since the factual knowledge the interviewee is assumed to possess about a certain topic rather than his subjective opinion are to be extracted.

2. In terms of the reference point, questions can be hypothetical or reality-based. Hypothetical questions are difficult to interpret due to the non-committal answer of the interview partner. They are not rooted in an actual observation of the interview partner, but draw on his knowledge and experience to judge the likely outcome of a certain situation. The majority of the questions in an expert interview therefore should be reality-based questions that are directed at the actual behavior of an economic agent or at a specific situation.

3. Questions can also be structured according to the answer that is expected. Narrative questions are aimed at inviting the interview partner to elaborate on a certain topic by sharing in-depth knowledge. Detail questions serve the purpose of confirming prior information, or of providing very specific detail that has been missing so far. The answers evoked by detail questions tend to be short and to the point.

4. Guiding questions can help to structure the course of an interview. Introductory questions are meant to break the ice at the beginning of the interview, and will therefore tend to be questions the interviewee feels comfortable with. Filter questions are employed to signal the level and degree

6.4 The Data Collection

of knowledge the interviewee possesses and to indicate which parts of the questionnaire can be sensibly applied. The purpose of primary questions is to evoke detailed answers to complex topics. Secondary questions represent means of further inquiry when the answers to primary questions are not satisfactory.

For this qualitative analysis, a questionnaire with 16 questions is designed. The number of questions is determined both by the informational need as well as by a time limit of approximately one hour (Gläser/Laudel (2004), p. 157). The questionnaire is adapted to the type of interviewee by selecting the relevant questions from the pool of the 16 questions. The majority of the questions are fact-based questions that are based on real-life observations of the interview partner. Both narrative and detail questions are used, as well as introductory questions and filter questions. Each primary question is followed by a list of possible secondary questions. They are intended as back-up questions in case the primary question does not yield the expected level of detail.

An example of the questionnaire is shown in the appendix of this chapter (see section 6.7.2). The questions are in German as this is the language in which all interviews are conducted. The four parts of the questionnaire refer to the four key questions, and each question is classified according to the categories outlined above.

6.4.5 Conduct of Data Collection

In order to ask for an interview, letters are sent out to the selected thirteen interview partners in order to introduce the topic and ask for an appointment (see section 6.7.1 in the appendix for a sample of the letter). All interview partners voluntarily agreed to the interview. Eleven interviews are conducted as personal interviews and two are realized via telephone since a personal appointment could not be scheduled.

In parallel, the university charters and laws governing the universities are obtained. They provide both a basis for the preparation for the interviews and they deliver important information on the formal structure of decision-making at the three universities.

All interviews are fully transcribed and the protocols are sent to the interview partners for release.[10] The protocols of the interviews provide the basis for the analysis of the information collected. The next section gives an overview of the different data evaluation methods with a focus on qualitative content analysis.

6.5 Evaluating and Interpreting Qualitative Research

The data generated by expert interviews is the transliteration of the spoken word during the interview in the form of a text. In general, evaluation methods can be distinguished into quantitative and qualitative approaches. Quantitative analysis allocates text fragments (i.e. words, sentences, or paragraphs) to predetermined categories and analyzes the frequency of occurrence of certain characteristics (Lamnek (1995b), pp. 185-196; Bortz/Döring (2002), pp. 147-153).

In qualitative analysis, three broad methodological approaches can be distinguished: Sequential analysis, coding, and qualitative content analysis. Sequential analysis uses the text as the basic data throughout the entire evaluation and interpretation process. A theoretically constructed model of the world is validated with the text as the primary data. The analysis emphasizes the chronological dimension of the data and the events studied (Gläser/Laudel (2004), p. 43. For a detailed overview of the different methods within sequential analysis, see Flick (2002), pp. 287-307).

Textual coding is often used in the context of theory-generating research questions. Text fragments are marked and indexed with a code belonging to various categories, which are later aggregated into more abstract concepts, ultimately leading to the formulation of a set of propositions (see Flick (2002), pp. 259-278

---

[10] Due to the anonymity and confidentiality of the study, the transliterations of the interviews cannot be provided in the appendix.

6.5 Evaluating and Interpreting Qualitative Research

for different coding methodologies and a detailed overview of the step by step procedure).

Qualitative content analysis evolved from the basis of quantitative analysis. It incorporates the informational significance of certain characteristics into the analysis and thus does not focus exclusively on their frequency of occurrence, as quantitative methods do. The main difference between sequential analysis and coding, and qualitative context analysis is the extraction of information that is relevant in the context of the research question from the original text. The extraction is carried out with a system of categories that is developed on the basis of the theoretical background, ensuring a theory-based research approach. Through interpretative aggregation of the extracted text, the material is reduced in size and condensed in terms of its meaning. The summarized material provides the foundation for the interpretation of the empirical data that is aimed at providing an answer to the research question. The analysis only draws on the original interview transcripts in cases of ambiguity (Gläser/Laudel (2004), pp. 193-200. See also Flick (2002) and Mayring 2003).

Qualitative content analysis has three main advantages. They provide the rationale for applying this method to evaluate the data collected from the expert interviews in this study. Firstly, it calls for the extraction of the relevant information from the original text. The interpretation of the information is then performed on the basis of the extracted and summarized data. For the large amounts of texts that results from the transcription of the interviews, this method has the advantage of condensing the relevant information and thus reducing the data basis for the interpretation.

The second advantage refers to the fact that the text is analyzed with a set of predetermined categories. The influence factors lined out in the conceptual model provide a first start to formulating the categories for the qualitative content analysis. This ensures a theory-based approach of the analysis. While the category system is predetermined, this does not imply that it is not flexible. During the extraction, the category system can be expanded to include effects that are visible from the texts but are not yet reflected in a category. Flexibility and openness are also guaranteed by extracting data on mostly nominal scales, i.e. by describing differences rather than classifying them based on restrictive ordinal or cardinal scales.

The third characteristics of qualitative content analysis is that is follows a clearly defined procedure that can be reconstructed by other researchers. Its three steps include extracting the data, adjusting the extraction for mistakes and redundancies, summarizing and sorting it, and finally, interpreting the data. Qualitative content analysis thus incorporates the basic principles of qualitative research outlined in section 6.3.2, openness, a theory-based approach, and a rule-based procedure (Gläser/Laudel (2004), pp. 197-200).

The evaluation of the data generated by the expert interviews is performed with the help of the software program Microsoft Excel, which allows for the necessary flexibility and traceability of the different steps. Nine separate Excel sheets are designed, eight of them representing the variables of the conceptual model, and one of them to extract the proposals for institutional and organizational improvements to the decision-making and governance system made by the experts.[11] A sample of an evaluation sheet is included in section 6.7.3 of the appendix of this chapter.

The thirteen interview transcripts are scanned for information regarding the causes and effects of faculty participation in university decision-making. Each relevant statement is copied into a separate line and the indicators of the factors are filled in accordingly. After all relevant information is extracted from the interview texts, the next step involves processing the extract to correct for mistakes and redundancies, and to adjust for more standardized formulations of the same issues. As a result, the original extraction is further condensed and reduced to 21 pages of summarized extraction. A sample of a summary page is shown in section 6.7.4 of the appendix. The third step of the qualitative content analysis involves the

---

[11] The ideas of the experts concerning organizational and institutional reform are not evaluated with qualitative content analysis. Rather, their proposals are incorporated into the policy recommendations that are given in section 8.3.

interpretation of the information based on the summarized information extracted from the interviews.

6.6 Conclusion

This chapter provides a basic overview of the relevant empirical research methodologies and tools. The differences between quantitative and qualitative empirical research are described, and the methods available for collecting, evaluating, and interpreting qualitative data are pointed out. The research question of the study of university decision-making in Germany requires a qualitative empirical approach. Data is collected through expert interviews and it is evaluated with qualitative content analysis. The set-up and conduct of the empirical study as pointed out above provides the basis for the interpretation of the data collected. The insights into decision-making in German universities and the impact of faculty participation are illustrated in the next chapter.

6.7 Appendix

6.7.1 Letter to Interview Partners

Oestrich-Winkel, den 13. April 2005

Sehr geehrte/r,

ich wende mich heute mit einer Bitte an Sie. Meine Doktorandin Jutta Merschen führt im Rahmen ihrer Dissertation Experteninterviews zum Thema "Leitungs- und Entscheidungsstrukturen in Universitäten" durch, um ihre theoretisch erarbeiteten Hypothesen zu überprüfen. Ein besonderer Fokus liegt auf der Partizipation von Fakultätsmitgliedern an der universitären Entscheidungsfindung.

Wie Sie vielleicht auch in Ihrem Alltag als Hochschulpräsident spüren, spielt die Ausgestaltung von Leitungs- und Entscheidungsstrukturen in Universitäten eine immer wichtigere Rolle. Universitäten erhalten von der Politik mehr und mehr Autonomie zugewiesen und müssen diese neu gewonnene Freiheit effektiv einsetzen, damit sie im Wettbewerb um die besten Köpfe und um finanzielle Ressourcen bestehen können. Manche Entscheidungen müssen schnell getroffen werden, sollen aber trotzdem auf einer möglichst breiten Informationsbasis stehen. Ebenso wichtig ist die Akzeptanz der Entscheidungen bei Fakultät und weiteren Anspruchsgruppen, damit ihre Umsetzung eine realistische Chance hat. Die Herausforderungen, die sich in diesem Kontext stellen, möchte Frau Merschen mit ihrem Forschungsvorhaben beleuchten.

Ziel ihrer Untersuchung ist es dabei, die Entscheidungsprozesse und -strukturen in drei ausgewählten Universitäten zu erforschen. Dazu will Frau Merschen die Entscheidungsprozesse und -strukturen in ihren Hauptmerkmalen vergleichen, die Auswirkungen der partizipativen Entscheidungsstruktur identifizieren und Entwicklungstendenzen in der Gestaltung universitärer Entscheidungsstrukturen erfassen. Dabei möchte Frau Merschen durch ein Gespräch mit Ihnen die universitätsinterne Perspektive beleuchten. Darüber hinaus plant sie ein Interview mit

6.7 Appendix

einem Mitglied Ihres Hochschulrates, um somit auch einen Einblick in die externe Sichtweise zu gewinnen.

Vor diesem Hintergrund bitte ich Sie sehr herzlich, Frau Merschen durch Ihre Gesprächsbereitschaft behilflich zu sein. Ihre Angaben während des Interviews werden selbstverständlich streng vertraulich behandelt und ausschließlich in anonymisierter, aggregierter Form zur Analyse verwendet. Frau Merschen wird sich in den nächsten Tagen gerne telefonisch mit Ihnen in Verbindung setzen, um einen etwa 1-stündigen Termin abzusprechen.

Als kleines Dankeschön für Ihre Unterstützung senden wir Ihnen selbstverständlich gerne eine Zusammenfassung der Ergebnisse zu.

In der Hoffnung auf Ihr Entgegenkommen verbleibe ich mit herzlichem Dank für Ihre Bemühungen und kollegialem Gruß,

Prof. Ulrich Hommel, Ph.D.

Rektor der European Business School

6.7.2 Interview Questionnaire

Leitfaden Rektor

Question	Comment
Part I – Participative Elements of Decision-Making	
1. Wie sehen die Entscheidungsstrukturen an Ihrer Hochschule aus? • Wer trifft an welcher Stelle welche Entscheidung?	Introductory question, fact-based question
2. Wie ist der zeitliche Ablauf der Entscheidungsprozesse gestaltet? • Wie unterscheiden sich die Prozesse je nach Art der Entscheidung?	Fact-based question
3. Welche Entscheidungen trifft die Hochschulleitung alleine und bei welchen Entscheidungen sind die Professoren beteiligt?	Fact-based question, filter question
4. Wie ist die Fakultät an der Entscheidungsfindung beteiligt? • Unterrichtungs-, Informationsrecht, Anhörungs-, Vorschlagsrecht? Beratungsrecht, Vetorecht, Mitbestimmungsrecht, alleiniges Entscheidungsrecht?	Fact-based question, filter question
5. Mit welchem Verfahren trifft die Fakultät Entscheidungen? • Nur mehrheitlich im Senat oder gibt es auch Einzelentscheidungen?	Fact-based question
6. Was bedeutet für Sie eine gelungene Entscheidung? • Was sind die wichtigsten Faktoren, die dazu beitragen?	Fact-based question
Part II – Preferences and Motives of the Actors	
7. Warum beteiligen sich Professoren an der universitären Entscheidungsfindung? • Welche Rolle spielen Punkte wie die Beeinflussung der Universität, Pflichtgefühl, Machtanspruch oder Einbringung von Wissen? • Welche Art von Professor ist meistens in der Entscheidungsfindung involviert (Alter, Fachbereich)?	Fact-based question

Fig. 6.4 The Interview Questionnaire - I

6.7 Appendix

Question	Comment
8. Was für Interessen vertritt ein Professor in der Entscheidungsfindung? • Verfolgen die Professoren eher ihre eigenen Interessen, Fachbereichsinteressen oder die Interessen der gesamten Universität? • Ist Professoren die Gesamtreputation der Universität wichtiger oder ihre individuelle Reputation? • Gibt es Interessenskonflikte unter den Professoren?	Fact-based question
9. Welche Interessenskonflikte sind in der Vergangenheit schon mal zwischen Hochschulleitung und Fakultät in der Entscheidungsfindung aufgetreten? • Um welche Entscheidung ging es? • Wie wurden diese gelöst?	Narrative question
Part III – Effects of Faculty Participation	
10. Welche Auswirkungen hat die Tatsache, daß die Fakultät (primär) Mehrheitsentscheidungen trifft? • Auf den Prozess / das Ergebnis? • Werden Koalitionen gebildet? • Kosten die Mehrheitsentscheidungen mehr Zeit als Einzelentscheidungen? • Was passiert mit den „Verlierern" in kollektiven Entscheidungsprozessen?	Fact-based question
11. Wie erfolgt in der gemeinsamen Entscheidungsfindung der Informationsaustausch zwischen Hochschulleitung und Fakultät? • Haben Professoren vielleicht in einigen Bereichen einen besseren Einblick (z.B. Berufungsentscheidungen)? • Wurde eine Entscheidungsgrundlage durch die Information, die die Fakultät kommuniziert hat, verbessert? Inwiefern? • Ist es wichtig für Professoren, daß sie ihre Information beisteuern können?	Fact-based question, depends on answer to question no. 1, 2 and 42

Fig. 6.5 The Interview Questionnaire - II

Question	Comment
12. Wie beurteilen Sie die Wirkung des Mitspracherechts der Professoren auf ihre Motivation für ihre tägliche Arbeit? ▪ Auf das Arbeitsklima? ▪ Gibt es weitere positiven Effekte? ▪ Welche Effekte wären zu erwarten, wenn man ihnen das Entscheidungsrecht entzöge?	Fact-based question
13. Gab es schon mal kritische Entscheidungen, die nicht zugunsten der Professoren gefällt wurden? Was waren die Auswirkungen? ▪ Wie äußerte sich dies (schlechte Stimmung, Demotivation, schlechtere Leistung)? ▪ Wie wurde diese Entscheidung getroffen (mit Fakultätsbeteiligung oder ohne)?	Fact-based question
14. Welche Faktoren der Mitbestimmung beurteilen Sie als positiv, welche als negativ? ▪ Überwiegt eine Auswirkung? ▪ Ist eine Änderung wünschenswert?	Opinion-based question
Part IV – Potential for Improvement	
15. Wie stellen Sie sich das ideale Entscheidungssystem für Ihre Hochschule vor, unabhängig von Rahmenbedingungen? ▪ Wie beurteilen Sie die Auswirkungen einer Einführung eines Vorstand-Aufsichtsratsmodells? ▪ Sind externe Experten statt Professoren in der Leitung einer Hochschule denkbar?	Hypothetical question
16. Engen Sie politischen Rahmenbedingungen in der Ausübung der Hochschulleitung ein? ▪ Hätten Sie gerne mehr Spielraum?	Fact-based question
17. Haben sich die Entscheidungssysteme in den letzten Jahren verändert? Wie? ▪ Zentralisierung vs. Dezentralisierung? ▪ Wer waren die „Change Agents"? ▪ Was war das Ziel und ist dieses erreicht?	Fact-based question

Fig. 6.6 The Interview Questionnaire - III

6.7 Appendix

6.7.3 Evaluation Sheet

Faculty

No.	Univ.	Type	Page	Topic	Statement	Characteristics/Self-Conception		Personal Preferences	Motives in Decision-Making	Applicability	Effect	Impact
						Type	Content					
4				Characteristics	Die Motivation der Professoren ist ein ganz eigenes Thema, ein ganz eigener Aspekt. Im Grunde sind ja die Professoren unsere Führungskräfte. In den Gesprächen mit den Professoren bezeichne ich sie immer als unsere Top-Manager. Die müssen die Geschichte vorantreiben, und erstellen. Von daher sollte ihre gewollte Leistung zielorientiert erbringen und erstellen. Motivation natürlich primär die sein, neben den persönlichen Motivationsfaktoren wie Lohn und Gehalt, dass sie sich den Zielen der Hochschule verschrieben und an deren Erreichung mit aller Kraft und Energie mitwirken. Das ist eigentlich die Hauptmotivation für ihre Tätigkeit.	Charac.	Faculty are elite workers of the university	University objectives as primary source of motivation		Special case	Faculty should derive motivation from developing the university	
7				Characteristics	Die Mitbestimmung ist es nicht, es ist mehr. Die Professorenschaft an der [...] hat sich über die Historie gesehen schon immer als die tragende Säule der Hochschule verstanden und hat in ihrem Engagement die ganzen Entwicklungen vorangetrieben und hat zum Teil auch Probleme gelöst. Insofern ist die Motivation an der [...] nicht von der Mitbestimmung abhängig. Das ist eher etwas, was in einem solchen Privatwirtschaftsunternehmen per se die grundlegende Entscheidung ist, dass man, wenn man hier her kommt, hier etwas machen kann, gestaltend tätig sein kann und auch verantwortlich tätig sein muss. Sie kommen gar nicht raus aus dieser Notwendigkeit, man kann sich nicht hinter irgendwelchen Senatsmitgliedern verstecken. Insofern ist die Mitbestimmung selbst nicht der treibende Grund für das Engagement, sondern das sehe ich eher in diesen persönlichen Entwürfen, der in-trinsischen Motivation, die einzelne verfolgen.	Self-Conc.	Faculty are elite workers of the university			Special case	Faculty contribute to the development of the university and thus claim participation right	Positive
5				Characteristics	Die Professoren haben, wie alle Menschen auch, die natürliche Präferenz zu einer persönlichen Optimierung ihrer Situation, solange keine Dialogvorgaben und keine Kontrollmöglichkeiten da sind. Dann kommt der menschliche Faktor zum Tragen und dann macht ein Professor mehr nebenher. Unsere Professoren haben ja viel Freiheit, fast so wie an der öffentlichen Universität und machen alle mögliche andere Sachen. Veranstaltungen, Lehrveranstaltungen, Ausbildungsveranstaltungen und ähnliches und ob sie nun da mehr machen oder zu viel machen und zu wenig für die Hochschule, muss ja irgendjemand kontrollieren.	Charac.	Faculty are free scholars	Private preferences in conflict w/ university objective	Interested in own wellbeing	Typical for faculty	Control mechanism needed to mitigate possible shirking behavior	Negative

Fig. 6.7 An Evaluation Sheet for the Variable 'Faculty'

6.7.4 Summary Sheet

Faculty

Topic	Content	Preferences	Motives	Effect	Sources
Characteristics	Faculty are elite employees of the university	- University objectives as primary source of motivation		- Faculty should derive motivation from developing the university - Faculty contribute to the development of the university and thus claim participation right	II, III
	Faculty are free scholars	- Private preferences in conflict with university objective		- Control mechanism needed to mitigate possible shirking behavior - Academic freedom as a motivation for becoming a professor	II, III
	Faculty cannot be forced to engage in decision-making / self-organization			Asymmetry in the allocation of rights and duties	XIII
	Faculty do not want to be ruled, but accept limited authority			Faculty accepts sensible centralization	V
	Faculty has desire to participate			- Faculty strives to be involved in decision-making - Participation has a motivational effect on faculty - Faculty strives to be involved in decision-making - Individual decision for commitment - No abolishment of the senate by law	I, III, X

Fig. 6.8 The Summary Sheet for the Variable 'Faculty'

7 Empirical Insights into University Decision-Making

7.1 Introduction

This chapter delivers an insight into the results of the qualitative study on university decision-making in Germany. From the outset, the explanatory scope of the results is limited to the sample of the universities studied. As will become evident throughout the presentation, some more general implications can also be deducted.

The results are presented in four steps. Firstly, a brief overview of the formal decision structures of the three different universities is given. This is a prerequisite for understanding the effects of faculty participation that can be observed in practice, which are illustrated in the second step. Thirdly, the factors of the conceptual model are examined for their explanatory value, and fourthly, the underlying relationships for the observed effects are illustrated. The informational basis for the interpretation is provided by the extracted and summarized data from the interview transcripts as well as by the university charters and laws. The latter are used predominantly for the brief description of the governance systems of universities in Germany which follows in the next section.[1]

7.2 Overview of the Governance Systems in Practice

Each of the three universities is led by a faculty-elected president and a small management board consisting of a number of vice presidents with clearly assigned tasks, such as international relation, research, or teaching. The size and composition of the management boards depend on the respective university charter or on the respective state law.[2]

The president and the management board have certain specified decision rights (including decisions on faculty appointments and staff hiring, financial issues, the

---

[1] An in-depth comparative study of the different university charters lies outside the scope of this dissertation.
[2] The typical university (TP) and the public university with special legal clause (SP) are bound to general clauses in the state laws. University PR can choose its own organizational form in accordance with its supervisory board.

development of the university, etc.). Another set of decision rights lies with the academic senate (including the right to decide on the university charter, on the establishment of academic clusters, etc.). Following a case decision by the Federal Constitutional Court of Germany in 1973, faculty must always have the majority in the academic senate. Since many decisions in the senate are taken by simple majority, faculty thus has formal control over the senate in all of the three sample universities. When the ultimate decision authority lies with the management, the senate usually has information and consultation rights. In any case, the senate can always issue a statement on any topic that concerns the university in general. In addition to the academic senate, informal faculty bodies exist where faculty members discuss the agenda of the senate in order to determine their position.

For some decisions, supervisory boards retain certain rights. The role of the supervisory board differs from university to university. University PR has a strong supervisory board that can veto practically any decision taken by management and the senate. In both public universities, the supervisory board has been endowed with some of the decision rights that were formerly located at the level of the State Ministry. Especially for university SP, the supervisory board acts as a control body that must approve certain university decisions. In the university TP, the supervisory board has more of a consultative function. In summary, the authority of university decision-making is allocated to university management on the one side and to the academic senate on the other side. The role of the supervisory board differs in the three universities studied.

Following these descriptions, the term 'faculty participation' can be further specified. It refers to the fact that by controlling the academic senate, faculty controls a number of important decisions in the university.[3] Faculty therefore effectively participates in university decision-making by being able to take certain decisions with the faculty majority in the senate. Speaking in the terms of Aghion/Tirole (1997), the formal authority over university decisions is divided

---

[3] Faculty only holds control over the senate if all faculty members vote together, effectively forming a majority coalition.

between university management and the academic senate depending on the type of decision.

7.3 The Effects of Faculty Participation

7.3.1 Overview

On the basis of these institutional descriptions, the results from the interpretation of the extracted information can be presented. If not explicitly noted otherwise, the following results apply to all three universities. The analysis is supported with direct quotes from the interviews and with references to the interview transcripts. In order to get an impression of the original wording, the quotes are presented in German, and a translation is provided in a footnote.

Taking into account all universities and all interview partners, the trade-off hypothesis that predicted both positive as well as negative effects of faculty participation in university decision-making can be confirmed. There are three different areas where effects of faculty participation can be distinguished: Academic working environment, academic quality, and managerial professionalism. Academic quality and managerial professionalism refer to the dimensions of university reputation developed as an indicator of university reputation in section 3.2.4. Since the interview partners frequently mention effects that cannot be clearly allocated to either category, a new category is created for all references to the organizational culture and working environment of the university. This is an example of the richness of qualitative data and of the flexibility of qualitative content analysis, which allows to incorporate unforeseen information. For all three areas, positive as well as negative effects are reported by multiple interview partners, both internal as well as external. The effects in the three different areas are separately discussed in the following.

7.3.2 The Effects on the Academic Working Environment

The positive effects of faculty participation on the academic working environment center around the positive motivational effects of faculty involvement in the decision-making process.

> "Ich glaube, dass es insgesamt an der Universität wichtig ist, dass man das Gefühl hat, dass die Entscheidungen irgendwie fair laufen. Von daher hat es einen großen Einfluss auf das Arbeitsklima, dass man weiß, daß die großen Entscheidungen von Professorenvertretern zumindest mitbestimmt werden."[4]

These effects are present when faculty participates formally by having a decision right or when faculty is invited to take part in discussions informally. Participative decision-making through collective bodies creates a sense of community between faculty members and the rest of the university so that a decision taken jointly can improve the atmosphere and can provide new spirit to the university community. Since faculty tend to listen more to colleagues than to other constituencies, faculty members can serve as mediators when conflicts between faculty and university management arise.[5]

This statement is a variation of the monitoring argument raised in section 3.5.3, proposing that faculty is a better monitor of faculty activities due to the insight into the academic production process. The evidence suggests that faculty has an intrinsic understanding of the preferences of other faculty members - while not necessarily sharing them - due to the fact that they belong to the same constituency. When this knowledge is employed for the benefit of the university, positive effects on the academic working environment result.

The existence of participative management structures also has an indirect positive effect on the academic working environment since they ensure the absence of centralized authority. If management were to take autocratic decisions that are not in the interest of faculty, this would lead to less cooperation between faculty

---

[4] I believe that it is important in a university that decisions are being taken fairly. The knowledge that the most important decisions are taken with the participation of faculty has a large impact on the working environment.
[5] Source: Interview partners I, V, VII, and VIII.

7.3 The Effects of Faculty Participation

and management. Participative discussion, on the other hand, can contribute to upholding the academic spirit and the motivation of faculty to become engaged for the university's purposes. Participative decision-making encourages cooperative behavior between university management and faculty.

"Aber wenn diese Entscheidung einfach vom Präsidenten zentral gefällt worden wäre, [...] ohne Diskussion, hätte es wahrscheinlich Ärger gegeben."[6]

Contrary to the positive impact on the working environment, faculty participation can, however, also negatively influence the organizational culture of the university. Some of these effects are diametrically opposed to the positive effects. Due to the different personal interests that arise in collective decision-making, participative discussions resemble personal feuds rather than focus on the exchange of objective arguments. Instead of exchanging reasonable arguments, personal offenses take place and the academic culture of debate deteriorates. This demotivates the faculty members involved in participative decision-making as well as university management.[7]

Another negative effect arises in the collective decision-making process. Due to the fact that faculty needs to vote unanimously to pass senate decisions, a faculty coalition needs to be forged. In order to ensure that this coalition holds, suboptimal compromises are sometimes made within the faculty group, pressuring minority groups into making a decision that leaves them worse off than others. The losers in this bargaining process often feel they are being treated unfairly and suffer from a lack of motivation.[8]

"Der eine ist dafür, der andere ist dagegen, dann muß man ihn irgendwie überstimmen [...]. Es wird mit unlauteren Mitteln, mit Halbwahrheiten gekämpft usw. Nach einer Zeit ist die Stimmung nicht mehr die beste."[9]

---

[6] If this decision had been taken centrally by the president without prior consultation, this would have caused aggravation.
[7] Source: Interview partners I, III, V, VIII, and XI.
[8] Source: Interview partners I, III, V, VIII, and XI.
[9] One faculty member is for a certain proposal, the other one is opposed and has to be overruled. Unfair means and factoids enter the discussion process and after a while, the atmosphere deteriorates.

Except for the last point, the evidence presented so far is in line with the theoretical arguments proposed in section 3.5. The negative effects that can be observed from coalition building and strategic voting, however, illustrate that costs inflicted by unfavorable decision-making also exist in participative decision-making. The reason seems to lie in the heterogeneous interests of faculty members. Conflicting interests can lead to majority coalition decisions that are to the disadvantage of the minority faculty group.

Despite these observations, it can still be argued that the commitment problem of ex-post detrimental decision-making is more severe under autocratic decision-making than under faculty participation. The reason for this conclusion is that the divergence of interests between university management and faculty can be assumed to be higher than among faculty members. Nevertheless, conflicts of interest also seem to exist within faculty groups, especially concerning financial decisions. This is an important insight: While faculty participation may alleviate the commitment problem between management and faculty, i.e. preventing the manager from implementing decisions that are detrimental for faculty as a whole, faculty participation cannot rule out that decisions that are detrimental to a minority of faculty are implemented.

7.3.3 The Effects on Academic Quality

Turning to the effects of faculty participation on academic quality, ambiguous effects can be observed. On the positive side, the academic insight faculty can provide on research and teaching topics in their respective fields leads to better academic decisions where this knowledge is crucial, e.g. the establishment of a new degree program, the creation of a new department, or the restructuring of the departments into more focused units.[10]

---

[10] Source: Interview partners IX and XI.

7.3 The Effects of Faculty Participation

"Natürlich ist ein Forschungsschwerpunkt einer Universität nicht ohne die Mitwirkung der Hochschullehrer zu entscheiden. Das kann kein Management, das kann keine Universitätsverwaltung tun, sondern das müssen die Hochschullehrer tun.[11]

Contrary to the theoretical propositions, no references are made to possible effects that the quality of academic work, i.e. the quality of research or the quality of teaching, is influenced by the fact that faculty participates in decision-making. The argument that academic quality is higher under a participatory decision-making system is based on the monitoring effect, assuming that faculty could be a better monitor of the academic performance of faculty than university management. While faculty indeed is the more knowledgeable monitor, the incentives to engage in self-monitoring are not strong enough. Instead of monitoring colleagues, faculty appears to be more inclined to protect faculty members that are showing low performance.[12]

The arguments that faculty as a residual claimant should be interested in improving the academic performance of his institution are subdued by the solidarity between faculty members. One interview partner aptly summarized this behavior by the proverb 'There is honor among thieves'.[13] This behavior may in part be encouraged by the currently dominant compensation system in German universities that does not reward individual performance.[14]

The aspect of protectionist behavior becomes especially pronounced in the discussion of the negative effects faculty participation has on academic quality. Due to the fact that faculty needs to preserve its narrow voting majority by unanimous voting in the senate, it cannot make tough decisions on other faculty members that have shown low performance.[15]

---

[11] Decisions about the creation of academic clusters cannot be made by management or administration without the participation of faculty. Faculty input is needed in these decisions.
[12] Source: Interview partners II, VII, IX, and XI.
[13] Source: Interview partner XI.
[14] Until recently, faculty in Germany was independent of actual performance. Starting in January 2005, all new faculty are paid a base salary and a performance-based bonus from a department-wide bonus pool. It can therefore be expected over the next years that competition among faculty will increase and with it the incentive to monitor colleagues. Due to a lack of experience with the new model, no conclusive evidence can be gathered at the moment.
[15] Source: Interview partners II, VII, IX, and XI.

"Es war meiner Ansicht nach dadurch schlimm, dass die Professoren in diesen Gremien die ganz knappe Mehrheit hatten und sich immer zusammenschließen mussten, um sich durchsetzen zu können. Sie haben daher auch ihre schwarzen Schafe schützen müssen, um weiter die Mehrheit zu behalten. Das war außerordentlich kontraproduktiv."[16]

The incentives faculty has to engage in monitoring stem from the potential improvement of university reputation and faculty reputation if low performance is detected and ameliorated. The incentives that speak against such behavior is that the faculty member who engages in monitoring himself can become the target of intensified monitoring once he has detected shirking and has brought it to the attention of fellow colleagues and university management. Protecting faculty colleagues instead of effectively monitoring them is ultimately a form of rational self-protection. Another related impediment to effective monitoring is that the impact of detecting bad performance is limited due to the fact that professors in Germany are civil servants that receive a fixed salary and cannot be dismissed. As pointed out earlier, a reform of the civil servant status and the compensation system has been initiated. Its effects have yet to be seen before any conclusions can be drawn.

The second negative effect faculty participation is observed to have on academic quality is the lack of incentive congruity in decisions on academic topics. Due to the personal interests of the different faculty members, the best academic decision for university reputation is not necessarily taken. Rather, personal and departmental academic interests often dominate the academic senate. This observation confirms the basic assumption this dissertation follows that economic agents tend to strive to pursue their personal interests (see section 2.2.2). For faculty, achieving personal reputation is often more important than the reputation of the university as a whole, although faculty reputation depends on institutional reputation to a certain degree.[17]

---

[16] In my perception, the narrow majority that faculty had in collective decision-making made the matter worse as faculty had to build coalitions in order to implement their preferred decisions. This had the detrimental effect of having to protect the black sheep in the faculty community.

[17] Source: Interview partners II, VII, IX, and XI. See also section 7.4.1 for the discussion of the characteristics of the prototypical faculty member.

7.3.4 The Effects on Managerial Professionalism

Turning to the third area of effects, the observations show faculty participation to have positive and negative effects on managerial professionalism. On the positive side, participative decision-making allows the incorporation of a larger degree of relevant knowledge and experience, thus improving the informational base on which decisions are founded.[18] Through discussions moderated by a strong and responsible university president, participative decision-making can yield timely and sound decision-making.

> "Ein zentraler positiver Punkt an Mitbestimmung ist, dass wir alle Menschen mit begrenztem Horizont sind. [...] Durch die aktive Mitbestimmung und Partizipation erhält man natürlich alle möglichen Gesichtspunkte zum selben Thema. Er enthebt nicht von der Verantwortung, daraus eine Entscheidung zu machen, aber die Entscheidung ist dann durch Wissen geprägt und nicht durch Zufall."[19]

On the negative side, the lack of project management and clearly assigned responsibility makes participative decision-making inefficient and ineffective. The inefficiency results from the large amount of time it takes to reach a decision, the long discussions and the multiple discussion of the same topic. The ineffectiveness of participative decision-making relates to the strategic direction of the decisions which often appear to oppose the apparent changes in the educational landscape, either by retaining the status quo or by taking decisions that slow down the reform process.[20]

> "Diese Gremienstruktur führt eher zu Nicht-Entscheidungen als zu Entscheidungen. [...] Und wenn sich etwas tat, sind das Kompromissentscheidungen gewesen, die nicht unbedingt zielführend waren."[21]

---

[18] Source: Interview partners III, IV, VII, VIII, an IX.
[19] One key issue about faculty participation is that all decision makers have limited knowledge. Through active participation, more information can be gathered on any topic. The responsibility to finally come to a decision remains, but the decision can be based on knowledge instead of leaving it to chance.
[20] Source: Interview partners I, III, V, VII, X, XI, XII, and XIII.
[21] Collective decision-making results more in non-decision-making than in actual decision-making. Those decisions that were taken in the end usually undermined the original intent."

"Was ich gerade im akademischen Kontext immer wieder beobachtet habe, ist, dass kein Zwang zum wirtschaftlichen Handeln da ist. Es gibt keine direkte Korrelation zwischen der Dauer einer Diskussion, der Dauer eines Prozesses und den assoziierten Kosten."[22]

Conflicting personal interests and egos, the absence of hierarchical structures, and a lack of economic understanding lead to decisions that are not in the best interest of the university.

7.3.5 Summary of the Effects

In summary, both positive and negative effects of faculty participation in university decision-making are present in all three universities. Three different areas of effects can be distinguished: The academic working environment, the academic quality, and managerial professionalism. The following table summarizes the effects that can be observed in practice.

Area	Positive Effects	Negative Effects
Academic working environment	<ul><li>Sense of community is established in the university</li><li>Faculty performs a mediating role between university management</li><li>Cooperation between university management and faculty is fostered</li></ul>	<ul><li>Deterioration of academic "culture" through bargaining and entrenched interests</li><li>Suboptimal compromises in collective decision-making demotivate faculty to participate</li></ul>
Academic quality	<ul><li>Better informational basis in academic decisions as faculty members contribute specific expertise</li></ul>	<ul><li>Coalition building in collective decision-making compromises academic quality</li><li>Protectionist behavior on behalf of faculty reduces incentives</li></ul>
Managerial professionalism	<ul><li>Better informational basis in decision-making in general as faculty members contribute their insight</li></ul>	<ul><li>Length of time needed to reach decisions impedes management</li><li>Partisan decision making is not in the best interest of the university</li></ul>

Fig. 7.1 The Effects of Faculty Participation in University Decision-Making

At this point, two preliminary conclusions could be proposed. Firstly, the negative effects of faculty participation in university decision-making appear to

---

[22] In the academic context, I have often noticed a lack of awareness for economic constraints. There is no direct correlation between the length of discussion processes and the associated costs."

be more tangible than the positive effects. The impact of the positive effects, however, should not be underestimated, and a more thorough understanding of the underlying reasons is needed before recommendations can be made. Due to the qualitative nature of this study it cannot be determined which effect is dominant in the university. Both effects, however, have a significant impact on the operation of the university. Any structure that mitigates the negative effects while promoting the positive effects is beneficial for the performance of the university as a whole.

The second plausible conclusion relates to the fact that significant differences between the universities fail to materialize. This can be regarded as a positive signal for the general character of this study. Since the differences in the legal and organizational structure of the universities do not yield fundamentally different effects, the explanatory value of the variable 'Institutional framework of the university' is unlikely to be very high. In order to give a deeper insight into the relationships that lie behind the effects outlined above, each of the factors is examined for its explanatory value in the next section.

7.4 The Explanatory Value of the Variables

7.4.1 The Impact of the Factor 'Faculty'

Of the seven explanatory factors, the characteristics, preferences, and motives of faculty and university management, and the formal and informal design of the decision structures of the university are expected to provide the greatest insight into the underlying reasons for the effects of faculty participation.

Consistent with the theory proposed in section 3.3.2, faculty perceive themselves, and are described by non-faculty interview partners, as the elite workers of the university.[23] They are free scholars, primarily striving for academic freedom and the fulfillment of their basic tasks, research and teaching.[24] As such, the

---

[23] Source: Interview partners II and III.
[24] Source: Interview partners II, III, VI, IX, XI, XII, and XIII.

development of their university as well as the academic work are the sources of the job motivation of faculty.

Faculty regard participation in decision-making as a responsibility and as a duty toward the university, which is derived from their superior knowledge and insight into the academic production process. The desire to participate is motivated by the notion that the ability to influence the relevant decisions secures academic freedom.[25]

While faculty do not want to be ruled by an autocratic management body, it is not their primary objective to run the university, either. Such a management task would conflict with their preferences for academic instead of administrative work. A certain degree of centralization of decision rights and duties with university management is therefore regarded as beneficial if it frees up faculty time for academic tasks.[26] However, it can be noted that a natural sense of skepticism is inherently installed in faculty when faced with management intervention. In general, a university led by an autocratic management is not considered an acceptable organizational form by faculty or by the university.

The characteristics of faculty point to a dilemma with regard to faculty participation in decision-making. On the one hand, it is maintained that formal faculty authority over decisions concerning research and teaching as well as a decentralized decision structure with a weak management are a natural privilege of faculty. On the other hand, the time the decision-making processes take away from research and teaching is regarded as a serious drawback of faculty participation.

Creating a strong university management and administration would involve transferring some decision rights to management, and this would give faculty more time available for the academic tasks since they would be less involved in decision-making than under a weak management. This observation throws a different light on the argument concerning the importance of influencing costs (see section 3.5.4). From a theoretical perspective, it can be argued that when

---

[25] Source: Interview partners I, VI, X, XI, and XIII.
[26] Source: Interview partners V, VI, and IX.

faculty does not possess formal decision rights, they would still participate in the decision-making process through extensive lobbying or influencing activities. The empirical evidence suggests, however, that this is not necessarily the case and that faculty would spend less time in the decision-making process if they did not possess formal authority. While faculty would probably remain involved in decision-making due to their intrinsic motivation, it is estimated that this informal participation process would require less faculty time.

Not only faculty characteristics, but also faculty information and faculty motives offer valuable insights into the underlying reasons of the effects of faculty participation. Faculty is generally attributed with superior information in regards to research, teaching, department capabilities and resources, and appointment decisions.[27] When faculty participate in decision-making, they share this knowledge in the decision-making process, thus improving the informational basis of decisions. Ceteris paribus, this leads to better decision-making.

In regards to the motives faculty members have in decision-making, no conclusive statement can be made. Faculty interests are manifold: They strive to represent the objectives of the group that elected them into the academic senate and to advocate the interest of their department as well as looking after the well-being of the entire university. In general, it can be stated that faculty members are self-interested economic agents.[28] Their personal interests, however, may at time coincide with the interests of special groups, departments or the entire university, so that faculty may act as a proponent of these respective groups in the senate.

All of these interests represent legitimate claims faculty may choose to support. The priorities in decision-making are particular to each faculty member and preferences may shift depending on the situation and the respective decision. The diversity of preferences, however, induces constant clashes and conflicts of interests. As a result of the apparent lack of coherence and a joint objective, these disagreements may lead to a demotivation of management and faculty.

---

[27] Source: Interview partners I, II, IV, V, IX, X, and XI.
[28] Source: Interview partners I, II, III, IV, V, VIII, XI, XII, and XIII.

It is evident that the self-perception, preferences, motives, and interests of faculty influence the effects of their participation in university decision-making, both academically and from an organizational point of view. A preliminary conclusion infers that faculty possesses superior information and knowledge about certain decisions. This can be regarded as a reason for the existence of faculty participation and for the positive effects on the quality of decision-making. On the other hand, the preference structure of faculty members also gives rise to less beneficial effects of faculty participation on the academic working environment. They are interrelated with university management and the decision structures of the university, so that these factors must be taken into account before any conclusion can be drawn.

7.4.2 The Impact of the Factor 'University Management'

In all of the universities analyzed, university management consists mostly of professors, some of whom suspended their academic duties for the duration of their management turn, while others perform both management and professorial duties on a part-time basis. Despite their faculty origin, university managers perceive themselves, and are regarded by other constituencies, as the professional managers of the university.[29] This is especially relevant for the president of the university, which requires a full-time position that cannot be combined with extensive academic activities in research and teaching. Management is the advocate of the well-being of the entire university, and is more interested in sustaining the entire organization rather than encouraging partisan interests.[30]

In terms of their role in the university, the communication and moderation function of university management is strongly emphasized. Management is regarded as the key driver of university development and internal reform. Their task is to initiate projects and decisions, and to promote the development of the university.[31] Management is thus responsible for the memos and papers that pro-

---

[29] Source: Interview partners I and V.
[30] Source: Interview partners I and IV.
[31] Source: Interview partners VII, X, XI, and XIII.

vide the basis for any decision in the academic senate. Once such a proposal has been drafted, communication processes are initiated with all constituents of the university, and especially with faculty members since they hold the voting majority in the senate. University managers cannot make decisions against all other constituents of the university since such decisions would be very difficult to implement against the will of the entire university community.[32] Therefore, university management must seek to explain their ideas to the constituencies and lobby for support. A mixture of assertiveness and consensus is needed to take controversial decisions.

The information university management possesses about the different objectives and interests of the university members, about the academic production process as well as about the functioning of the academic and administrative departments of the university depends both on the complexity of the university as well as on the capabilities and experience of university management. While no conclusive statement can be made regarding the degree of insight university management has, the widespread notion that academic outcome is difficult to evaluate for university management appears to be valid.[33] University managers themselves believe the faculty has superior knowledge on these aspects.

The ideal management style is described as a participative, cooperative approach, including faculty and the constituencies of the university in the management processes. While management has the right and the responsibility to initiate progress, open communication structures, both formal and informal, as well as moderated discussion processes characterize the management approach in the three universities studied.[34]

The way university management fulfills its role as a communicator of its proposals, trying to persuade the constituencies of the right course of action, influences the effects of faculty participation. A management approach that combines both intensive, cooperative discussion as well as centralized decision-making re-

---

[32] Source: VII, X, and XIII.
[33] Source: Interview partners I and IV.
[34] Source: Interview partners IV, VII, XI, and XII.

sponsibility seems to take advantage of the positive aspects of faculty participation in decision-making while mitigating the negative effects.[35]

The above discussions of the factors 'Faculty' and 'University Management' provide the basis for understanding the effects of faculty participation. Further insight is expected from the factor 'Decision Structures', which refers to the rules that govern decision-making at the university.

7.4.3 The Impact of the Factor 'Decision Structures'

One fundamental insight with regard to decision structures is that not only the formally prescribed processes are relevant, but also their practical implementation. University management tends to ask faculty for their opinion on a certain decision even if there does not exist a formal participation rule. De facto participation is therefore more widespread in the university than can be concluded from the study of the formal decision structures as set out in the university charter or the respective laws.[36] Voluntarily involving faculty members is conditional on the perception of the university manager as a networker and communicator of ideas. The integration of constituencies into the process of finding the best alternative and making a decision leads to a broader backing of the decision and causes less resistance in the implementation of the decision.

Informal preliminary discussions, however, do not only take place between management and faculty, but also between faculty members in order to bargain about the joint position faculty represents in the senate. These informal faculty meetings yield considerable power over the decision since faculty effectively provides the majority in the senate so that any decision can be determined by faculty coalitions.[37] These coalitions, however, tend to favor the interests of faculty over

---

[35] Source: Interview partner IV.
[36] I, IV, VIII, and XIII.
[37] This seems to be especially applicable in the university PR as interview partners I, II, and III point out.

the interests of the university as a whole, so that decisions can become biased toward the welfare of one constituency while neglecting overall welfare.[38]

This problem is discussed as the incentive problem in section 3.5.4. Due to the fact that diverging interests and de facto domination of the senate give faculty the authority to implement decisions, they can accept proposals that are in their own best interest while not necessarily taking into account the effects of a decision on university reputation or other constituencies. These conflicts become more severe if different coalitions within the faculty group pursue differing objectives. Since faculty has to be united for making a decision with a simple majority in the academic senate, coalitions may evolve that are based on the smallest common denominator.

In such a setting, the role of the president in the decision-making process is of vital importance. If the president is involved in moderating the discussions both between faculty members and within the academic senate, he can uphold the interests of the university and can mediate between conflicting objectives. Since responsibility over the decision-making process is often allocated to the president, he has the authority to take the final decision after discussing it with the constituencies. This strengthens the positive effects of faculty participation (better information, faculty motivation, less resistance, etc.) while mitigating the effects of long, tiresome discussions that are driven by private interests.[39]

Two insights evolve from the discussion of the decision processes in real-life situations. Firstly, people are considered to be at least as important as decision structures.[40] University presidents have to be respected personalities in order to be able to effectively communicate and discuss with the constituencies of the university. Secondly, responsibility plays a big role in decision-making. Since responsibility cannot be allocated to groups, the academic senate cannot make responsible decisions in the sense that it can be held accountable for the implica-

---

[38] Source: Interview partners I and VIII.
[39] Source: Interview partners II, IV, VII, VIII, X, and XI.
[40] Source: Interview partners I and III.

tions of the decisions.[41] Incentives for good decision-making only exist when the president is personally responsible for the decision-making and can be dismissed from office for bad performance.

7.4.4 The Impact of Other Factors

The allocation of responsibility to the president of the university evolved over the last few years, as the information extracted with respect to the institutional change in the universities reveals. In the last decade, public university policy underwent several reforms when the Federal Ministry of Education as well as the State Ministries began to realize that they could no longer effectively control the university. A lack of information, insight, and resources, combined with a changing environment in the market for higher education necessitated alternative forms of external university governance. The trend that is visible from recent legislative reforms (see section 1.1) is to give the university an increasing level of autonomy over decision-making, over the design of organizational structures as well as over the development of their academic programs. This involves delegating decision rights to university management, especially giving the president new control and decision rights that previously resided in the Ministries.[42] It also involves the creation of supervisory boards that take over the control function from the Ministry.

In order to develop a responsible, empowered president, the delegation of authority from the Ministries to the university level is accompanied by a tendency within the university to centralize decision power with the management. While this does not necessarily imply that decision rights of faculty are formally restricted, the role of university management is nevertheless developing from a representative function into a true management role with initiation and implementation rights.[43] This implies that faculty members have to give up their notion of the university as an "Ordinarienuniversität" run after the interests of the professors.

---

[41] Source: Interview partners VII, X, and XI.
[42] Source: Interview partners IV, VII, IX, X, XI, and XII.
[43] Source: Interview partners IV, VII, IX, X, XI, and XII.

7.4 The Explanatory Value of the Variables

In principle, faculty appear to be willing to do this since this reduces the time they need to spend in decision-making.[44] Problems arise in the change process when the concession of decision rights by faculty and the state to the university management is perceived to be asymmetric. When faculty feel their rights are being curtailed while the Ministry still enjoys and makes use of effective intervention rights, distrust and demotivation results.[45] Such problems obstructed the change process in the past. In the meantime, such conflicts seem to have abated and faculty largely perceive the current assignment of rights as fair.

In regards to future institutional change, the trend of giving autonomy to universities and university boards is expected to continue. As the competition for the best students, faculty, and staff is likely to increase in the future, flexible structures are necessary in order for universities to be able to react quickly on an individual basis, taking into account the respective framework in which the university operates.[46]

Generational succession is another source of change. New cohorts of professors have been educated in a more competitive educational market and have already experienced stronger management bodies than the incumbent professors. Therefore, the general acceptance of competition among faculty is assumed to rise and professional university management structures are increasingly regarded as the logical consequence of the changes in the educational landscape in Germany.[47] Yet, fundamental institutional change, such as the implementation of new organizational structures, is likely to be triggered by outside parties, i.e. the state as the ultimate principal of public universities.

Contrary to the expectation raised in the conceptual model, the factors 'Institutional Framework of the University System', 'Institutional Framework of the University', and the variable 'Communication' do not yield significant insights into the reasons underlying the effects of faculty participation in university decision-

---

[44] Source: Interview partner V.
[45] Source: Interview partner XIII.
[46] Source: Interview partners IV, VI, VII, IX, X, XI, XII, and XIII.
[47] Source: Interview partner XI.

making. The general importance of functioning communication structures has already been pointed out in the prior discussion of the characteristics of university management. To a great extent, the task of university management includes communicating its proposals for developing the university to faculty, the senate, and other constituencies. In order to achieve this, open and trustworthy communication between university management and faculty channels are crucial.[48]

No relevant differences between the effects of faculty participation in university PR versus the universities SP and TP could be discovered. Thus, it can be inferred that faculty participation seems to come with benefits and costs regardless of the institutional form of the university. The information extracted for the variable 'Institutional Framework of the University System' does not show that the legal framework of the German university system has a significant impact on the different effects of faculty participation either. A comparative study between different "Bundesländer" may be able to find significant differences between the German states, thus helping to clarify the importance of the legal system in which universities operate. Such an analysis clearly lies beyond the scope of this study.

The above discussion of the information extracted for the factors concerning faculty, university management, decision structures, and institutional change provides many detailed, but dispersed insights into the reasons that underlie the observed effects of faculty participation. In the third step of qualitative content analysis, these insights are used to develop a better, if preliminary understanding of the relationships between the influence factors.

---

[48] Source: Interview partners II, III, IV, V, and VIII.

7.5 A First Classification of the Underlying Reasons of Faculty Participation

7.5.1 Conditions and Relationships between Influence Factors and Effects

In sections 7.3 and 7.4, the effects of faculty participation that can be observed in universities in Germany are described, and the influence factors are illustrated. The missing link between the influence factors and the effects are interdependent relationships between them.

One strategy for the identification of possible relationships between explanatory factors and the effects that are to be explained is to classify the conditions for the different factors according to their impact on faculty participation (Gläser/Laudel (2004), pp. 244-245). Conditions can be assigned to one of five categories:

1. Necessary conditions have to be present in order for an effect to occur at all.

2. Sufficient conditions bring about a certain effect regardless of the other conditions.

3. Facilitating conditions strengthen a certain effect.

4. Obstructive conditions weaken a certain effect.

5. Prohibiting conditions prevent a certain effect from happening irrespective of other conditions.

As summarized by figure 7.1, there are six different effects of faculty participation in university decision-making. They include positive and negative effects on the academic quality, the academic working environment, and on managerial professionalism. For the purpose of this section, the positive and the negative effects will be treated in conjunction. The objective is to identify the different conditions that can evoke or prevent the emergence of positive and negative effects. These conditions illustrate the causal reasons of faculty participation.

To avoid duplicating the conditions, only the necessary, sufficient, and facilitating conditions of the positive and negative effects are outlined. The conditions for the positive and negative effects are reciprocal since the facilitating conditions of the positive effects tend to be obstructive conditions of the negative effects. If the conditions for the positive effects of faculty participation are fulfilled, this implies that the negative effects are concurrently subdued, and vice versa.

In order for the positive effects of faculty participation pointed out in the figure 7.1 above to materialize in general, faculty must have an incentive to participate in decision-making at all, and the decision structures must allow participative elements such as delegating formal or real authority over certain decisions to faculty. These are the basic necessary conditions of the positive effects. Two further necessary conditions apply to the decision structures: The existence of clearly assigned decision rights, and the allocation of responsibility to the university management. If these four necessary conditions are not fulfilled, the empirical evidence shows that the positive effects of faculty participation in university decision-making are very unlikely to arise.

On the basis of these four necessary conditions, a number of facilitating conditions exist that strengthen the positive effects. For university management, they include an open management approach that actively and seriously involves faculty in decision-making, a self-perception as a communicator rather than an autocratic decision-maker, and a strong personality of the university president. Functioning communication channels between management and faculty as well as other constituencies also facilitate the task of university management.

On the side of faculty, a facilitating condition of the positive effects of faculty participation is the general willingness to accept a strong, responsible president and to work together with university management to advance the objectives of the university. This in turn is facilitated when the overall reputation of the university features strongly in the preferences of the faculty members involved in decision-making. The positive effects of faculty participation in regard to the informational basis of decision-making can only be realized if faculty in fact possesses an informational advantage over university management and administrative staff in at least some decision areas. Together with the necessary condition that faculty has an intrinsic incentive to participate in decision-making at all, the possession of superior information on the side of faculty can thus be regarded as a sufficient condition for the positive informational effects of faculty participation. Whenever faculty is allowed to participate and contribute their valuable knowledge to the decision-making process, this can be assumed to have a positive impact on decision-making.

Turning to the conditions that facilitate the emergence of negative effects of faculty participation, the first two necessary conditions again refer to the basic motivation of faculty to participate in decision-making, and the ability to participate through appropriate decision structures. The third necessary condition is the existence of diverging interests between university management and faculty and/or between faculty members. If all parties involved in decision-making had similar interests, then participative decision-making would be quick and effective.[49]

One condition that facilitates the emergence of negative effects is the narrow majority margin that faculty members enjoy in collective decision making since this encourages coalition building and may compromise the quality of decision-making. The lack of responsibility in decision-making is a second facilitating condition that also strengthens the likelihood for negative effects to appear.

The table depicted in figure 7.2 summarizes the conditions underlying the possible effects of faculty participation in university decision-making that can be detected in the empirical material. It also includes the contrary effect for each condition where applicable, so that the table draws a complete picture of the interdependencies between the conditions.

---

[49] See also the discussion of an agency problem in section 2.3 and Arrow's conditions for consensus decision-making in section 3.5.4.

Condition	Positive Effects on			Negative Effects on		
	Academic working environment	Academic quality	Managerial professionalism	Academic working environment	Academic quality	Managerial professionalism
Faculty conditions						
Willingness to participate		Neccesary			Necessary	
Acceptance of strong university management	Facilitating		Facilitating			Obstructive
University reputation part of faculty preference structure		Facilitating			Obstructive	
Superior knowledge		Sufficient				
Diverging interests	Obstructive				Necessary	
University management conditions						
Open management approach	Facilitating			Obstructive		
Self-perception as communicator	Facilitating		Facilitating			
Strong personality of president	Facilitating		Facilitating			Obstructive
Structural and procedural conditions						
Participatory elements in university decision-making		Neccesary			Necessary	
Clearly assigned decision rights		Necessary				Obstructive
Allocation of responsibility to university management	Neccesary			Obstructive		
Narrow faculty majority in senate	Obstructive		Obstructive		Facilitating	
Functioning communication channels		Facilitating				

Fig. 7.2 The Conditions Underlying Effects of Faculty Participation in University Decision-Making

7.5 A First Classification of the Underlying Reasons of Faculty Participation

Due to the primary nature of this study, the conditions discovered in the empirical material may not represent all existing conditions. Furthermore, the conditions outlined are of abstract, general nature. Further empirical research is needed in order to refine both the scope of the conditions as well as their level of detail.

Based on the above discussions, it can be concluded that the factors capturing the attributes of faculty, university management, the decision structures, and, to a lesser degree, the communication structures of the university and the change of the institutional framework influence the effects of faculty participation in university decision-making. As pointed out above, this conclusion is necessarily preliminary due to the limited scope of the study.

An impact of the variables describing the institutional framework of the university system and the institutional framework of the university could not be established. While the factual existence of such causal relationships between faculty participation and the institutional frameworks cannot be excluded, this study could not detect them.

Since the attributes of the variables are not available in numerical but rather in verbal form, they cannot be arranged on ordinal or cardinal scales. Thus, the relationships cannot be generalized in a form such that a certain variable can be assumed to have a positive or a negative effect. A statement on the influence of a variable can only be made in the context of the conditions outlined above, i.e. if the variable 'Faculty' shows the attribute 'Acceptance of centralized university management', then the positive effects of faculty participation are likely to arise.

The fact that all three university types showed very similar effects of faculty participation and the conclusion that the variable 'Institutional framework of the university' does not have a significant value in explaining the effects of faculty participation suggest that the results of this study are generalizable within the "Bundesland" studied. The assessment that the institutional framework of the university system does not indicate a causal relationship with the effects of faculty participation could imply that the results may even be representative for the

German university landscape. This conjecture is supported by the fact that the external experts, who have a knowledge of the effects of faculty participation in other states of Germany as well, confirmed the basic insight gained in the sample universities. As already pointed out above, an extensive comparative study across the German higher education landscape would be necessary to validate the general character of the implications of this study.

7.6 Conclusion

This chapter outlines the results of the first qualitative empirical study on university governance in Germany. The objective of the study is to describe and explain the effects of faculty participation in university decision-making. Due to its explorative character, a qualitative empirical approach is selected. Data is collected in thirteen expert interviews conducted with the help of a detailed questionnaire. The data gathered is processed and evaluated in accordance with the qualitative content analysis methodology.

The results presented above confirm the general hypothesis this dissertation proposes: There exists a trade-off of the effect of faculty participation in university decision-making. Faculty participation in German university practice comes with benefits but also with costs. A number of necessary, sufficient, facilitating, and obstructive conditions for the emergence of these effects can be identified. The reasons for the emergence of the effects of faculty participation can be found in the preferences and the behavior of the economic agents in the university, most notably university management and faculty, as well as in the design of the decision structures.

Concerning the theoretical arguments for the existence of the effects of faculty participation in university decision-making proposed in section 3.5, the arguments raised for the negative effects appear to be largely confirmed through the empirical study. The costs of collective decision-making, and the problem of diverging interests between the university in general and faculty in decision-making (see

7.6 Conclusion

section 3.5.4) are reflected in the causal conditions identified for the negative effects.

As summarized below, the results of the empirical study are ambiguous with regard to the arguments for the positive effects pointed out in section 3.5.3 – monitoring, commitment, and information. Faculty members indeed possess superior information about important decisions, and their participation thus improves the informational basis of university decision-making.

The commitment argument proposes that faculty participation alleviates the risk imposed by an autocratic management of making decisions that are detrimental to faculty. The threat of such a commitment problem does play a role, and it seems to provide faculty with a strong motivation to become involved in decision-making at all. However, even faculty members can take decisions by majority vote that discriminate against the minority interests and that may not be in the best interest of the university in general.

The monitoring argument, suggesting that faculty performance improves when colleagues engage in peer monitoring cannot be confirmed by the empirical evidence. On the contrary, participating in decision-making seems to give faculty the possibility to protect their peers instead of closely monitoring them. Despite the fact that faculty has the best insight into the academic production process and is therefore best capable of monitoring the performance of fellow faculty members, the incentives that the residual claimant status provides to faculty are apparently not strong enough. Faculty members rather follow their personal interests for personal academic reputation than performing the unrewarding task of monitoring the performance of colleagues. Contrary to the corporation, the internal peer performance pressure that emanates from professors thus seems to be limited. A reason for this may lie in the civil servant status that the majority of faculty members enjoy which safeguards faculty against sanctions for low performance. Consequently, the task of monitoring faculty performance in practice lies with the university management although their capabilities for evaluating the value of research and teaching output are limited.

Due to the nature of this study, the insights are novel from a scientific perspective. However, there is ample room for further research. On the qualitative side, the relationships that impact the effects of faculty participation in university decision-making can be studied in more depth, thus refining the degree of detail. Secondly, the scope of the study can be broadened in terms of the number of states and universities studied and with regard to the type of experts selected for the interview. Including deans, professors, and students may yield even more conclusive insights and generalizable results.

Thirdly, on the basis of the qualitative insight, a representative quantitative study of the German university governance system could be conducted. Equipped with a solid understanding of the underlying reasons for the effects of faculty participation in university decision-making, an effort could be made to detect the relationship between university decision systems and university performance. In a final step, the insights gained on the German university system could then be compared to findings across America and Europe. It becomes clear from this discussion that the empirical knowledge about governance and decision structures of universities is still at a very early stage. This promises important and significant insights of further research conducted in this area.

8 Final Conclusion

8.1 Summary

Universities are some of the most important organizations in modern societies. They provide the institutional framework for the creation and transfer of knowledge. A well-functioning system of higher education is often considered to be a prerequisite for economic growth and prosperity. Similar to the corporate world, the management and governance structures of the university can be regarded as an important driver of organizational performance. Surprisingly, little rigorous analysis has been conducted in this area. While the governance structures of corporations have been studied in depth both by economic as well as management science, researchers have shunned their own institutional framework.

This thesis contributes to the general literature on university governance by analyzing the inner workings of the university, its governance, and its decision structures within an economic framework. This framework is based on the research paradigm of the New Institutional Economics, and draws on agency and governance theory. A key characteristics of university governance structures is that they contain many elements that allow for stakeholder participation in governance and decision systems. Participation rights are held especially by faculty members, the elite workers of the university. The participatory decision-making system of universities thus lies at the heart of the analyses in this thesis.

Consequently, the research questions this dissertation addresses are concerned with the description and explanation of faculty participation in university decision-making and the effects it has on the university. The answers to these questions are presented in chapters 2 through 8. The methodological approach of this dissertation draws on theoretical argumentation, formal mathematical modeling, and empirical analysis of university decision-making in Germany. The three parts of this dissertation can be considered as separate, self-contained papers. They are linked by the overarching research question and draw on each other, but differ in their methodological viewpoint.

In part I of the dissertation, the university is defined as a non-profit degree-granting organization offering research, teaching and services to society. The university consists of a number of internal and external stakeholders with diverging interests. For the purpose of analyzing the effects of organizational and governance structures on the university, only the internal constituencies are relevant. Among them, principal-agent problems can be identified between the financial sponsor of the university and university management, between university management and administrative staff, and between university management and faculty. These relationships are characterized by moral hazard and other difficulties such as a lack of performance measurement.

In order to mitigate the agency problems, governance mechanisms come into play when complete contracts between the principal and the agent cannot be written. Governance can be regarded as the sum of the mechanisms designed to act as checks and balances on agent behavior. From a theoretical perspective, the special decision-making system of the university can be considered as such a governance mechanism.

With regard to the participative decision structures of the university, this thesis develops the argument that faculty participation in university decision-making exists as an internal governance mechanism to mitigate the agency conflicts between university management, faculty, and administrative staff. Faculty participation acts as a check to prevent university management from making decisions that are detrimental to the university in general and faculty in particular. Faculty can also be regarded as monitors of the performance of fellow faculty colleagues and administrative staff since they have the best insight into the academic production process.

Qualified performance monitoring through faculty is one argument for positive effects of faculty participation. Other benefits of faculty participation include the superior information faculty can provide about research and teaching, thus enhancing the informational basis on which decisions are made. Furthermore, faculty participation serves as a commitment device to the university manager,

8.1 Summary

discouraging decisions that are detrimental to faculty. This participatory role leads to an increase in faculty motivation and academic quality.

However, faculty participation does not only come with benefits, but with costs as well. These disadvantages center around the argument that collective decision-making is less efficient compared to autocratic, management-dominated decision-making. In decision-making, faculty is led by personal interests, which do not necessarily coincide with the interests of the university manager or the other constituencies of the university. A lack of incentive compatibility may therefore induce faculty to take decisions that are not in the best interest of the university.

On the basis of these arguments in favor of both positive and negative effects, the trade-off of faculty participation in university decision-making on university performance was identified. In the optimal allocation of decision rights across the different decision types, the positive effects overcompensate the negative effects of faculty participation, implying a favorable impact of faculty participation on the university in general.

The mathematical model of faculty participation in university decision-making that is developed in part II of the dissertation addresses the question of the optimal allocation of decision authority from a formal perspective. The optimal organizational setting is derived mathematically by translating the verbal arguments raised in part I into technical notation. Faculty participation in university decision-making is regarded as the delegation of authority from the principal - the university manager - to the agent, faculty. The model of faculty participation in university decision-making thus draws on previous economic models of intra-firm strategic delegation.

Two related models of faculty participation in the university are developed. They constitute the first attempt to formally depict the effects of faculty participation in university governance. Two organizational settings are distinguished by the models: A setting of university control, where the formal right to decide on a certain issue lies with the principal, and faculty control, where this right has been irrevocably delegated to faculty.

Both models show that faculty is more likely to engage in the decision process when formal authority has been delegated to him. When the university manager retains formal authority over the decision herself, faculty is less likely to conduct an extensive search for the best alternative since this search is costly to him. Still, faculty has an incentive to provide his (costly) information about the possible alternatives because it may be optimal for the university manager to rely on faculty to effectively make the decision. In this situation, faculty is regarded to have real authority, although formal authority still resides with the university manager.

In the initiative model, the optimal allocation of formal authority from a total welfare perspective depends on the magnitude of the decision payoffs to the university manager and to the agent. There are economic environments where delegation of authority is both efficient and feasible. When a certain decision is more important to faculty, i.e. faculty payoff from the decision is higher than the payoff for the university manager, formal authority should be optimally allocated to faculty, and vice versa.

In the second model, the proposal model, the optimal allocation of formal authority in terms of total welfare depends on the efficiency factor that is introduced into the cost function of faculty. The model is illustrated by example of a decision where faculty is assumed to be less efficient in providing the necessary information concerning the given decision than university management, e.g. in financial or organizational decisions. The model suggests that formal authority should be delegated to faculty when faculty inefficiency is high. Due to the high costs, faculty will exert only little information searching effort. The university manager, on the other hand, will compensate for this by showing high effort herself. She is therefore very likely to hold real authority over the decision. The key insight of the proposal model is that effective control over a decision, i.e. real authority, is more important than formal authority. When assessing an organizational setting, not only the formal rules have to be taken into account, but also the de facto distribution of authority.

8.1 Summary

Part III of the dissertation turns from theoretical argumentation to practical evidence by conducting the first empirical study on university decision-making in Germany. A qualitative approach is selected to describe the effects of faculty participation in university governance and to explain why they emerge. Data is collected through expert interviews and the evaluation is performed on the basis of qualitative content analysis.

The main hypothesis of this thesis - the existence of a trade-off of effects of faculty participation in university governance - is validated by the empirical analysis. The information gathered in the expert interviews confirms that faculty participation comes with both benefits and costs. Both positive and negative effects arise in three areas: Academic working environment, academic quality, and managerial professionalism.

The positive effects of faculty participation concentrate on the quality of participative decision-making, which is assumed to be higher than without participation due to the incorporation of the knowledge faculty members possess. With regard to the academic working environment, the role faculty play in decision-making contributes to the creation of a sense of academic community and cooperation.

On the negative side, suboptimal compromises, a deterioration of the academic culture of debate, coalition building, and partisan decisions can occur when entrenched bargaining positions dominate the decision-making process. The length of time needed in collective decision-making is also viewed as a negative effect of faculty participation since this takes away time from faculty that cannot be used for conducting research or teaching.

In order to explain the underlying causal reasons of the effects of faculty participation, conditions are identified for the positive and negative effects. These conditions provide an insight into the causal relationships between the effects of faculty participation and the characteristics of faculty and university management, and the design of the decision structures. The open, participative university decision-making process is the central mechanism that translates the causes into their effects.

Most of the theoretical propositions of part I are confirmed by the empirical evidence. Discrepancies arise with regard to the monitoring argument and the influencing costs, where the theory predicts an outcome different from the observed phenomena in the real world. The empirical analysis conducted in this thesis can be regarded as a starting point for the exploration of university governance structures in Germany.

This concludes the summary of the findings of this dissertation. The next section summarizes the main limitation that has to be imposed on the results and implications of this dissertation.[1]

8.2 Limitations

In the literature on corporate governance, one of the foremost objectives in both theoretical and empirical studies is the analysis of the effects of governance structures on corporate performance. Corporate performance is approximated with indicators such as shareholder value, shareholder return, or profitability measures. By establishing a relationship between corporate governance mechanisms and the respective performance indicators, the effectiveness of the respective mechanism in the mitigation of the corporate agency conflicts is determined.

This study on university governance, on the other hand, cannot examine the impact of university governance mechanisms on its performance, neither theoretically nor empirically. Despite describing and explaining the effect on the university that faculty participation in university governance as a mechanism of university governance has, a precise relationship to university performance is not established. The reason for this limitation lies in the lack of an accepted, objective performance measure for the university. As discussed in detail in section 3.2.4, no consistent indicator exists to evaluate and rank universities according to their performance.

Without an in-depth examination of the performance drivers and possible means of measuring them adequately, any aggregation of different outcome and

---

[1] See the concluding sections of each part for specific limitations in the theoretical, the mathematical, and the empirical part of the dissertation.

impact indicators for the university (e.g. academic publications, graduate salaries) is necessarily arbitrary. This dissertation proposes to regard university prestige as the overarching performance measure of the university, yet a precise formulation of this indicator cannot be given. Therefore, a comprehensive study and the development of universally accepted measures of university governance are a prerequisite for the analysis of the effects of university governance mechanisms on the performance of the university.

Consequently, it must be stated that this dissertation cannot develop a unified theory of university governance because the link to university performance is not yet fully explored. The merits of the three parts of this study lie in the analysis of university governance and university decision-making from three different angles in order to broaden and deepen the existing knowledge.

Despite the fact that more research needs to be carried out before the internal organization of an organization as complex as a university will be fully understood, a number of policy implications can be derived from the results of this dissertation.

8.3 Policy Recommendations

The objective of this dissertation is not only to address university decision-making from an academic standpoint, but also to provide policy recommendations in order to improve the institutional and organizational framework in which public universities in Germany operate. More specifically, the recommendations are aimed at improving the decision structures in German universities by strengthening the positive effects of faculty participation in university decision-making while mitigating the negative effects.

Due to the limited scope of this dissertation, the given recommendation should be regarded as a starting point for the discussion of the optimal organization of the university on the basis of the insights of theoretical and empirical research. They do not outline a comprehensive policy program that is ready to implement. The objective is rather to summarize the practical conclusions that can be derived on the basis of the discussions in parts I to III of this dissertation. The general nature of the recommendation leaves room for flexible adaptation to the specific legal environment in the different states and the relevant institutional setting of the individual universities.

In general, soft and hard actions can be proposed. Soft measures refer to a change in the academic culture of the university. While this measure may be hard to implement, both organizational theory as well as the experts interviewed for the empirical part of the dissertation suggest the positive impact of a strong and positive organizational culture. It can serve as an intangible commitment and control device, mitigating diverging interests and providing implicit rules and norms to the university community. A sense of community and joint purpose is especially important for the university due to its multitude of internal and external stakeholders and their diverse claims toward the university.

Proposing a general 'cultural improvement program' for the university goes beyond the claim this dissertation can make . The point is rather that organizational culture matters in the university as much as in other organizations. Therefore, university management should devote time and effort to analyzing, understanding the organizational culture of their institution in order to be able to shape it in accordance with the specific needs of the university.

Hard policy measures refer to changes to the organizational structures of the university. More concrete proposals can be recommended in this regard. When discussing organizational change, the legal framework in which universities operate has to be taken into account since most of the formal structures of the universities in Germany are specified by law. Recent legislative reforms (e.g. in the states of Bavaria, Berlin, Hesse, Rhineland-Palatinate) have shown that universities in general are becoming more and more autonomous. Authority over decision-making in such areas as examination and admission regulations or faculty appointment is increasingly being allocated to the university management and in particular to the president of the university. All experts agreed that this trend is likely to continue. Future legislation may become more specific, differentiating universities

8.3 Policy Recommendations

from each other by drafting individual laws for specific universities or certain types of universities like the State of Hesse has pioneered this with the Technical University of Darmstadt. The following recommendation rests on the assumption that the general tendency to allocate authority to the universities will not be reversed.

As decision rights are delegated from the Ministry to the level of the university, the importance of good internal structures increases. The overarching policy recommendation this dissertation makes is the creation of a bipolar organizational structure with a strong university management board on the first level, and a professionalized department board for each of the different departments on the second level of the organizational 'hierarchy'.[2]

Each management board is supported by collective consultation and control bodies consisting of representatives of the different internal constituencies of the university, i.e. faculty, administrative staff, and students. These consultation bodies resemble the current institution of the academic senate, and are thus referred to as the university senate and the department senate. University management is monitored by a supervisory board made up of external experts from business, science, politics, and society.

On a more detailed level, the implementation of this policy recommendation has implications on the role of management and the senate bodies, their election procedures, and the distribution of decision rights.

University managers and department managers are full-time positions that run for a tenure of at least three years. Professors who take up such a position suspend their academic activities for the duration of their tenure on the respective management board.

The senates are collective bodies that are consulted before the university and department management can take any significant decision. The issue that is to be decided and the different decision options are presented to the senate and are

---

[2] For small universities that have only one department, only one layer of management is needed.

discussed with its members. The senate can issue a recommendation in favor of a certain alternative, but the responsibility to decide and to implement the respective alternative lies with the management board.

University managers are elected by the university senate, and are confirmed by the supervisory board. Department managers are elected by the department senate and are approved by the university management. The dismissal of a university manager or the entire board can be initiated by the supervisory board or the university senate and has to be confirmed by both bodies. On the departmental level, the dismissal of a manager has to be confirmed by university management and the department senate.

Candidates for both management boards can be recruited both from within as well as from outside the university. While currently most university managers and deans are professors, it is up to the respective senate to select a suitable candidate, who may well be a professional university manager. All of the experts interviewed in the empirical study regarded an academic education as a prerequisite for performing a management function in the university. Special education programs for university managers are already evolving in Germany (e.g. the University of Oldenburg offers a Master of Business Administration in Educational Management), so that the labor market for university managers will define the degree requirements that have to be fulfilled.

The members of the university senate and the department senates are elected by the respective constituency groups, i.e. faculty, students, and administrative staff each select their representatives. The members of the supervisory board of the university are nominated jointly by the State Ministry and the university senate.

Decision authority between university management and department management is allocated on the basis of subsidiarity. All decisions that affect only one department are taken by the respective department board, while all university-wide decisions are taken by university management. Decision rights are clearly distinguished and assigned, and are part of the university charter.

8.3 Policy Recommendations

Responsibility for decision-making lies with the university management and the department management, depending on who has authority over the respective decision. The university senate and the department senates do not have decision-making authority.

The senates have a control function over the management boards. Similar to the supervisory body, they have the right to demand information of the respective management board. In case of bad performance or shirking, the senates can ask the management board or certain managers to step down from their task.

Some of these elements outlined above are already incorporated in some of the State Acts of Higher Education in Germany. The innovation of these recommendations lies in the institution of professionalized department management boards and the exclusive allocation of decision responsibility with management boards. The senate is retained as an institution, but its consultative and controlling functions are emphasized while its decision-making authority is reduced.

On the basis of the results and implications of part I to III of this dissertation, the suggested reorganization of decision structures in German universities could provide an important step toward the mitigation of the negative effects of the current participative decision-making system while sustaining the positive effects. By retaining faculty participation through the consultation and discussion in the senates, the superior information the faculty possesses over research and teaching can be incorporated into the decision-making process. The positive effects of faculty participation on the creation of an academic community and on the cooperation between faculty members and management boards can be maintained since faculty can be assumed to be intrinsically interested in shaping the development of the university. Therefore, faculty members have an incentive to make use of the opportunities provided by the consultation, information, and control rights accorded to the senates.

The proposed reorganization has the benefit of mitigating at least some of the negative effects of the current model of faculty participation. While discussion may still be lengthy, the senates are not involved in decision-making and therefore do not need to build majority coalitions. Instead, senate members can focus on providing the best arguments to the management boards, who are ultimately responsible for decision-making. Without the pressure of having to reach a collective decision, suboptimal compromises driven by partisan interests as well as protectionist behavior among senate members should play less of a role when the management boards are ultimately responsible for the decisions. This also avoids decision processes that are too long because the management can always impose an ultimate deadline, leaving more time for faculty to carry out their actual tasks of research and teaching.

Implementing a new system of decision-making and control in the university needs a change agent. The experts interviewed for the empirical study suggest that change in public universities has to be initiated from the outside. The entrenched interest of the internal stakeholders of the university prevent the far-reaching reorganization that is needed to improve university governance.

Giving complete freedom to universities to organize themselves without providing a framework may be preferable from a theoretical perspective of decentralization and subsidiarity. Practical evidence seems to suggest, however, that such freedom may not necessarily lead to the emergence of the most efficient governance structures due to the multitude of stakeholders and the divergence of their claims and interests in the university. The lack of effective competition on the market of higher education also moderates the pressure placed on the internal constituencies of the universities to vote for change. Therefore, an external change agent is needed to initiate the necessary organizational reforms.

The natural change agent for public universities in Germany is the legislator, who can prescribe internal university reform by changing the according laws.[3] Such a reform of the State Acts on Higher Education has to be carefully prepared in order to ensure that a sufficient degree of flexibility is incorporated into the legal measures. Not every university is the same, so that decision and control

---

[3] Recent reforms in Germany on degree programs (e.g. the Bologna Process), on academic career tracks, and on compensation systems have all been initiated by the Federal Ministry of Education and Research, or by the respective State Ministries.

structures should be adaptable to reflect the specific circumstances and needs of the organization. The elements of the decision-making system outlined serve as a starting point for the design of the optimal policy of university organization. Similar to the proposed ideal decision process within the university, the process of legal reform should also be characterized by participative elements. Preparatory discussion and consultation with the affected stakeholders of the university can improve the acceptance and implementation of the new institutions.

The system of checks and balances devised above necessarily builds on the principles of trust and sincerity, which have to be reflected in the personalities of the managers. As Popper (1992, p. 151) pointed out, governance systems do not only have to be well designed, but also have to be well staffed. This thesis has delivered a theoretical and scientific approach to the design of the optimal governance structure of the university. Finding the right people for the right job, however, remains an art.

Bibliography

AAUP. 1971. Report of subcommittee T. *AAUP Bulletin*, **57**(Spring), 69–124.

Ackroyd, Pamela, & Ackroyd, Stephen. 1999. Problems of university governance in Britain - Is more accountability the solution? *The International Journal of Public Sector Management*, **12**(2), 171–185.

Aghion, Philippe, & Bolton, Patrick. 1992. An incomplete contracts approach to financial contracting. *Review of Economic Studies*, **59**(3), 473–494.

Aghion, Philippe, & Tirole, Jean. 1997. Formal and real authority in organizations. *Journal of Political Economy*, **105**(11), 1–29.

Agrawal, Anup, & Knoeber, Charles R. 1996. Firm performance and mechanisms to control agency problems between managers and shareholders. *Journal of Financial and Quantitative Analysis*, **31**(3), 377–397.

Ahrens, Joachim. 2002. *Governance and economic development*. Cheltenham: Edward Elgar.

Akerlof, George A. 1970. The market for lemons: Quality uncertainty and the market mechanism. *Quarterly Journal of Economics*, **84**(3), 488–500.

Alchian, Armen A. 1965. Some economics of property rights. *Il Politico*, **30**(4), 816–829.

Alchian, Armen A. 1969. Corporate management and property rights. *Pages 337–360 of:* Manne, Henry G. (ed), *Economic policy and regulation of corporate securities*. Washington, D.C.: American Institute for Public Policy Research.

Alchian, Armen A., & Demsetz, Harold. 1972. Production, information costs, and economic organization. *The American Economic Review*, **62**(5), 777–795.

Alchian, Armen A., & Demsetz, Harold. 1973. The property rights paradigm. *Journal of Economic History*, **33**(1), 16–27.

Arrow, Kenneth, & Debreu, Gerard. 1954. Existence of a competitive equilibrium for a competitive economy. *Econometrica*, **22**(3), 265–290.

Arrow, Kenneth J. 1963. *Social choice and individual values.* 2nd edn. New York: Wiley.

Arrow, Kenneth J. 1969. The organization of economic activity: Issues pertinent to the choice of market versus non-market allocation. *Pages 39–73 of:* U.S. Joint Economic Committee, 91st Congress, 1st Session (ed), *The analysis and evolution of public expenditure - The PPB system*, vol. 1. Washington D.C.: U.S. Government Printing Office.

Arrow, Kenneth J. 1994. Methodological invidividualism and social knowledge. *The American Economic Review*, **84**(2), 1–9.

Backes-Gellner, Uschi. 1989. Zum Verhältnis von Lehre und Forschung in sozialwissenschaftlichen Fachbereichen. *Pages 51–76 of:* Helberger, Christof (ed), *Ökonomie der Hochschule I*. Berlin: Duncker & Humblot.

Backes-Gellner, Uschi, & Sadowski, Dieter. 1991. Zur Lage der deutschen Universität - Eine organisationsökonomische Zwischenbilanz. *Pages 9–37 of:* Helberger, Christof (ed), *Ökonomie der Hochschule II*. Berlin: Duncker & Humblot.

Bailey, Stephen K. 1973. A comparison of the university with a government bureau. *Pages 121–136 of:* Perkins, James A. (ed), *The university as an organization*. New York: McGraw-Hill.

Bainbridge, Stephen M. 1997. Privately ordered participatory management: An organizational failures analysis. *University of California at Los Angeles Law School Working Paper*, 1–87.

Baker, George P., Jensen, Michael C., & Murphy, Kevin J. 1988. Compensation and incentives: Practice vs. theory. *The Journal of Finance*, **43**(3), 593–616.

Baker, George P., Gibbons, Robert, & Murphy, Kevin J. 1999. Informal authority in organizations. *Journal of Law, Economics and Organization*, **15**(1), 56–73.

Baker, George P., Gibbons, Robert, & Murphy, Kevin J. 2002. Relational contracts and the theory of the firm. *The Quarterly Journal of Economics*, **117**(1), 39–84.

Baron, David P., & Myerson, Roger B. 1982. Regulating a monopolist with unknown costs. *Econometrica*, **50**(4), 911–930.

Barrett, Arnold L. 1963. University governance: Some omitted aspects. *Academy of Management Journal*, **6**(2), 170–172.

Barzel, Yoram. 1982. Measurement Cost and the Organization of Markets. *Journal of Law & Economics*, **25**(1), 27–48.

Bayerisches Hochschulgesetz, in the version of October 2, 1998, last changed March 24, 2004.

Becker, William E. Jr. 1975. The university professor as a utility maximizer and producer of learning, research, and income. *The Journal of Human Resources*, **10**(1), 107–115.

Ben-David, Joseph. 1971. *American higher education - Directions old and new*. New York: McGraw-Hill.

Berle, Adolf A., & Means, Gardiner C. 1932. *The modern corperation and private property*. New York: Macmillan Publishing Co.

Bess, James L. 1998. Contract systems, bureaucracies and faculty motivation - The probable effect of a no-tenure policy. *The Journal of Higher Education*, **69**(1), 1–22.

Besse, Ralph M. 1973. A comparison of the university with the corporation. *Pages 107–120 of:* Perkins, James A. (ed), *The university as an organization*. New York: McGraw-Hill.

Böhm, Franz. 1933. *Wettbewerb und Monopolkampf*. Berlin: Carl Heymann.

Böhm, Franz, Eucken, Walter, & Großmann-Doerth, Hans (eds). *Die Ordnung der Wirtschaft als geschichtliche Aufgabe und rechtsschöpferische Leistung*. Stuttgart: Kohlhammer.

Birnbaum, Robert. 1989a. The latent organizational functions of the academic senate. *The Journal of Higher Education*, **60**(4), 423–443.

Birnbaum, Robert. 1989b. Presidential succession and institutional functioning in higher education. *The Journal of Higher Education*, **60**(2), 123–132.

Blair, Margaret M., & Stout, Lynn A. 1999. A team production theory of corporate law. *Virginia Law Review*, **85**(2), 247–328.

Bohren, Oyvind, & Odegaard, Bent A. 2003. Governance and performance revisited. *European Corporate Governance Institute Working Paper Series, Finance Working Paper No. 28/2003*, 1–32.

Bolsenkötter, Heinz. 1976. *Die Ökonomie der Hochschule - Band I*. Baden-Baden: Nomos Verlagsgesellschaft.

Borooah, Vani K. 1994. Modelling institutional behaviour: A microeconomic analysis of university management. *Public Choice*, **81**(1-2), 101–124.

Bortz, Jürgen, & Döring, Nicola. 2002. *Forschungsmethoden und Evaluation für Human- und Sozialwissenschaftler*. 3rd edn. Berlin: Springer.

Bowen, Howard R. 1969. University governance: Workable participation, administrative authority and the public interest. *Labor Law Journal*, **20**(8), 517–528.

Brennan, H. Geoffrey, & Tollison, Robert D. 1980. Rent seeking in academia. *Pages 3–15 of:* Buchanan, James M., Tollison, Robert D., & Tullock, Gordon (eds), *Toward a theory of the rent-seeking society*. College Station: Texas A&M University Press.

Brown, William O. Jr. 1997. University governance and academic tenure - A property rights explanation. *Journal of Institutional and Theoretical Economics*, **153**(3), 441–461.

Brown, William O. Jr. 2001. Faculty participation in university governance and the effects on university performance. *Journal of Economic Behavior & Organization*, **44**, 129–143.

Brüsemeister, Thomas. 2000. *Qualitative Forschung - Ein Überblick.* Wiesbaden: Westdeutscher Verlag.

Buchanan, James M., & Tullock, Gordon. 1962. *The calculus of consent - Logical foundations of constitutional democracy.* Ann Arbor: University of Michigan Press.

Bundesamt, Statistisches. 2003. *Bericht zur finanziellen Lage der Hochschulen.* Wiesbaden: Statistisches Bundesamt.

Burgess, Simon, & Metcalfe, Paul. 1999a. Incentives in organisations - A selective overview of the literature with application to the public sector. *University of Bristol CMPO Working Paper Series No. 00/16*, 1–84.

Burgess, Simon, & Metcalfe, Paul. 1999b. The Use of incentive schemes in the public and private sectors - Evidence from British establishments. *University of Bristol CMPO Working Paper Series No. 00/15*, 1–43.

Burkart, Mike, Gromb, Denis, & Panunzi, Fausto. 1997. Large shareholders, monitoring, and the value of the firm. *The Quarterly Journal of Economics*, **12**(3), 693–728.

Carmichael, H. Lorne. 1988. Incentives in academia: Why is there tenure? *Journal of Political Economy*, **96**(3), 453–472.

Cater, Bruce, & Lew, Byron. 2002. A theory of academic tenure. *Trent University at Peterborough, Department of Economics Working Paper*, 1–19.

Chalmers, Alan F. 1999. *Wege der Wissenschaft.* 3rd edn. Berlin: Springer.

Chandler, Alfred D. 1962. Organizational capabilities and the economic history of the industrial enterprise. *Journal of Ecoomic Perspective*, **6**(3), 79–100.

Cheung, Steven N.S. 1968. Private property rights and sharecropping. *Journal of Political Economy*, **76**(6), 1107–1122.

Cheung, Steven N.S. 1969. *The theory of share tenacy*. Chicago: University of Chicago Press.

Cheung, Steven N.S. 1970. The structure of contract and the theory of a non-exclusive resource. *Journal of Law & Economics*, **13**(1), 49–70.

Chiang, Alpha C. 1984. *Fundamental methods of mathematical economics*. 3rd edn. Singapore: McGraw-Hill.

Coase, Ronald H. 1937. The nature of the firm. *Economica*, **4**(16), 386–405.

Coase, Ronald H. 1959. The federal communications commission. *Journal of Law & Economics*, **2**(1), 1–40.

Coase, Ronald H. 1960. The problem of social cost. *Journal of Law & Economics*, **3**(1), 1–44.

Coelho, Philip R. P. 1976. Rules, authorities, and the design of not-for-profit firms. *Journal of Economic Issues*, **X**(2), 416–428.

Colesa, Jerilyn W., McWilliams, Victoria B., & Senc, Nilanjan. 2001. An examination of the relationship of governance mechanism performance. *Journal of Management*, **27**(1), 23–51.

Cont, Walter A. 2001. Monitoring timing an collusion in hierarchies. *Universidad Nacional de la Plata, Department of Economics Working Paper*, 1–54.

Corson, John J. 1973. Perspectives on the university compared with other institutions. Pages 155–169 of: Perkins, James A. (ed), *The university as an organization*. New York: McGraw-Hill.

Coupé, Tom. 2003. Human, all too human - On the behavior of scientists and universities. *Ecares Université Libre de Bruxelles Working Paper*, 1–45.

Cowley, W. H. 1980. *Presidents, professors, and trustees.* San Francisco: Jossey-Bass Publishers.

Davis, Lance E., & North, Douglass C. 1971. *Institutional change and American economic growth.* Cambridge: Cambridge University Press.

De Boer, Harry. 1998. Vom partizipatorischen System zum Managerialismus? Internationale Trends in der Leitung von Hochschulen. *Pages 59–83 of:* Müller-Böling, Detlef, & Fedrowitz, Jutta (eds), *Leitungsstrukturen für autonome Hochschulen.* Gütersloh: Bertelsmann Stiftung.

De Groof, Jan, Neave, Guy, & Svec, Juraj. 1998. *Democracy and governance in higher education.* Legislating for higher education in Europe, vol. 2. The Hague: Kluwer Law International.

Dearlove, John. 1998. The deadly dull issue of university "adminstration"? Good governance, managerialism and organising academic work. *Higher Education Policy*, **11**(1), 59–79.

Dearlove, John. 2002. A continuing role for academics - The governance of UK universities in the post-Dearing era. *Higher Education Quarterly*, **56**(3), 257–275.

Demsetz, Harold. 1964. The exchange and enforcement of property rights. *Journal of Law & Economics*, **7**(2), 11–26.

Demsetz, Harold. 1966. Some aspects of property rights. *Journal of Law & Economics*, **9**(2), 61–70.

Demsetz, Harold. 1967. Toward a theory of property rights. *American Economic Review*, **57**(2), 347–359.

Denzin, Norman K., & Lincoln, Yvonna. 1998. *Collecting and interpreting qualitative materials.* Thousand Oaks: Sage.

Dewatripont, Mathias, Jewitt, Ian, & Tirole, Jean. 1999. The economics of career concerns, part II - Application to missions and accountability of government agencies. *Review of Economic Studies*, **66**(1), 199–217.

Dewatripont, Mathias, Jewitt, Ian, & Tirole, Jean. 2000. Multitask agency problems: Focus and task clustering. *European Economic Review*, **44**(4-6), 869–877.

Dilger, Alexander. 2001. Was lehrt die Prinzipal-Agenten-Theorie für die Anreizgestaltung in Hochschulen? *Zeitschrift für Personalforschung*, **15**(2), 132–148.

Dixit, Avinash, Grossman, Gene M., & Helpman, Elhanan. 1997. Common agency and coordination: General theory and application to government policy making. *Journal of Political Economy*, **105**(4), 753–769.

Dohmen, Thomas J. 2002. Building and using economic model - A case study analysis of the IS-LM model. *Journal of Economic Methodology*, **9**(2), 191–212.

Downs, Anthony. 1957. *An economic theory of democracy*. Cambridge: Cambridge University Press.

Dunleavy, Patrick. 1991. *Democracy, bureaucracy and public choice*. London et al.: Prentice Hall.

Ehrenberg, Ronald G. 1999. Adam Smith goes to college - An economist becomes an academic administrator. *Journal of Economic Perspectives*, **13**(1), 99–116.

Ehrenberg, Ronald G., Pieper, Paul J., & Willis, Rachel A. 1995. Would reducing tenure probabilities increase faculty salaries? *NBER Working Paper Series, Working Paper No. 5150*, 1–32.

Englmaier, Florian. 2005. *The effects of preference characteristics and overconfidence on economic incentives*. Ph.D. thesis, Ludwig-Maximilians-Universität München.

Erlei, Mathias, Leschke, Martin, & Sauerland, Dirk. 1999. *Neue Institutionenökonomik.* Stuttgart: Schäffer-Poeschel.

Eucken, Walter. 1947. *Nationalökonomie - wozu?* Godesberg: Küpper.

Eucken, Walter. 1990. *Grundsätze der Wirtschaftspolitik (1st edn 1952).* Tübingen: Mohr Siebeck.

Eurydice. 2000. *Two decades of reform in higher education in Europe: 1980 onwards.* Brussels: Eurydice.

Fama, Eugene F. 1980. Agency problems and the theory of the firm. *Journal of Political Economy,* **88**(2), 288–307.

Fama, Eugene F., & Jensen, Michael C. 1983a. Agency problems and residual claims. *Journal of Law & Economics,* **26**(2), 327–349.

Fama, Eugene F., & Jensen, Michael C. 1983b. Separation of ownership and control. *Journal of Law & Economics,* **26**(2), 301–325.

Fama, Eugene F., & Jensen, Michael C. 1985. Residual claims and investment decisions. *Journal of Financial Economics,* **14**(1), 101–119.

Faria, Joao R. 2001. Rent seeking in academia - The consultancy disease. *The American Economist,* **45**(2), 69–74.

Faria, Joao R. 2002a. Is there a trade-off between domestic and international publications? *The University of Texas at Dallas, School of Social Science, Political Economy Working Paper 11/02,* 1–19.

Faria, Joao R. 2002b. Scientific, business and political networks in academia. *Research in Economics,* **56**(2), 187–198.

Faria, Joao R. 2003. What type of economist are you - r-strategist or K-strategist? *Journal of Economic Studies,* **30**(2), 144–154.

Faria, Joao R. 2005. Is there a trade-off between domestic and international publications? *Journal of Socio-Economics*, **34**(2), 269–280.

Feltham, Gerald A., & Xie, Jim. 1994. Performance measure congruity and diversity in multi-task principal-agent relations. *The Accounting Review*, **69**(3), 429–453.

Fershtman, Chaim. 1985. Managerial incentives as a strategic variable in duopolistic environment. *International Journal of Industrial Organization*, **3**(2), 245–2553.

Fershtman, Chaim, & Judd, Kenneth L. 1987. Equilibrium incentives in oligopoly. *American Economic Review*, **77**(5), 927–940.

Fershtman, Chaim, Judd, Kenneth L., & Kalai, Ehud. 1991. Observable contracts - Strategic delegation and cooperation. *International Economic Review*, **32**(2), 551–559.

Flick, Uwe. 2002. *Qualitative Sozialforschung - Eine Einführung*. 6th edn. Reinbek bei Hamburg: Rowohlt Taschenbuch Verlag.

Foss, Nicolai. Coase vs. Hayek - Economic organization in the knowledge economy. *Department of Industrial Economics and Strategy, Copenhagen Business School Working Paper*, 1–50.

Frey, Bruno S., & Eichenberger, Reiner. 1992. Economics and economists - A European perspective. *American Economic Review*, **82**(2), 216–220.

Frey, Bruno S., & Eichenberger, Reiner. 1993. American and European economics and economists. *Journal of Economic Perspectives*, **7**(4), 185–193.

Friedman, Milton. 1953a. *Essays in positive economics*. Chicago: Chicago University Press.

Friedman, Milton. 1953b. The methodology of positive economics. *Pages 3–43 of:* Friedman, Milton (ed), *Essays in positive economics*. Chicago: University of Chicago Press.

Furubotn, E G., & J., Pejovich N. 1973. Property rights, economic decentralization and the evolution of the Yugoslav firm. *Journal of Law & Economics*, **16**(2), 275–302.

Furubotn, Eirik G., & Pejovich, Svetozar. 1972. Property rights and economic theory - A survey of recent literature. *Journal of Economic Literature*, **10**(4), 1137–1162.

Garvin, David A. 1980. *The economics of university behavior.* New York: Academic Press.

Gibbard, Allan, & Varian, Hal R. 1978. Economic models. *The Journal of Philosophy*, **75**(11), 664–677.

Gibbons, Robert. 1992. *A primer in game theory.* Hertfordshire: Harvester Wheatsheaf.

Gibbons, Robert. 2003. Team theory, garbage cans and real organizations - Some history and prospects of economic research on decision-making in organizations. *Industrial and Corporate Change*, **12**(4), 753–787.

Gilligan, Thomas W. 1993. Information and the allocation of legislative authority. *Journal of Institutional and Theoretical Economics*, **149**(March), 321–341.

Glaeser, Edward L. 2002. The governance of not-for-profit firms. *Harvard Institute of Economic Research, Discussion Paper No. 1954*, 1–62.

Glaeser, Edward L., & Shleifer, Andrei. 1998. Not-For-Profit Entrepreneurs. *Harvard University, Department of Economics Working Paper*, 1–26.

Glaser, Barney G., & Strauss, Anselm L. 1967. *The discovery of grounded theory - Strategies for qualitative research.* Chicago: Aldine Atherton.

Gläser, Jörg, & Laudel, Grit. 2004. *Experteninterviews und qualitative Inhaltsanalyse.* Wiesbaden: VS Verlag für Sozialwissenschaften.

Goldberg, Victor. 1976. Regulation and administered contracts. *Bell Journal of Economics*, **7**, 426–452.

Gomez-Mejia, Luis R., & Balkin, David B. 1992. Determinants of faculty pay - An agency theory perspective. *Academy of Management Journal*, **35**(3), 921–955.

Gordon, Scott. 1991. *The history and philosophy of social science*. London: Routledge.

Grant, Robert M. 1996. Toward a knowledge-based theory of the firm. *Strategic Management Journal*, **17**(Winter Special Issue), 109–122.

Gross, Edward, & Grambsch, Paul V. 1974. *Changes in university organization, 1964-1971*. New York: McGraw-Hill.

Grossman, Sanford J., & Hart, Oliver. 1983. An analysis of the principal-agent problem. *Econometrica*, **51**(1), 7–46.

Grossman, Sanford J., & Hart, Oliver. 1986. The costs and benefits of ownership - A theory of vertical and lateral integration. *Journal of Political Economy*, **94**(4), 691–719. m.

Hansmann, Henry B. 1980. The role of nonprofit enterprise. *The Yale Law Journal*, **89**(6), 835–901.

Harris, Milton, & Holmström, Bengt. 1982. A theory of wage dynamics. *Review of Economic Studies*, **49**(3), 315–333.

Harris, Milton, & Raviv, Artur. 1978. Some results on incentive contracts with applications to education and employment, health insurance, and law enforcement. *American Economic Review*, **68**(1), 20–30.

Harris, Milton, & Townsend, Robert M. 1981. Resource allocation under asymmetric information. *Econometrica*, **49**(1), 33–64.

Harris, Milton, & Weiss, Yoram. 1984. Job matching with finite horizon and risk aversion. *Journal of Political Economy*, **92**(4), 758–779.

Hart, Oliver. 1995. Corporate governance - Some theory and implications. *The Economic Journal*, **105**(430), 678–689.

Hart, Oliver, & Holmström, Bengt. 2002. A theory of firm scope. *Massachusetts Institute of Technology, Department of Economics Working Paper 02-42*, 1–44.

Hart, Oliver, & Moore, John. 1990. Property rights and the nature of the firm. *Journal of Political Economy*, **98**(6), 1119–1158.

Hart, Oliver D. 1983. Optimal labour contracts under asymmetric information. *Review of Economic Studies*, **50**(1), 3–35.

Hartmann, Yvette E. 1998. *Controlling interdisziplinärer Forschungsprojekte - Theoretische Grundlagen und Gestaltungsempfehlungen auf der Basis einer empirischen Untersuchung*. Stuttgart: Schäffer-Poesche.

Hausman, Daniel M. 1992. On the conceptual structure of neoclassical economics - A philosopher's view. *Pages 25–32 of:* Hausman, Daniel M. (ed), *Essays in philosophy and economic methodology*. Cambridge: Cambridge University Press.

Hennig-Thurau, Thorsten, Walsh, Gianfranco, & Schrader, Ulf. 2003. VHB-JOURQUAL: Ein Ranking von betriebswirtschaftlichrelevanten Zeitschriften auf der Grundlage von Expertenurteilen. *Bauhaus-Universität Weimar, Fakultät für Medien, Working Paper Nr. 1 - Juni 2003*, 1–36.

Hoenack, Stephen A. 1994. Economics, organizations, and learning - Research direction for the economics of education. *Economics of Education Review*, **13**(2), 147–162.

Hoenack, Stephen A., & Collins, Eileen L. (eds). 1990. *The economics of American universities - Management, fiscal operations, and fiscal environment*. Albany: State University of New York Press.

Holmström, Bengt. 1979. Moral hazard and observability. *The Bell Journal of Economics*, **10**(1), 74–91.

Holmström, Bengt. 1980. On the theory of delegation. *Kellogg School of Management CMS-EMS Discussion Paper 438*, 1–33.

Holmström, Bengt. 1982. Moral hazard in teams. *The Bell Journal of Economics*, **13**(2), 324–340.

Holmström, Bengt, & Milgrom, Paul. 1987. Aggregation and linearity in the provision of intertemporal incentives. *Econometrica*, **55**(2), 303–328.

Holmström, Bengt, & Milgrom, Paul. 1991. Multitask principal-agent analyses - Incentives contracts, asset ownership, and job design. *Journal of Law, Economics and Organization*, **7**(Special Issue: Papers from the Conference on the New Science of Organization), 24–52.

Holmström, Bengt, & Milgrom, Paul. 1994. The firm as an incentive system. *The American Economic Review*, **84**(4), 972–991.

Holmström, Bengt, & Myerson, Roger B. 1983. Efficient and durable decision rules with incomplete information. *Econometrica*, **51**(6), 1799–1819.

Holmström, Bengt, & Tirole, Jean. 1989. The theory of the firm. *Pages 61–133 of:* Schmalensee, Richard, & Willig, Robert D. (eds), *Handbook of industrial organization*. Amsterdam: North Holland.

Holmström, Bengt, & Tirole, Jean. 1993. Market liquidity and performance monitoring. *Journal of Political Economy*, **101**(4), 678–709.

Homann, Karl, & Suchanek, Andreas. 2000. *Ökonomik - Eine Einführung*. Tübingen: Mohr Siebeck.

Hommel, Ulrich, & Pritsch, Gunnar. 1997. Anreizprobleme zwischen Management und Unternehmenseignern - Implikationen für Investoren und Shareholder Value. *Pages 1–40 of:* Achleitner, Ann-Kristin, & Thoma, Georg F. (eds), *Handbuch Corporate Finance, 9. Ergänzungslieferung*. Köln: Gabler Verlag.

(HRK), Hochschulrektorenkonferenz. 2005. *Hochschulkompass*. http://www.hochschulkompass.de edn. Accessed on September 20, 2005.

Hume, David. 2000. *A Treatise of human nature (1st edn 1739)*. Oxford: Oxford University Press.

Ito, Takatoshi, & Kahn, Charles M. 1986. Why is there tenure? *University of Minnesota Department of Economics Center for Economic Research Discussion Paper No. 228*, 1–26.

Itoh, Hideshi. 1994. Job design, delegation and cooperation - A principal-agent analysis. *European Economic Review*, **38**(3-4), 691–700.

James, Estelle, & Neuberger, Egon. 1981. The university department as a non-profit labor cooperative. *Public Choice*, **36**(3), 585–612.

Jensen, Michael C. 1983. Organization theory and methodology. *The Accounting Review*, **68**(2), 319–339.

Jensen, Michael C., & Meckling, William H. 1976. Theory of the firm - Managerial behaviour, agency costs, and ownership structure. *Journal of Financial Economics*, **3**(4), 305–360.

Jensen, Michael C., & Meckling, William H. 1992. Specific and general knowledge, and organizational structure. *Pages 251–274 of:* Werin, Lars, & Wijkander, H. (eds), *Contract economics*. Cambridge, Mass.: Basil Blackwell.

Jick, Todd D. 1983. Mixing qualitative and quantitative methods - Triangulation in action. *Pages 135–148 of:* Maanen, John van (ed), *Qualitative methodology*. London: Sage.

Jost, Peter-J. 2001. Die Prinzipal-Agenten-Theorie im Unternehmenskontext. *Pages 11–43 of:* Jost, Peter-J. (ed), *Die Prinzipal-Agenten-Theorie in der Betriebswirtschaftslehre*. Stuttgart: Schäffer-Poeschel.

Jost (ed), Peter-J. 2001. *Die Prinzipal-Agenten-Theorie in der Betriebswirtschaftslehre*. Stuttgart: Schäffer-Poeschel.

Kahn, Charles M., & Huberman, Gur. 1988. Two-sided uncertainty and "up-or-out" contracts. *Journal of Labor Economics*, **6**(4), 423–444.

Kaplan, Gabriel E. 2002. Preliminary results of the 2001 Survey on Higher Education Governance. *Harvard University and AAUP*, 1–22.

Kim, Jongwook, & Mahoney, Joseph T. 2005. Property rights theory, transaction costs theory, and agency theory - An organizational economics approach to strategic management. *Managerial and Decision Economics*, **26**(4), 223–242.

Kockesen, Levent, & Ok, Efe A. 2004. Strategic delegation by unobservable incentive contracts. *Review of Economic Studies*, **71**(2), 397–424.

Koopmans, Tjalling C. 1957. *Three essays on the state of economic science*. New York: McGraw-Hill.

Kovac, Vesna, Ledic, Jasminka, & Rafajac, Branko. 2003. Academic staff participation in university govenance - Internal responses to external quality demands. *Tertiary Education and Management*, **9**(3), 215–232.

Küpper, Hans-Ulrich. 1997. *Controlling*. 2nd edn. Stuttgart: Schäffer-Poeschel.

Kuhn, Thomas S. 1976. *Die Struktur wissenschaftlicher Revolutionen*. 2nd edn. Frankfurt am Main: Suhrkamp.

Laffont, Jean-Jaques, & Tirole, Jean. 1986. Using cost observation to regulate firms. *Journal of Political Economy*, **94**(3), 614–641.

Laffont, Jean-Jaques, & Tirole, Jean. 1988. The dynamics of incentive contracts. *Econometrica*, **56**(5), 1153–1175.

Laffont, Jean-Jaques, & Tirole, Jean. 1990. Adverse selection and renegotiation in procurement. *Review of Economic Studies*, **57**(4), 597–625.

Lakatos, Imre. 1974. Falsifikation und die Methodologie wissenschaftlicher Forschungsprogamme. *Pages 89–189 of:* Lakatos, Imre, & Musgrave, Alan (eds), *Kritik und Erkenntnisfortschritt*. Braunschweig: Vieweg.

Lamnek, Siegfried. 1980. *Sozialwissenschaftliche Arbeitsmethoden.* Weinheim: Beltz Psychologie Verlags Union.

Lamnek, Siegfried. 1995a. *Qualitative Sozialforschung.* 3rd edn. Vol. 1 Methodologie. Weinheim: Beltz Psychologie Verlags Union.

Lamnek, Siegfried. 1995b. *Qualitative Sozialforschung.* 3rd edn. Vol. 2 Methoden und Techniken. Weinheim: Beltz Psychologie Verlags Union.

Laver, Michael. 1997. *Private desires, political action.* London: Sage Publications.

Lazear, Edward P. 1979. Why is there mandatory retirement? *Journal of Political Economy*, **87**(6), 1261–1284.

Lazear, Edward P. 1981. Agency, earnings profiles, productivity, and earnings restrictions. *The American Economic Review*, **71**(3), 606–620.

Li, Hao, Rosen, Sherwin, & Wing, Suen. 2001. Conflicts and common interests in committees. *Amercian Economic Review*, **91**(5), 1478–1597.

Macho-Stadler, Inés, & Pérez-Castrillo, David. 1997. *An introduction to the economics of information.* Oxford: Oxford University Press.

Mankiw, N. Gregory. 2001. *Principles of economics.* 2nd edn. Orlando: Hartcourt College Publishers.

Mantzavinos, Chrysostomos. 2001. *Indidivuals, institutions and markets.* Cambridge: Cambridge University Press.

Mas-Colell, Andreu, Whinston, Michael D., & Green, Jerry R. 1995. *Microeconomic theory.* Oxford: Oxford University Press.

Masten, Scott E. 2000. Commitment and political governance: Why universities, like legislatures, are not organized as firms. *University of Michigan Business School at Ann Arbor Working Paper*, 1–33.

Mayring, Philipp. 2002. *Einführung in die qualitative Sozialforschung*. Weinheim: Beltz Verlag.

Mayring, Philipp. 2003. *Qualitative Inhaltsanalyse*. Weinheim: Beltz Verlag.

McCormick, Robert E., & Meiners, Roger E. 1988. University governance - A property rights perspective. *Journal of Law & Economics*, **31**(2), 423–442.

McKenzie, Richard B. 1996. In defense of academic tenure. *Journal of Institutional and Theoretical Economics*, **152**(2), 325–341.

McPherson, Michael S., & Schapiro, Morton Owen. 1999. Tenure issues in higher education. *Journal of Economic Perspectives*, **13**(1), 85–98.

McPherson, Michael S., & Winston, Gordon C. 1983. The economics of academic tenure - A relational perspective. *Journal of Economic Behavior & Organization*, **4**(2), 163–184.

Menger, Carl. 1871. *Grundsätze der Volkswirtschaftslehre*. Wien: Wilhelm Braumüller.

Menger, Carl. 1969. *Untersuchungen über die Methode der Sozialwissenschaften und der politischen Ökonomie insbesondere (1st edn 1883)*. 2nd edn. Gesammelte Werke, Vol. II. Tübingen: Mohr Siebeck.

Meyer, Matthias. 2003. *Die Heuristik des normative Prinzipal-Agenten Modells*. Ph.D. thesis, Ludwig-Maximilian-Universität München.

Milgrom, Paul. 1988. Employment contracts, influence activities, and efficient organization design. *Journal of Political Economy*, **96**(1), 42–60.

Milgrom, Paul, & Roberts, John. 1988. An economic approach to influence activities in organizations. *American Journal of Sociology*, **94**(Supplement), S154–S179.

Milgrom, Paul R., & Roberts, John. 1992. *Economics, organization and management*. Upper Saddle River: Prentice Hall.

Mirrlees, James A. 1976. The optimal structure of incentives and authority within an organization. *The Bell Journal of Economics*, **7**(1), 105–131.

Mises, Ludwig von. 1933. *Grundprobleme der Nationalökonomie*. Jena: Gustav Fischer.

Mises, Ludwig von. 1996. *Human action - A treatise on economics (1st edn 1949)*. San Francisco: Fox & Wilkes.

Mittelstraß, Jürgen. 2003. Universität und Universalität. *Frankfurter Allgemeine Zeitung*, **10**, 8.

Müller-Böling, Detlef. 1994. Von der Gelehrtenrepublik zum Dienstleistungsunternehmen? *Forschung & Lehre*, **7**, 272–275.

Müller-Böling, Detlef, & Fedrowitz, Jutta. 1998. *Leitungsstrukturen für autonome Hochschulen*. Gütersloh: Verlag Bertelsmann Stiftung.

Müller-Böling, Detlef, & Küchler, Tilman. 1998. Zwischen gesetzlicher Fixierung und gestalterischem Freiraum: Leitungsstrukturen für Hochschulen. *Pages 13–36 of:* Müller-Böling, Detlef, & Fedrowitz, Jutta (eds), *Leitungsstrukturen für autonome Hochschulen*. Gütersloh: Verlag Bertelsmann Stiftung.

Mora, José-Ginés. 2001a. Governance and management in the new university. *Tertiary Education and Management*, **7**(2), 95–110.

Mora, José-Ginés. 2001b. International seminar on university governance and management - An overview. *Tertiary Education and Management*, **7**(2), 91–92.

Morgan, Mary S., & Morrison, Margaret C. 1999. Models as mediating instruments. *Pages 10–37 of:* Morgan, Mary S., & Morrison, Margaret C. (eds), *Models as mediators*. Cambridge: Cambridge University Press.

Mussa, Michael, & Rosen, Sherwin. 1978. Monopoly and product quality. *Journal of Economic Theory*, **18**(2), 301–317.

National Center for Education Statistics (NCES). 2001. *Postsecondary Institutions in the United States*. Washington D.C.: NCES.

North, Douglass C. 1990. *Institutions, institutional change and economic performance*. Cambridge: Cambridge University Press.

Olsen, Trond E., & Torsvik, Gaute. 2000. Discretion and incentives in organizations. *Journal of Labor Economics*, **18**(3), 377–404.

Olson, Mancur. 1965. *The logic of collective action*. Cambridge, Mass.: Harvard University Press.

Ortmann, Andreas. 1997. How to survive in postindustrial environments: Adam Smith's advice for today's colleges and universities. *The Journal of Higher Education*, **69**(5), 483–501.

Ortmann, Andreas, & Squire, Richard. 2000. A game-theoretic explanation of the administrative lattice in institutions of higher education. *Journal of Economic Behavior & Organization*, **43**(3), 377–391.

Oster, Sharon M. 2000. Privatizing university services. *Proceedings of the Forum on Higher Education*, 9–21.

Osterloh, Margit, Frey, Bruno S., & Frost, Jetta. 1999. Was kann das Unternehmen besser als der Markt? *Zeitschrift für Betriebswirtschaft*, **69**(11), 1245–1262.

Perkins, James A. 1973. Organization and functions of the university. *Pages 3–14 of:* Perkins, James A. (ed), *The university as an organization*. New York: McGraw-Hill.

Persson, Torsten, & Tabellini, Guido. 1994. *Political economics - Explaining economic policy.* Cambridge, Mass.: MIT Press.

Pfnister, Allan O. 1970. The role of faculty in university governance. *The Journal of Higher Education,* **41**(6), 430–449.

Picot, Arnold. 1991. Ökonomische Theorien der Organisation - Ein Überblick über neuere Ansätze und deren betriebswirtschaftliches Anwendungspotential. *Pages 143–170 of:* Ordelheide, Dieter, Rudolph, Bernd, & Büsselmann, Elke (eds), *Betriebswirtschaftslehre und ökonomische Theorie.* Stuttgart: Schäffer-Poeschel.

Popper, Karl. 2002. *Logik der Forschung (1st edn 1935).* 10th edn. Tübingen: Mohr Siebeck.

Popper, Karl R. 1992. *Die offene Gesellschaft und ihre Feinde.* 7th edn. Tübingen: Mohr Siebeck.

Pratt, John W., & Zeckhauser, Richard J. 1985. *Principals and agents - The structure of business.* Cambridge, Mass.: Harvard University Press.

Psacharopoulos, George. 1985. Returns to education - A further international update and implications. *The Journal of Human Resources,* **20**(4), 583–604.

Psacharopoulos, George (ed). 1987. *Economics of education: Research and studies.* Oxford: Pergamon Press.

Richardson, Hugh. 1999. Incentives in academics - Moral hazard and tenure. *Pacific University, Forest Grove, Department of Business and Economics Working Paper,* 1–16.

Richter, Rudolf, & Furubotn, Eirik G. 2003. *Neue Institutionenökonomik.* 3rd edn. Tübingen: Mohr Siebeck.

Robbins, Lionel. 1984. *Essays on the nature and significance of economic science.* 3rd edn. London: MacMillan Press.

Robbins, Stephen P. 1990. *Organization theory - Structure, design, and applications.* Englewood Cliffs: Prentice Hall.

Rogoff, Kenneth. 1985. The optimal degree of commitment to an intermediate monetary target. *Quarterly Journal of Economics*, **100**(4), 1169–1189.

Ross, Stephen A. 1973. The economics theory of agency - The principal's problem. *The American Economic Review*, **63**(2), 134–139.

Roth, Erwin, & Holling, Heinz (Eds). 1999. *Sozialwissenschaftliche Methoden - Lehr- und Handbuch für Forschung und Praxis.* 5th edn. München: Oldenbourg.

Rubinstein, Ariel. *Modeling bounded rationality.* Cambridge, Mass.: MIT Press.

Salanié, Bernard. 1997. *The economics of contracts - A primer.* Cambridge, Mass.: MIT Press.

Samuelson, Paul A. 1973. *Economics - An introduction analysis.* 9th edn. New York: McGraw-Hill.

Sappington, David. 1983. Limited liability contracts between principal and agent. *Journal of Economic Theory*, **29**(1), 1–21.

Schenker-Wicki, Andrea. 1996. *Evaluation von Hochschulleistung.* Wiesbaden: Deutscher Universitäts-Verlag.

Schmidt, Klaus M. 1995. *Lecture notes: Vertragstheorie für Doktoranden.*

Schmidt, Klaus M. 1997. Managerial incentives and product market competition. *Review of Economic Studies*, **64**(2), 191–213.

Schmitz, Patrick W. 2001. The hold-up problem and incomplete contracts - A survey of recent topics in contract theory. *Bulletin of Economic Research*, **53**(1), 1–17.

Schnell, Rainer, Hill, Paul B., & Esser, Elke. 2005. *Methoden der empirischen Sozialforschung.* 7th edn. München: Oldenbourg.

Schweizer, Urs. 1999. *Vertragstheorie*. Tübingen: Mohr Siebeck.

Shavell, Steven. 1979. Risk-sharing and incentives in the principal-agent relationship. *Bell Journal of Economics*, **10**(1), 55–73.

Shepsle, Kenneth A., & Boncheck, Mark S. 1997. *Analyzing politics - Rationality, behavior, and institutions*. New York: W. W. Norton & Company.

Shleifer, Andrei, & Vishny, Robert W. 1997. A survey of corporate governance. *Journal of Finance*, **52**(2), 737–783.

Simon, Herbert A. 1955. A behavioral model of rational choice. *Quarterly Journal of Economics*, **69**, 99–118.

Simon, Herbert A. 1957. *Models of man*. New York: Wiley.

Sinclair-Desgagné, Bernard. 1999. How to restore higher powered incentives in multitask agencies. *Journal of Law, Economics, and Organization*, **15**(2), 418–433.

Siow, Aloysius. 1998. Tenure and other unusual personnel practices in academia. *Journal of Law, Economics and Organization*, **14**(1), 152–173.

Sklivas, Steven D. 1987. The strategic choice of managerial incentives. *RAND Journal of Economics*, **18**(3), 452–458.

Smith, Adam. 1999. *The wealth of nations (1st edn 1776)*. London: Penguin Books.

Spence, A. Michael. 1973. Job market signaling. *Quarterly Journal of Economics*, **87**(3), 355–374.

Spence, A. Michael. 1974. *Market signaling - Information transfer in hiring and related processes*. Cambridge, Mass.: Harvard University Press.

Spence, Michael, & Zeckhauser, Richard. 1971. Insurance, information, and individual action. *The American Economic Review*, **61**(2), 380–387.

Spöhring, Walter. 1989. *Qualitative Sozialforschung*. Stuttgart: Teubner.

Stegner, Achim. 2000. *Ansätze und Perspektiven einer anspruchsgruppenorientierten Hochschulgestaltung*. Aachen: Shaker.

Stuchtey, Tim. 1999. Müssen Professoren Beamte sein? Eine Analyse der Anreizstruktur mit Hilfe der Property Rights Theorie. *Wirtschaftswissenschaftiche Fakultät der Humboldt Universität Berlin Working Paper 1999/08*, 1–10.

Toma, Eugene F. 1986. State university boards of trustees - A principal-agent perspective. *Public Choice*, **49**(2), 155–163.

Tropp, Gerhard. 2002. *Kennzahlensysteme des Hochschul-Controlling*. Ph.D. thesis, Ludwig-Maximilians-Universität München.

Tullock, Gordon. 1993. Are scientists different? *Journal of Economic Studies*, **20**(4/5), 90–106.

University of Mannheim. 2003. *Press release, February 18, 2003*. http://www.uni-mannheim.de/pressestelle/p/pressemitteilungen/2003/2003_01/2003_pm_09.html. Accessed on September 21, 2005.

Varian, Hal. 1997. How to build an economic model in your spare time. *Pages 256–271 of:* Szenberg, Michael (ed), *Passion and craft - Economists at work*. Ann Arbor: University of Michigan Press.

Vickers, John. 1985. Delegation and the theory of the firm. *Economic Journal*, **95**(380a), 138–147.

Vladeck, Bruce C. 1976. Why nonprofits go broke. *The Public Interest*, **42**(4), 86–101.

von Hayek, Friedrich August. 1937. Economics and knowledge. *Economica*, **4**(13), 33–54.

von Hayek, Friedrich August. 1945. The use of knowledge in society. *The American Economic Review*, **35**(4), 519–530.

von Hayek, Friedrich August. 1960. *The constitution of liberty*. Chicago: University of Chicago Press.

von Hayek, Friedrich August. 1973. *Law, legislation and liberty*. London: Routledge.

Váradi, Balázs. 2001. *Essays in the economics of education and non-profits*. Ph.D. thesis, Yale University.

Waldman, Michael. 1990. Up-or-out contracts - A signaling perspective. *Journal of Labor Economics*, **8**(2), 230–250.

Walsh, Carl E. 1995. Optimal contracts for central bankers. *American Economic Review*, **85**(1), 150–167.

Ward, Andrew. 1999. Washington University uses bonds to avoid tapping its endowment. *Bond Buye*, **330**(37061), 1–2.

Waugh, William L. Jr. 2003. Issues in university governance: More "professional" and less academic. *Annals of the American Academy*, **585**(1), 85–97.

Weigel, Wolfgang. 2003. Theory of tenure. *German Working Papers in Law and Economics No. 19*, 1–19.

Williams, Fred. 2003. Schools facing new budget problems to make up for endowment losses. *Pensions & Investments*, **31**(4), 30.

Williamson, Oliver E. 1963. Managerial discretion and business behavior. *The American Economic Review*, **53**(5), 1032–1057.

Williamson, Oliver E. 1975. *Markets and hierarchies - Analysis and anti-trust implications: A study in the economics of internal organization*. New York: Free Press.

Williamson, Oliver E. 1976. Franchise building for natural monopolies in general and with respect to CATV. *Bell Journal of Economics*, **7**, 73–104.

Williamson, Oliver E. 1985. *The economic institutions of capitalism - Firms, markets relational contracting*. New York: Free Press.

Williamson, Oliver E. 1986. *Economic organization*. Brighton: Wheatsheaf.

Williamson, Oliver E. 1991. Comparative economic organization - The analysis of discrete structural alternatives. *Administrative Science Quarterly*, **36**(2), 269–296.

Williamson, Oliver E. 1996. *The mechanisms of governance*. Oxford: Oxford University Press.

Wolff, Birgitta. 1999. Zum methodischen Status von Verhaltensannahmen in der Neuen Institutionenökonomik. *Pages 133–145 of:* Edeling, Thomas, Jann, Werner, & Wagner, Dieter (eds), *Institutionenökonomie und Neuer Institutionalismus*. Opladen: Leske + Budrich.

Yoder, Dale. 1962. The faculty role in university governance. *Academy of Management Journal*, **5**(3), 222–229.

ibidem-Verlag
Melchiorstr. 15
D-70439 Stuttgart

info@ibidem-verlag.de

www.ibidem-verlag.de
www.edition-noema.de
www.autorenbetreuung.de

www.ingramcontent.com/pod-product-compliance
Lightning Source LLC
Chambersburg PA
CBHW051804230426
43672CB00012B/2630